THE DYNAMICS OF
INTERNATIONAL LAW

Paul F. Diehl and Charlotte Ku's new framework for international law divides it into operating and normative systems. The authors provide a theory of how these two systems interact, which explains how changes in one system precipitate changes and create capacity in the other. A punctuated equilibrium theory of system evolution, drawn from studies of biology and public policy studies, provides the basis for delineating the conditions for change and helps explain a pattern of international legal change that is often infrequent and sub-optimal, but still influential.

PAUL F. DIEHL is Henning Larsen Professor of Political Science and University Distinguished Teacher/Scholar at the University of Illinois at Urbana-Champaign.

CHARLOTTE KU is Assistant Dean for Graduate and International Legal Studies at the University of Illinois College of Law, and Co-Director of the Centre on Law and Globalization, a partnership of the American Bar Foundation and the University of Illinois College of Law.

THE DYNAMICS OF INTERNATIONAL LAW

PAUL F. DIEHL

and

CHARLOTTE KU

CAMBRIDGE UNIVERSITY PRESS

Cambridge, New York, Melbourne, Madrid, Cape Town, Singapore,
São Paulo, Delhi, Dubai, Tokyo

Cambridge University Press
The Edinburgh Building, Cambridge CB2 8RU, UK

Published in the United States of America by Cambridge University Press, New York

www.cambridge.org
Information on this title: www.cambridge.org/9780521198523

First published 2010

Printed in the United Kingdom at the University Press, Cambridge

A catalogue record for this publication is available from the British Library

ISBN-13: 978-0-521-19852-3 Hardback
ISBN-13: 978-0-521-12147-7 Paperback

CONTENTS

ACKNOWLEDGEMENTS

The authors would like to thank a number of individuals and organizations that assisted in the completion of this work. The following individuals read or commented on different parts of the manuscript: Lee Alston, Karen Alter, Amitai Aviram, Robert Beck, Bear Braumoeller, Edwina Campbell, Xinyuan Dai, John Gamble, Tom Ginsburg, Lawrence LeBlanc, Sara McLaughlin Mitchell, Ron Mitchell, Robert Pahre, Anne Peters, Emilia Powell, Steve Rothman, Tatiana Vashchilko, Jana von Stein, and Thomas Ulen. Two anonymous reviewers for Cambridge University Press also provided encouragement and useful suggestions for revision.

The authors would also like to thank Todd Allee, Karen Alter, William Bernhard, Xinyuan Dai, Michael Findley, Tom Ginsburg, Robert Pahre, Gisela Sin, Tracy Sulkin, Isabelle van Damme, and Rick Wilson for their literature suggestions. Research assistance was provided by Michael Findley and Daniel Zamora, the latter through support from the Summer Research Opportunities Program (SROP) at the University of Illinois. Special thanks to the Cambridge University Faculty of Law, the Squire Law Library, and the Lauterpacht Centre for International Law for support and assistance to Dr. Ku in the preparation of a portion of this manuscript during her time as Acting Director of the Lauterpacht Centre for International Law. Gratitude is also given to Delinda Swanson for her efforts in the formatting and final preparation of the manuscript.

Various segments of this manuscript were presented before a variety of groups and the authors received valuable feedback from the audiences: Rice University Department of Political Science, Leiden University Public International Law Program, Cambridge University Lauterpacht Centre for International Law Speakers Series, University of Illinois School of Law Faculty Retreat, Northwestern University School of Law,

Oxford University Public International Law Speakers Series, and University of Iowa Shambaugh Conference.

Our appreciation also goes to Finola O'Sullivan, Editorial Director, Law at Cambridge University Press for her encouragement and support of this project.

1

Introduction

The study of international law has, in some ways, undergone dramatic changes over the past centuries, but it has also stayed remarkably the same. The subject matter with international legal components has expanded dramatically and the depth of international law's reach has also increased. From an early reliance on theological writings and natural law, international law has evolved substantially to include a variety of sources for rules, most notably custom and treaties. Early international law focused extensively on the territory of states and the regulation of the use of armed force. Today, its parameters have broadened to include human rights, the environment, and trade, among other emerging areas (see UNGA, 2006). As a result, the practice and practitioners of international law have also increased substantially, providing previously unavailable pools of data and experience to analyze and to test. There has also been an explosion of institutions – notably, the recent growth in the number of international judicial institutions – as well as international processes for scholars to examine. Thus, international law has expanded in volume, content, structure, and process, but the methods of scholarly inquiry have not kept pace.

The predominant mode of international legal analysis is still descriptive and expositive. International law scholars typically seek to uncover what international rules exist (e.g., see chapter 3 of Arend, 1999) with a view to suggesting where rules may need modification in order to be effective. Although there are a variety of approaches to this method, the primary purpose of these inquiries is to determine the present state of the law, and to examine such rules within a given political environment. This method of divining the law or searching for it in treaties and other documents dates back hundreds of years. Another important framework is primarily prescriptive, undertaking critique and analysis as a basis for advocating what the law *should be* in light of perceived inadequacies or failure rather than describing what it is. In neither approach is there an ability to explain or predict the actual development of international law and the dynamics behind the evolution; notable exceptions are Charney (1993), Goldsmith and Posner (2005), Raustiala (2005), Guzman (2008), Helfer (2008a), and Trachtman (2008). This book provides a new framework to analyze international legal processes that is specifically designed to help us understand the tremendous changes that have occurred in international law over the last sixty-plus years as well as ones that are likely (or not) in the future. Consistent with that framework, we offer a theory of legal change, focusing largely on factors endogenous to the international legal system. The orientation of the book, however, is not to offer an analysis of one (e.g., human rights) or even a handful of international legal concerns – the trees – but rather the international legal system writ large – the forest.

We begin with a more dynamic and interactive orientation to studying international law. We agree with treatise writers who see international law as the basis for political discourse among members of the international system (see for example, Schachter, 1991; Henkin, 1968 and 1995; Friedmann, 1966; Fawcett, 1968; Janis, 1993; Cassese, 1986; Higgins, 1994; and Shaw, 2008). This discourse does not necessarily imply or guarantee consensus, but it does foster the ongoing interaction needed to provide conceptual clarity in determining legal obligations and in generating the capacity to implement them. In playing this role, international law performs two distinct functions: one is to provide the parameters and mechanisms for cross-border interactions, and the other is to shape the values and goals these interactions promote. We call the first set of functions the *operating system* of international law, and the second set the *normative system*.

The book examines the basic components of the operating and normative systems to construct a dynamic framework for analyzing and understanding international law. The operating system deals with the basic "structures" of international law. It functions in some ways (but not others) as a constitution does for domestic political systems by allocating power, identifying legitimate actors, specifying sources of law, and providing remedies and enforcement mechanisms. It serves as a general repository of modes or techniques for change available to the entire system no matter what the specific subject matter. For example, rules on criminal and court jurisdictions determine which actors have access to what venues in addressing violations of torture proscriptions. Thus, the operating system is concerned with creating and maintaining the modalities that can create and give effect to international law's norms. The normative system of international law includes the values and goals that guide the conduct of states in the international system. It establishes general standards in the international arena whereby the values of the international system are identified and general prescriptions and proscriptions for behavior are established. For example, the prohibition of genocide is a legal norm that is designed to restrict state behavior.

Using the framework provided by the specification of the operating and normative systems, we seek to understand how these two systems interact and thereby explain and predict when and how changes in one system precipitate changes and create capacity in the other system. To do so, we construct a punctuated equilibrium theory of system evolution, drawn from studies of biology and public policy studies. That theory provides the basis for delineating the conditions for change and helps explain a pattern of international legal change that is often infrequent and suboptimal. A norm that functions at a suboptimal level is quite different from a norm that does not exist. Nonetheless, the popular perception that suboptimality creates is that international law does not exist or does not function.

Implications

There are several theoretical and policy implications that flow from this new framework. First and most broadly, we hope to marry international legal scholarship with social scientific research. The former has too often been characterized by static analyses whose purpose is to assess the status of legal norms, with little or no concern for the behavior of states over time or broad theoretical generalizations. Our framework and accompanying theory of legal change is predicated on the assumption that general patterns of behavior on legal issues exist across different time periods and within different contexts. These patterns are further conditioned by what precedes and what follows. Accordingly, our analysis seeks to provide greater explanatory depth beyond asking what the law is to include what cumulative effects the law has and what prospects exist for changes in the future.

The movement away from pure description also presents the potential for international relations theory. More broadly then, our framework and theory answer the call to bridge international legal and international relations theories. Too often, such calls have occurred more frequently (Beck, 1996; Slaughter, 1998; Ku and Weiss, 1998; Yasuaki, 2003) than efforts to fulfill those suggestions. Thus, we aspire to develop explanations for international legal phenomena with a general theory of legal change and specific arguments for particular kinds of legal change. The application of theoretical expectations to empirical cases in those chapters illustrates the application of social science to international legal problems, as well as the breadth of our approach to international law writ large.

Just as the study of international law has been stilted by lacking reference to international relations, so too has the latter been limited by largely ignoring international law. As Joyner (2006: 248) notes:

> Academicians who study either international law or international politics share a dirty little secret: both groups know that the presence of international law is critical for international relations to occur, and both know that the practice of international politics is essential for international law to evolve and function. But each is reluctant to admit the necessity of the other.

Illustrative of this, most scholarship has been devoted to how international norms arise (e.g., Klotz, 1995; Finnemore, 1996), with special attention to the moral character of the norm and how it became accepted broadly by the international community. Such scholarship has not often paid attention to the ways in which the international community has sought to ensure that such norms actually influence state behavior or the needed capacity to give norms effect. Either this was assumed to be a tautology (some argue that behavior modification is an essential component of a norm – see Goertz and Diehl, 1992) or it was dismissed as a fundamentally different question. Our analysis seeks to extend the concern with how norms develop to include how the international legal system gives them effect, or in a number of cases does not provide this service, as well as why this is the case.

Although not exclusively concerned with international "regimes" (for a review, see Hasenclever, Mayer, and Rittberger, 1997), our framework and accompanying theory have implications for how regimes are designed and what mechanisms exist for their maintenance. As Slaughter (1998: 385) indicates, "effective regime design requires a theory of why states cooperate through institutional arrangements and why those arrangements might not succeed." We hope to offer some insights on when states will build institutional as well as other mechanisms to ensure that regime norms are not empty ideals. In effect, operating system provisions become a necessary part of the legal regime in a given issue area. Thus, understanding how normative change prompts operating system change (and vice versa) could be a key component of understanding the development and ultimately the effectiveness of international regimes.

Although integrating international law and international relations scholarship is an important contribution, we were initially motivated by two central and more specific concerns in the scholarship of international law. First, we found existing frameworks and taxonomies for international legal scholarship inadequate. In a number of cases, no framework or taxonomy is specified. To the extent that one is evident, directly or indirectly, it tends to emphasize the descriptive and static qualities of international law. Our review of international legal scholarship below lays bare these limitations. This stifles the specification of theoretical questions and thereby inhibits the empirical examination of propositions derived from models that seek to offer answers to those questions. Problems with those frameworks in particular make it difficult to carry out queries related to how and why international law evolves.

Our dynamic framework for international law also allows scholars to raise (and answer) new questions that are impossible in static frameworks. For example, why are new legal norms and standards created in the international system when that system lacks the capacity to ensure compliance with those norms or mechanisms for compliance arise only decades later? A number of human rights provisions have been adopted in the last sixty years, such as the Convention on the Elimination of Discrimination Against Women (CEDAW), but few legal avenues are available to ensure their precepts are followed. Such vital questions never crop up if the overarching framework for analysis is purely descriptive or prescriptive.

Second, we move beyond the specification of a framework for analyzing international law and develop both a general theory of legal change and specific models for particular kinds of institutional and normative change. Understanding when and how change occurs can provide important insights into the capacity of any individual norm to meet its objectives. Current legal scholarship does not generally posit causal relationships, much less subject them to empirical examination. In particular, legal change is not generally the focus of those efforts. Furthermore, broad treatments of international law (e.g., Guzman, 2008; Goldsmith and Posner, 2005) rely extensively on conventional and exogenous influences, such as the power or interests of leading states. Although we don't dismiss such influences, we place considerable emphasis on some of the endogenous or internal components of the international legal system as impetuses for change. To the extent that they evaluate disputes and the resolution of disputes as part of an ongoing cycle of normative change in the international system, international relations scholars are looking within the system. Nevertheless, their work touches on the evolutionary cycles of specific norms to explain change within the entire system (Sandholtz and Stiles, 2009). In contrast to other works, we offer a general theory of legal change and then provide specific models that are derived from that theory to account for specific incidences of change.

The framework and theory presented here do more than make scholarly contributions to international legal and relations study. Our emphasis on the dynamics of international law allows us to offer some policy-relevant conclusions. Barrett's (2003) analysis and subsequent approach to climate change provides an example of how understanding the international legal operating system can assist with more effective treaty design. He points to the inherent difficulties in the effective monitoring and implementation of the Kyoto Protocol. Barrett's approach is to find ways to build a climate change treaty that draws on existing practices within the international system that can work to enforce the treaty's obligations. His approach is therefore to rely on the existing operating system in this case, the setting of technology and building incentives to comply with these standards as a means to achieving compliance. "International agreements need to be self-enforcing, and so must restructure incentives" (Barrett, 2003: 398) to take advantage of structures and procedures in the system that already work for other rules.

Our framework and theory provide insights into the kind of changes in international law one might anticipate. For example if a new human rights provision, such as one recognizing new rights for ethnic groups, is adopted, what kind of institutions or processes might be adopted to give that new norm effect? When might limited changes occur (or none at all) such that the norm becomes little more than an ideal rather than a reality in the international legal system? Yet the failure to give the norm effect in our "operating system" does not necessarily mean it will remain unobserved or without influence. As we note in Chapter 4, there are adaptive mechanisms that serve to supplement the international legal system or compensate for its inadequacies. Policymakers may be cued to when they will need to build in compliance or other mechanisms in a treaty as opposed to when they can rely on extant process when adopting a new norm.

Our analyses in subsequent chapters might also help national leaders and international lawyers recognize when adopting new processes, such as an adjudicatory structure or allowing universal jurisdiction for some crimes, will have a spillover effect in the creation of new norms, unintended at the time that the court or legal principle was created. In this way, the expansion of international law into a given topic area does not have to begin with grand forethought, but may be facilitated (or inhibited) by the presence of structures and processes already operating in other subject areas (see Aviram, 2004). For example, allowing individuals or corporations to have greater legal standing to file claims or assert rights, independent of their home states, might have the effect of expanding the rights and responsibilities of those actors in other areas of the law.

In the following sections, we provide an overview of international legal scholarship, with special emphasis on the frameworks used to analyze law in the world community and models of legal change implied or derived from those frameworks. We begin with a brief summary of the major approaches from the early days of international law. This is not intended to be a comprehensive review, covering all approaches and ideas since the beginning of international law (see Nussbaum, 1954 for such a survey). Rather, we note several of the highlights in order to place our approach in contrast to that early work and to establish our place in the progression of international legal scholarship. We then describe more modern approaches, focusing on those found exclusively in international legal study as well as those designed to study legal systems and processes more generally. The purpose of such an exercise is more than for the simple edification of the reader. Presenting these approaches allows us to identify the inherent limitations of these approaches, as well as providing segues for the presentation of our new framework and theory, which is designed in part to address the problems with past approaches, in Chapter 2.

Historical antecedents from antiquity to the early modern period

In the pre-modern, early history of international relations, efforts to understand relations beyond a particular nation were often closely associated with religion, ecclesiastical study, or philosophy, and relations were framed as those between the preferred self and outsiders or barbarians. In his study of international law in antiquity, Bederman (2001: 287) concluded that even though there was "no single, cohesive body of rules for a law of nations, recognized by all States in antiquity or that such rules were proximate to those that we regard today as being part of 'modern' international law . . . there was a common *idea* held in antiquity that international relations were to be based on the rule of law."

Ancient efforts to address international relations were all based on some belief in a universal order. As Kennedy (1986: 96) explained: "primitives elaborated a coherent vision of authority in radically diverse theoretical and doctrinal texts." The well-developed and widely recognized system of law used by the Roman Empire may have provided international law analysis with something of a false start because of its use of the term *jus gentium*, Latin for the "law of nations" and referring to law governing interactions with outsiders. At best, this might have covered "inter-municipal" relations, but did not include a "broad conception of the family of nations" (Nussbaum, 1954: 9; see also Walker, 1893). Thus, to the extent that any theoretical structure for international law existed, it was based on a crude "us versus them" conception.

The fall of the Roman Empire limited the further development of international law, and eventually led to a consideration of a legal order based largely on natural law. Accordingly, the framework for analyzing international law was based on religion, most prominently Catholicism. The medieval collecting of the ecclesiastical decrees that guided the Catholic Church from its founding over time produced the Code of Canon Law. Because of the Catholic Church's reach, canon law became an important basis for activity following the decay and collapse of the Roman Empire. The components of canon law were promulgated to operate separately from any national law and derived from the Pope's authority as head of a universal church with authority over the entire Christian world. As supreme pontiff, all final legislative, executive, and judicial authority therefore resided with the Pope (see Arrieta, 2000 and Martin de Agar, 2007). To the extent that international law was part of canon law, it had little need for any separate intellectual basis or tenets. Indeed to have suggested a need would have been regarded as heretical. Such practices as regulating warfare through the Truces of God during the medieval period were therefore carried out as part of the Church's ecclesiastical authority with little further theoretical or doctrinal justification regarded as necessary.

The era in which canon law predominated did not provide a framework under which international law could be analyzed. The process of lawmaking was said to be divinely inspired and therefore not transparent. Furthermore, the idea that law could change was not recognized; only new revelations could produce additional legal rules.

St. Augustine's (354–430) work on just war perhaps can be seen as a turning point in moving international law from traditional religious dogma to something with a more reasoned basis (St. Augustine, 1958).

This was still in the mode of ecclesiastical inquiry, but it provided some doctrinal underpinning beyond correct conduct. Even this modest beginning, however, was constrained by an almost exclusive doctrinal focus on the prevention of war as was also the case with the work of Thomas Aquinas and other scholastics. Nevertheless, there was now at least an external and visible standard by which to judge the legality of actions, albeit one still heavily influenced by religious precepts.

In the realm of political philosophy, Niccolò Machiavelli (1469–1527) and Jean Bodin (1530–96) provided alternatives to religious hierarchy and doctrine as the bases for human behavior and the exercise of power. Bodin introduced the concept of sovereignty "as the absolute and perpetual power over the people, unrestrained by human law" (Bodin, 1992). The power of the state thus became the centerpiece around which law might be analyzed. The study of international law in these conceptions was somewhat divorced from religious roots, but still lacked a coherent framework to understand its origins and evolution. At best, more rationalist standards replaced religious ones in what was still an exercise in normatively evaluating international law rather than scientifically explaining it.

The Spanish Dominican Francisco Vitoria (1480–1546) and the Spanish Jesuit Francisco Suárez (1548–1617) worked in the area of theology, but provided some further elaboration in areas that touch on international law. The notable shift was away from discerning moral principles or rational calculations for the purpose of identifying international law. Instead, scholars and other analysts should look to the *practice* of states to identify international law, a precursor to the development of positivism. Thus, the analytical framework for international law was shifting away from religious and philosophical texts to patterns in real world events. This also opened up the possibility for changes in the law over time (from practice) as opposed to immutable and divine truths as the basis for law.

This brings us to the work of Hugo Grotius (1583–1645), a colorful and talented figure who is widely cited as the "father of international law." Ironically, it may have been his deep-seated desire to find a way to reconcile the Protestants and the Catholics that caused him to adopt neutrality with regard to aspects of religious doctrine that has made his work valuable as a foundation for international law. Accordingly, Grotius saw law as secular and did not assign any special role for religious officials. He did give credence to Roman jurists, but for the strength of the legal reasoning rather than from some privileged position (Nussbaum, 1954).

Grotius (see Grotius, 1925) referred to continued practice for the *evidence* of law, but he grounded its *authority* primarily in consent, and so ultimately in the Moral Sense of Rational Humanity (Nussbaum, 1954: 107 and Walker, 1893: 104). The idea of consent as a central framework for detecting international law is a considerable break from religious conceptions of law granted from above. Grotius also saw international law as a unified whole rather than composed of disparate pieces, foreshadowing some conceptions of international law as a system, although Grotius never used those terms or developed such ideas further. Grotius is associated with the concept of the *Mare liberum* ("freedom of the seas") that advanced the interests of his Dutch masters, but would over time become international law in contrast to the rival concept of the *Mare clausum* ("closed seas") advanced by John Selden (Selden, 2003) on behalf of the English who were challenging Dutch maritime interests around the world. Although not embedded in their approaches *per se*, this is one of the first indications that "national interests," especially those of leading states, might be examined to understand international law, a conception that has found its way into some important later works (e.g., Goldsmith and Posner, 2005).

Although a philosopher and mathematician, Christian Wolff (1676–1756) further systematized international law and contributed the proposition that every right is based on a duty (Nussbaum, 1954; Wolff, 1934). Despite the lack of evidence or documentation in his work, Wolff's approach provided shape and definition to international law. Later writers, such as von Martens (Martens, 1803), would acknowledge Wolff's effort to produce "an organic, strictly scientific exposition of international law" (Wolff, 1934: xxxi). Again, this is a precursor to a system-level approach that is reflected in our theory. This effort also had the effect of separating international law from natural law and introduced positivism by taking into account agreements and customary practice (Wolff, 1934).

Appraising early efforts

The writings of towering figures such as Grotius and Wolff clearly shaped the early study and indeed the development of international law. Yet they tended to focus on establishing the ground rules for identifying the law rather than providing an analytical framework for understanding the process of that formation or the impact of the law on behavior. As such, pre-modern writers "tended to emphasize the moral imperative of law between nations and were part of a natural law tradition – a 'common law' of states backed up by religious and philosophical principles of good faith and goodwill between men and nations" (Bederman, 2002: 5). Rooted in tradition and authority, these issues generated few separate intellectual underpinnings or structures beyond the religious and the moral. If international law comes from religious principles, there is little debate permitted about its origins. If religious authorities are the sole legitimate interpreters of such principles, then no analytical framework is necessary to study or understand the law.

Once the universal authority of the Pope came under challenge with the Protestant Reformation, religious principles gave way to concern for reason, practice, and ultimately written agreements as sources of international law. This opened up the toolbox for scholars, who could now explore different elements as potential sources of international law. This scholarly focus was still heavily rooted in natural law and was again normatively driven, seeking as much to advocate what the law should be as what the law actually was. Ideas about a system of international law and the role of national interests in the formation of law were still, at best, nascent notions.

From an explanatory perspective, these early writings were even less fully developed as they provided little, if anything, to explain if international law affected behavior and how it might do so. Part of this is attributable to the exclusive emphasis on discerning the normative standards for behavior without concern for whether those precepts were followed or not. There also seemed a tacit assumption that the right doctrinal underpinnings could automatically bring to bear the capabilities necessary to carry out the tenets of international law. In fact, we know that this is not the case, but we also know that perfect performance all the time is not required to maintain the system. Furthermore, neither the volume of interactions nor the political structures of the times required elaborate theorizing because the authority of the Pope or others who had interests in orderly international relations had the ability simply to prescribe such an order.

International legal scholarship was also not generally concerned with change in international law. Basing international law on natural law and religious principles made such concerns moot; those sources were considered immutable and law only changed when competent authorities "discovered" or discerned new rules. With the later recognition of new sources of law, including custom and written agreements, the possibility of legal evolution could be addressed. So too might the rise of new topics on the legal agenda such as maritime law and peace. Yet despite such opportunities, scholars kept their concentration on static concerns of what the law was. To the extent that change was addressed, it was to understand change in the legal content or how the law *should* be further altered rather than *how* change occurred. This lack of attention to how change occurred may have stemmed from an assumption that there was little to study because the modes of change were so few and so widely accepted – as the outcome either of long practice or of specific negotiation and agreement.

As the level of global contacts increased with developments in technology that allowed for new discoveries, increased trading, and eventual occupation by Europeans around the world, so too did the number of legal questions raised about the bases for these actions. This growing number of cases and experiences started to provide an empirical basis for analysis that further shaped international legal study. The close ties between the origins of international legal study and theology or known points of political interest have been one of the weaknesses that deniers of international law use in arguing that international law had no basis or purpose beyond the specific interest of the entity advancing it or some specific need (see Carr, 1964; Morgenthau, 1948). In the next section, we review modernist approaches to the study of international law, ones that grew in parallel with international law itself.

Modernist approaches to international legal study

The increase in complexity in international relations and the waning of broadly accepted authority such as that of the Catholic Church were factors in efforts to provide a systematic basis for international law. The shift also coincided with new scientific discoveries and a general move towards developing a more scientific basis for human activity based on observation and research. "In international law too, theories had to be based upon the solid foundation of fact" (Nussbaum, 1954: 233). This epistemological shift further coincided with the political tenor of the times following a turning away from natural law's association with mob violence as it emerged from the French Revolution's efforts to promote the rights of man.

Despite a slow movement toward scientific analysis, the study of international law retained its moral imperative. For example, Jeremy Bentham (1748–1832) (Bentham, 1970) provided one such approach "as part of his general attempt to reorganize legal discourse and direct it towards laws as they *ought* to be. This involved not only an attempt to classify law rationally, but also a (positivist) conception of the nature of law in which the distinction between law as it *is* and law as it *ought* to be played a crucial role" (Sylvest, 2004: 13).

As the nineteenth century dawned, naturalists, positivists, and Grotians could be found writing about law (Oppenheim, 1955). The differences in their analytical frameworks were largely over where international law might be found, the traditional point of contention between scholars and philosophers. Natural law proponents saw international law as fixed and derivative from reason or religious principles; this provided only narrow spaces for legal change. Positivists emphasized law as created by humans, and thereby implicitly subject to change over time, although positivists did not necessarily have a theory about how and when such change would occur. Grotians drew from both schools.

Over time, "positivism gains slowly and gradually the upper hand, until at the end [by the end of the nineteenth century and the beginning of the twentieth], it may be said to be victorious, without, however, being omnipotent" (Oppenheim, 1955: 106). This, at least, provided some direction on where to look for the law, but there was still not an over-arching framework to assist that quest or to classify the results at the end of the hunt. A more scientific basis was needed.

The founding of scholarly associations, journals, and separate university chairs for the study of international law indicated international law's coming of age as a field of study and pursuit. Although much of this was driven by the desire to find rational and empirical bases for international law, it did not mean a complete break with the moral objectives advanced by the earlier writers. William Whewell (1794–1866), whose name would be associated with Cambridge's chair in international law, was a mathematician, a historian, and a philosopher of science whose "interest in international law seems to have derived from an ambition to find a place for international legal ideas in his general moral system" (Sylvest, 2004: 23). For Whewell, "the general progression of law (based on morality) ... tend[ed] towards justice" (Sylvest, 2004: 23) and for international law, "the increase of a regard for the authority for such [International] Law, [is] among the most hopeful avenues to that noble Ideal of the lovers of mankind, a perpetual peace" (Whewell, 1853: xii).

For others, the law of nature became the bridge between the natural law of the early writers and the positivism of the modern writers; they suggested that there was a state of nature either pre-dating positive law or that embraced positive law as part of a broader legal system, community, or society. This concept of evolution in law provided a scientific basis for the law of nature whereby "international jurists became empiricists who should identify and codify (or rewrite) these rules as civilization developed" (Sylvest, 2004: 39).

Whatever its shortcomings, this was one of the first explicit recognitions that international law could and should change over time. It also suggested that changes in international law would come from conditions in the international system and not through new derivations from natural law.

As the post-Napoleonic period gave rise to the ascendancy of positivism, particularly following the Crimean and Franco-Prussian Wars, so too did the two World Wars provide impetus for the further integration of international law into an overall legal system. The monist approach (the idea of one legal system rather than separate national and international systems), advocated by Scelle (1932), did not see any normative differences in municipal and international or private and public law (Koskienniemi, 2001). This was perhaps most succinctly expressed in Scelle's (1932) concept of *dédoublement fonctionnel* where "an individual has been put in a position of agent or administrator of two or more societies, that is where a national Parliament in approving a treaty legislated both for the national and the international society. In the same way – and controversially – national governments are also put in a position to administer international society" (Koskienniemi, 2001: 333). Such a perspective opens up a series of important questions about the role of domestic politics in international law and society as well as how what are now called "two-level games" (Evans, Jacobson, and Putnam, 1993) influence the development of international law. Yet such formulations at the time were little more than philosophical assertions rather than contentions about empirical reality. Later scholarly studies of institutions, for example on treaty ratification and domestic political influences in international negotiations (e.g., Konig and Hug, 2000; Pahre, 2006), are consistent with these frameworks, but cannot be traced back in a straight line to these formulations.

Writers in the modern era emphasized describing or documenting international law. Efforts at compiling digests and founding learned societies were meant to illuminate the breadth of acceptance of particular norms and to describe the actions taken by individual players. Competing frameworks were centered on the sources of international law, be they naturalist or more positivist (e.g., custom, treaties). There was little effort, however, directed at explaining the behavior of states beyond recording their actions. Furthermore, if any explanation was given for state actions, it normally focused only on the government's official foreign policy departments without attention to domestic politics or factors associated with material interests.

In the modern era, the normative tension was different than in earlier periods. The struggle was between conceptualizing the functions of international law as either (1) to serve as manager of international relations and to avoid the appearance of backing one value over another or (2) to advance particular values as central to any world order. In both approaches, universality was the goal in order to ensure the broadest level of participation and thereby create the widest generally recognized legal system. Post-modern scholarship, however, reminds us that the context of the lawmaking and implementation environment is important. These scholars point out that the exclusive focus on the managerial function or the value function is not only inadequate, but may, in fact, distort reality by failing to take into account the interactions that will have changed conditions over time (for a list of key scholars and works, see Kennedy and Tennant, 1994).

Although there had been high hopes that providing international law with a scientific and rational basis would serve as an effective alternative to war and a means to resolving conflicts, the two World Wars clearly showed the limits of that approach. The emphasis in international law then shifted toward process, structure, and new values such as the protection of individual human rights. Institutions at the international level as well as attachment to national legal systems would add depth and structure to the psychological awareness that international law is pervasive in international relations since antiquity.

Contemporary approaches

International law's historical development has been pushed along by the need to provide intellectual bases to increase the capacity for international law to meet the increasingly complicated needs of international life. From the viewpoint of the scholar, the increase in international activity has provided a rich body of experience to draw on for observation and analysis. The twentieth century and especially the last sixty years have seen a wealth of new frameworks or lenses under which to examine international law. We review these major approaches below, although our critiques of early frameworks as largely descriptive, static, atheoretical, and normative still largely apply to contemporary approaches.

Ratner and Slaughter (1999) surveyed what they term "methods" of international law analysis. Yet there is nothing on their list of methodologies that would be recognizable as such by social scientists. As the authors admit, they did not intend their review to encompass research design or traditional social science methods; rather their methodologies are more akin to theoretical or analytical approaches, better for understanding contemporary issues than constructing explanatory models.

Beck (1996) reviews many of the same approaches as Ratner and Slaughter (1999) and classifies them according to two dimensions. First, he identifies whether the approach is explanatory or prescriptive (normative), with more approaches falling in the latter category. Second, he notes whether the approach is empirical or critical. The former focuses on what the law is, without any judgments about its suitability or effectiveness. The latter includes approaches whose primary result is to provide a negative assessment of the state of international law, its origins, and the like.

Positivism

Positivism is not a new approach to international law, but rather a further development of the theoretical viewpoint that emerged in the nineteenth century. As with many other pre-modern and modern approaches, classical positivism focused on what the law is and can be within a given political and legal framework rather than what it should be based on reason or belief. Therefore it rejected the non-legal elements of other frameworks. The series of intellectual profiles published in the *European Journal of International Law* as part of a feature on the European tradition in international law provides several good examples of writers in the positivist tradition (see, for example, Giorgia on Dionisio Anzilotti (1992), Thierry on George Scelle (1990), Simma on Alfred Verdross (1995), Leben on Hans Kelsen (1998), and Gross's classic essay on the Peace of Westphalia (1948)). Positivism has had a largely descriptive goal, which is to depict the state of the law. In contrast, it does not have broader theoretical goals of explaining the law or its operations, much less predicting changes in its composition in the future. The positivist framework in its traditional formulation is state-centric, directing scholars to concentrate exclusively on states and their consent in seeking to identify international rules.

Simma and Paulus (1999) offer a number of modifications, promoting what they term "modern positivism." These include widening the focus on "state practice" to include a range of other evidence of law, including government documents and official statements; many of these are considered supplementary sources of law to traditional custom and treaties. There is also the recommendation that normative concerns not be abandoned, but only that they should not be a mechanism to define law or criticize its existence.

Positivism would be a suitable approach if one is interested only in detecting the existence of law (note some of the other approaches below would disagree), a traditional focus of legal scholarship. The narrow focus on states, however, makes it increasingly limited in identifying legal rules in a globalizing world. Yet broader aspirations to understand how law is made are all but assumed away or treated as exogenous under this framework. Furthermore, issues of compliance and process are largely ignored. Fundamentally, a positivist framework can neither anticipate nor account for change in the legal system well.

Policy and process approaches

A second influential approach is concerned with international law as policymaking. Most prominent of these frameworks is the so-called New Haven School, introduced by, and perhaps most closely associated with, the work of Myres McDougal and Harold Lasswell (McDougal and Lasswell, 1959; Lasswell and McDougal, 1992; see also Tipson, 1974 and more recently the special issue of the *Yale Journal of International Law*, 2007). The policy approach was prompted by the recognition that formal rules were limited in their effectiveness because they were "inconsistent, ambiguous, and full of omissions" (as quoted in Koskienniemi, 2001: 475). The New Haven School looks at the values, interests, goals, and other factors surrounding the actors in the system to understand how decision makers pursue common interests. Law is seen as a product of both legitimacy and its effect on behavior.

The New Haven School is an empiricist approach in the sense that it seeks to identify the law and evaluate the degree to which the law fulfills certain values (Lasswell and McDougal, 1992). Law is a process in which community members seek to promote a common interest (Wiessner and Willard, 1999). Yet such an evaluation takes place against a distinctly normative standard: a universal order of human dignity. Thus, this approach takes on a problem-solving orientation. McDougal and Lasswell (1959) describe five steps in the assessment process suggested by their framework: (1) clarifying the goal of human dignity; (2) describing the trend toward or away from that goal; (3) analyzing the factors that condition goal achievement; (4) projecting future developments; and (5) creating policy alternatives to ensure goal achievement. Clearly the goal is improving policymaking with the emphasis on the effects of law empirically in pursuit of normative goals. The gathering of facts and data is made in pursuit of this practical application – to guide decision makers (Wiessner and Willard, 1999).

Other approaches in the "legal process" tradition continued the New Haven School emphasis on community values and authoritative decisions by the international community. "The role of law is to provide an operational system for security values that we all desire – security, freedom, the provision of sufficient material goods. It is not, as is commonly supposed, only about resolving disputes" (Higgins, 1994: 1). Included in such frameworks is a different conception of what law is, beyond simply the state practice standard advocated by positivists. For example, Higgins (1968: 58) notes: "When . . . decisions are made by authorized persons or organs, in appropriate forums, within the framework of certain established practices and norms, then what occurs is *legal* decision-making. In other words, international law is a continuing process of authoritative decisions. This view rejects the notion of law merely as the impartial application of rules."

Instead of making a choice between a managerial function and a value-setting function of law, Higgins' approach allows for law to develop as it needs once issues have risen to the attention of decision makers whose authority derives from domestic and international political processes. In this way, international law concerns itself less with the formalities of law, but more with the process that facilitates legitimacy and observance for orderly international relations. Unlike previous approaches, there is also the recognition of a process, albeit not an explanatory one, of legal change.

The emphasis on legal process continued in the International Legal Process (ILP) approach (Chayes, Ehrlich, and Lowenfeld, 1968) and its derivatives (O'Connell, 1999). In doing so, the focus is not on the normative implications of the outcome, but on the mechanisms leading to outcomes. A concern for legal change receives more attention here than in previous approaches: "In the end, an understanding of the way law adapts to change may be more important for both student and practitioner than a study of what the law may say about the law at any single point in time" (Chayes, Ehrlich, and Lowenfeld, 1968: xv). ILP scholars thus were interested in the inner workings of the international law process, especially those most observable elements, including the formal institutions such as international organizations and state foreign ministries. A concern with policy improvement was not abandoned as one of the consequences of ILP analysis was purported to be improved efficiency in decision making. Nevertheless, variations in efficiency or effectiveness were neither modeled nor necessarily explained.

More recently, the notion of legal process has moved from lawmaking to the realm of implementation, particularly where the international has joined with the national to create something transnational (Koh, 2002). This approach has generated interest not only because the number of issues that have cross-border implications has increased, but also because of the dramatic growth in the number of actors at the local and national levels who now need to be involved to put international standards and obligations into effect. This orientation suggests that the focus of legal process be on "the pathways by which [the diverse sources of law] are internalized into our domestic legal systems" (Koh, 2002: 331).

From our vantage point, the policy and process approaches represent an advance over positivism in that they are concerned with more than identifying the content of the law. Most importantly, they recognize that law can and does change, and that the process of that change is impor tant. Nevertheless, they have a number of limitations at least for our purposes. First, the approaches in this section are still largely descriptive. Admittedly, they have a broader scope in going beyond the origins of the law to issues of implementation. Yet the focus is still on detailing how this process works rather than offering an explanatory framework. Second, and consistent with the first limitation, these related approaches are designed first and foremost to improve policymaking. With this charge, an emphasis on *causal* processes is shunted aside and evaluation rather than explanation is given the highest priority.

Legal pluralism

Related to some policy approaches, the legal pluralism school is based largely on the ideas of Robert Cover (see for example Cover, 1983), namely that norms are constructed through competition among various norm-generating communities. Adapted to international law by Berman (2005; 2007a; 2007b) and others, this approach focuses on the interaction of local, national, and international norms. That is, international norms are seen as the product of a political process similar to those described in models of American politics in which multiple actors compete to establish laws and the outcome is often a composite of the different preferences of key actors.

Yet, global pluralism adds another level, the international one, to the mix. As such, this framework deemphasizes the role of states in norm creation, or at the very least does not privilege them vis-à-vis other normative communities.

Global legal pluralists significantly create space for multiple actors, beyond states, to have influence in decision making, and while this may be obvious to some, it is not always reflected in other approaches. Nevertheless, this approach seems to confound norms and law, acknowledging the difference, but not necessarily distinguishing the different processes of creation and compliance that exist between the two. Furthermore, although there is reference to "spheres of complex, overlapping, legal authority" (Berman, 2007b: 320), there is no clear specification of the procedures that manage them, a necessary element to understanding how the multilevel legal systems work. Indeed, legal pluralism at best describes only situations in which such actions are governed by multiple legal regimes. Accordingly, this reflects only a subset of the international legal system.

Critical approaches

Growing out of post-modern and post-structuralist philosophy (e.g., Foucault) and interpretive approaches in other disciplines, critical legal studies have become increasingly prominent in law schools and in particular in the study of international law. Critical approaches, under which varieties of "New Stream" (Kennedy, 1997) or feminist theory (Charlesworth, Chinkin, and Wright, 1999) fall, begin with the premise, unlike earlier frameworks, that international law is not objective. Feminist and critical race scholars, for example, point out how the fundamental structure of the international system may bias it against particular issues or populations. Harking back to the early days of international law, other scholars that fall into this grouping are not content to see international law as primarily a manager of power relations, but seek to curb and to constrain such power. Works in this group critique the basic assumptions that international law is sterile and static, but also argue that it is fundamentally unjust and ineffective, at least with respect to the values espoused by these critics.

Many critical legal studies employ discourse analysis, focusing on the language, rhetoric, and debates surrounding international law (Kennedy, 1986). The purpose is to expose the alleged contradictions, hypocrisies, and failings of international law, often as means to criticize those in power and to highlight the plight of the dispossessed. As Koskienniemi (2001: 486) writes: "If law is only about what works, and pays no attention to the objectives for which it is used, then it will become only a smokescreen for effective power." For him, the purpose of law is to constrain power, not legitimize it (Koskienniemi, 2001: 493).

Whereas policy jurisprudence and earlier legal approaches saw international law as a unified system centered on some set of universal values, critical approaches emphasize the heterogeneity of the international system and specifically how cultural differences make it impossible for international law to reflect universal human values. Most scholars in this tradition argue that it is the dominance of certain structures (be they patriarchy or major powers) that suppresses those differences and such dominance is persistent over time. Even the forces of globalization are not said to alter the basic unjust legal system. For example, Sassen (2006: 17) writes that: "Globalization is a phenomenon of the combined capabilities or capacities of all that came before, states and international institutions. It is also the product of the global issues that are being pursued or performed within states. Nevertheless, the process is not an evolutionary one; rather, it is one where old processes may be constitutive of the new organizing logic" (see also Anghie, 2004 for similar arguments in the specific context of decolonization).

Among the most visible approaches within the critical category is feminist theory, recognizing that there are several variations and not all comport perfectly with critical assumptions (Charlesworth, Chinkin, and Wright, 1999). Still, feminist approaches primarily critique the present state of international law, but focus primarily on its intersection with gender. Much of this scholarship is dedicated to demonstrating how international law has excluded women or kept them in subservient roles. Thus, feminist scholars are as likely to discuss what law isn't ("silences") rather than what international law is. In some ways, the feminist scholars adopt a systemic approach in that patriarchic systems of governance and social relations are said to be responsible for the outcomes. As with other critical theory approaches, there is a normative element in that scholars are concerned with how to change the system in order to redress problems.

None of the critical approaches provides any building blocks for theoretical formulations on international law. Indeed, some proponents of this set of approaches would claim that such attempts are futile or only serve to perpetuate the injustices in the system. The normative element that was downplayed in the process and policy approaches is strongly evident here, both as the starting point of analysis and with respect to the prescribed changes to the international legal system.

Economic and rationalist approaches

If the previous approaches were those with strong normative components, approaches from a rational choice tradition are at the opposite end of the spectrum. In the study of law, the subfield of law and economics provided a new way to consider the origins and development of law. Using economic assumptions and models, scholars used market analyses to understand law (see Cooter and Ulen, 1987; Coase, 1960; Calabresi, 1961; Posner, 2007). Here international rules are understood as the product of the most efficient outcome in maximizing some value, most commonly economic wealth or some form of self-interest (see Goldsmith and Posner, 2005).

There are a variety of techniques that might be brought to bear from this perspective (a few are described in Dunoff and Trachtman, 1999; see also Trachtman, 2008). Some approaches (e.g., game theory) look at the strategic interaction of actors to understand how outcomes such as particular treaty configurations might be the result of bargaining processes. Others use ideas such as the reduction of transaction costs as rationale for why certain legal agreements – a trade treaty or a permanent legal forum – are made or created. Most rational choice models are applied to domestic legal systems, but a few deal with international law (e.g., Guzman, 2008). States are not necessarily exclusive actors in this approach, but they are important and generally are treated as unitary actors for analytical purposes.

International law as an efficient outcome privileges the interests of the actors in determining outcomes. Goldsmith and Posner (2005) posit that international law derives from state interests, especially those of leading states. Theirs is a simple, parsimonious framework in which to account for international law, although it does remain strictly state-centered and perhaps underspecified. The national interests model does provide a basis for understanding change in the law. Goldsmith and Posner illustrate that custom changes over time as a function of interest transformation, new payoff configurations, or power shifts; maximization of interests remains, but whose interests, what those are, and what new alternatives might exist account for alterations in international legal rules.

In a related scheme, scholars in the rational design tradition (Koremenos, Lipson, and Snidal, 2003; for a critique, see Duffield, 2003, Wendt, 2003,

Reus-Smit, 2004) also see the creation of international institutions as the product of a utility-maximizing process. Institutions are seen as rational, negotiated responses to problems: uncertainty, enforcement, and distribution problems to name a few. These scholars adopt an evolutionary perspective on change, noting that institutions are modified over time and actors choose to use certain institutions more often than others. They also note that institutions have some "stickiness" given that actors are risk adverse, institutions are resistant to change, and actors may not want to pay transaction costs associated with new or modified institutions. (The failed efforts to reform the United Nations Security Council with respect to voting power are a good example of this difficulty for institutions to change.) Of course, an institution in this conception is not always a legal one and it is not clear whether an exclusive focus on international legal entities would be as fruitful; as such, rational institutions have generated a series of heuristic propositions but not necessarily the hard empirical evidence to confirm their models.

The rational choice perspective is the one most aligned with a social scientific orientation toward international law. It does provide a basis for description, explanation, and prediction. Yet rational choice often wholly removes the normative component from the equation. Preferences are treated as exogenous and therefore are excluded from the explanation for why rules are created, except as some direct function of national interests. In that case, there is a limited difference with traditional realist thought as described below. Compliance also becomes reduced to efficiency and there is little room for explanations based on the "logic of appropriateness" (Wendt, 2003), that is, based on conceptions of right and wrong, rather than pure utility calculations. Rational choice perspectives also fail to account for a number of suboptimalities (described in the next chapter) in the international legal system. We borrow a number of ideas from this set of approaches, but we present a more sophisticated theory of international law and one with a less deterministic outlook.

General international relations theory

The study of international law is technically one of the subfields (along with, for example, political economy and war) of international relations scholarship. Yet historically, international legal scholarship has been concentrated in law schools and among practitioners. Social science analyses of international legal processes were rare, even as social science methods and models were applied to American public law with increasing frequency.

There are several reasons for this ignorance of international law in international relations (Diehl, 2001). Most notable was the dominance of realism as the guiding framework of international relationship scholarship. Most realist and neorealist conceptions of international relations treat international law as epiphenomenal. That is, international law is not an independent influence on state behavior, but rather only a reflection of the prevailing distribution of power and therefore reflective of the interests of leading states (see for example Mearsheimer, 1994–5). Thus, international law concerns as dependent variables became a largely uninteresting research agenda. Similarly, international legal factors as independent variables were irrelevant or at least weak surrogates for more central influences surrounding national interests. For theoretical and other reasons, there also were few data sets that incorporated international legal variables, thereby limiting the ability of those who wanted to include such factors in their multivariate models of international behavior.

International legal scholars have called on analysts to use international relations theory (Beck, 1996; Slaughter, 1997; Ku and Weiss, 1998; Simmons, 2001) for understanding international law. Abbott (1999) takes up that challenge and discusses the intersection of four international relations theories – realism, institutionalism, liberalism, and constructivism – and a particular problem in human rights laws. In most cases, such theoretical approaches offer important insights into individual phenomena in international law, ideas that could not be generated by the extant legal approaches reviewed above. Nevertheless, because these are theories for international relations writ large, they are less capable of addressing and accounting for processes unique to international law, and of course each has limitations even at the broader level of all international relations phenomena.

It is not so much that international relations theories can't provide valuable ideas and arguments about international law – indeed they can and they have. Rather, they are not substitutes for middle-level theory that incorporates the best of these approaches while remaining centered on international law as the focal point.

Some conclusions on extant frameworks

Although the preceding historical survey of international law's intellectual underpinnings recounts change and development, it also shows that until the 1990s writers remain focused on what the law *is* and what it *should* achieve rather than on understanding how it functions. The emphasis on the former has meant that scholars and practitioners have directed most of their attention to the legal output, rather than the processes that led to the formation of that output. In addition, understanding what the law is at a given point in time has led scholarship to have a static quality to it, largely ignoring how change has occurred over time and how it might change in the future. The latter emphasis on what the law should be produced scholarly writings with an overly prescriptive or normative bent. Accordingly, there has not been much concern with whether international law is effective in modifying actor behavior, much less with understanding the factors that influence that effectiveness or lack thereof. Combining these two effects, much of the debate then is over normative preferences (be they from critical theory, feminism, or liberalism); fundamentally, such debates are irreconcilable. Worse, there is no basis for assessing whether the prescriptions offered by one school of thought or another will even produce the desired outcomes.

The study of international law has evolved away from normative and static approaches in certain ways, but those elements still dominate contemporary study. Positivism, which developed over a broad period of time, moved some segments of legal study away from its origins in natural law and religion, attempting to eliminate the moral aspects of analysis. Yet even as positivism deemphasized normative elements, it reinforced the static aspects by focusing on the content of law and not how it was made. Even the policy or process approaches (e.g., New Haven School) did not provide the theoretical frameworks to model causal processes.

Several frameworks began to address explanations for the state of international law, but these usually did not do so in a social scientific fashion. Feminist and critical theorists accounted for law by reference to the interests of powerful actors. In a strange juxtaposition, so too did some realist and rational choice theorists, emphasizing the influence of major power interests in shaping the law, albeit without the pejorative attribution. In both cases, the explanations for international legal patterns are better seen as assumptions of the frameworks, rather than empirically based conclusions. Furthermore, in the case of critical and feminist approaches, they are merely precursors to critiques of the system and suggestions for change.

With some sporadic exceptions, past and current frameworks for studying international law lack several elements. First, they are incapable of accounting for change in the law, except in the most rudimentary way (e.g., the law changes when interests change). There are no dynamic elements to the way the law is formed and implemented, and therefore little sense of causal process. Second, there is little attention given to the effects of law – that is, what works and what does not. Only occasionally has scholarship (Chayes and Chayes, 1995) devoted some attention to compliance issues, but then often outside a broader theoretical framework.

In the remainder of this book, we first develop a new framework for international law that redresses these shortcomings. Then we propose a theory focused on accounting for change in international law. We consider both institutions and processes in describing and explaining that change. Our theory also provides a basis for understanding when and how international law is effective in modifying behavior. Finally, our approach also gives some insights into how international law might change in the future, not from a prescriptive perspective, but from an empirical one.

Overview of the remaining chapters

The remaining chapters of the book are dedicated to presenting our framework for analyzing international law, deriving models of change from that framework, and illustrating the resultant processes with cases and frequent examples from international law. Chapter 2 introduces and elucidates our framework. We begin by drawing a distinction between the operating and normative systems of international law. This is a fundamental distinction that sets the stage for the rest of our analysis. We then briefly trace the historical development in each of those systems, which is in the direction of expansion in both cases. The remainder of the chapter is devoted to presenting a theory of change in international law. The emphasis is on infrequent, rapid change in international legal systems, as opposed to conceptions that posit gradual or slow alterations in the law.

The framework and the resulting theory elucidated in Chapter 2 provide the theoretical lenses through which we can understand international law and its changes. The next three chapters address several of the dynamic processes that occur within international law and build specific models that derive from the overall theoretical framework. Chapter 3 explores, in a preliminary fashion, the conditions under which operating system changes occur in response to normative system changes. We present a number of theoretical arguments consistent with our framework on when and how adjustments occur. These processes are illustrated by reference to the norm to prohibit genocide and the subsequent steps taken by states to change international legal rules so that this norm influences state behavior.

Chapter 4 follows from the findings in Chapter 3 that not all normative system changes led to accompanying operating system changes, resulting in some sense in an "imbalance" between the systems. What happens when there is an imbalance between the operating and normative systems of international law? One obvious outcome is nothing; the imbalance remains, and the norms of the system are not given full effect. For example, human rights provisions abound, but can be widely ignored in the absence of enforcement mechanisms. In this chapter, however, we identify several other possibilities. Our contention is that adaptations occur that compensate for, or at least mitigate, the effects of the operating–normative systems imbalance. Specifically, we explore four kinds of extra-systemic (at least from the perspective of the international legal system) adaptations: (1) actions by NGOs and transnational networks; (2) internalization of international law; (3) domestic legal and political processes; and (4) "soft law" mechanisms. Our contention is that the international legal system is partly kept functioning by these actors and mechanisms, even though they technically fall outside the framework of the formal international legal system.

Chapter 5 reverses the causal arrow of Chapter 3 and examines how the operating system conditions the adoption of new rules in the normative system. This chapter identifies six different ways that extant provisions or changes in the international legal operating system condition international rule creation: (1) setting the parameters of acceptability; (2) clarifying credible commitment; (3) providing flexibility; (4) actor specification; (5) forum specification; and (6) direct law-making.

In Chapter 6, we summarize the results of our theoretical exercises and empirical applications. Yet this book is not merely intended to enlighten international legal scholarship. We also discuss the prospects and consequences of change in international law, with an eye to offering some policy-relevant advice to practitioners. Such prescriptions are not grounded in any particular normative viewpoint, but rather are dedicated to making international law more effective, whatever the normative values to be maximized. We conclude by highlighting three trends that represent challenges for international legal change in the future, specifically fragmentation, public–private partnerships, and the role of domestic institutions.

2

A new framework for analysis and a model for legal change

In the previous chapter, we reviewed a broad range of different frameworks over a long time period for the study of international law. Most, if not all, were static and descriptive, incapable of accounting for legal evolution and adaptation in the global arena. In this chapter, we develop our own theoretical framework for capturing this behavior and understanding international law. The heart of that approach is the bifurcation of international law into two subsystems, the operating and normative systems. The sections below describe those systems in detail as well as specifying their functions. We then briefly discuss how, and in what ways, those systems have expanded over the history of modern state relations, with an emphasis on more contemporary changes.

Our theoretical framework specifying the operating and normative systems permits us and others to address questions of change. Yet the framework itself, and indeed any framework *per se*, does not provide the answers to those questions. To achieve this, we must spell out a theory of how the two systems interact. Thus, the second part of the chapter provides the theoretical conception of how these systems influence each other. This is the basis for the precise elucidation of the conditions and forms associated with system changes that are examined in Chapters 3–5.

The operating system

The dual character of international law results from its Westphalian legacy in which law functions *between*, rather than *above*, states and in which the states carry out the legislative, judicial, and executive functions that in domestic legal systems are performed by separate institutions. The operating system of international law provides the platform and structure to govern and to manage international relations. The operating system manages international relations by setting out the consensus of its constituent actors (historically states have been the primary ones) on the distribution of authority and responsibilities for governance within the system. The capacity to govern can be expressed and recognized in terms of rights and duties. When international law provides a framework for international governance, it can function in similar ways internationally to how constitutions function domestically. For example, Dahl (1998) identified a number of items that constitutions generally specify and that comprise the capacity to govern, including several that are shared with international law: competent decisions, accountability, and ensuring stability to name a few.[1]

In order for international law's operating system to maintain vibrancy and resiliency, and to assure the stability necessary for orderly behavior, it must provide for a dynamic normative system that facilitates the competition of values, views, and actors. It does so by applying the functions as described above when including new actors, new issues, new structures, and new norms. Who, for example, are the authorized decision-makers in international law? Whose actions can bind not only the parties involved, but also others? How do we know that an authoritative decision has taken place? When does the resolution of a conflict or a dispute give rise to new law? These are among the key questions that the operating system answers.

The operating system may be associated with formal structures; the United Nations, the European Union, and other international organizations are often assigned lawmaking and monitoring roles by their members. Most obviously, the International Court of Justice is a formal institution with established rules and procedures for adjudicating disputes. Nevertheless, not all operating system elements are institutional, at least in a formal structural sense. For example, the Vienna Convention on the Law of Treaties entails no institutional structures, but does specify various operational rules (e.g., who can conclude treaties, what is a treaty, and rules on invalidity) about treaties and therefore the parameters of lawmaking.

The international legal operating system has a number of dimensions or components, typically covered in international law textbooks but largely unconnected with one another in those treatments: sources of law, actors/subjects, and jurisdiction, as well as courts and compliance

---

[1] We acknowledge that the analogy to constitutions is not perfect and constitutions perform other functions beyond those in the operating system of international law, including those that fall under the rubric of the normative system described below.

mechanisms. These general law topics often precede the discussion of more specific subject areas such as human rights, the use of force, trade, and the environment to name a few (see, for example, chapters 1–5 in Higgins, 1994, chapters 1–8 in Brierly, 1963, chapters 1–9 in Cassese, 1986, chapters 1–6 in Janis, 1988, and chapters 1–9 in Aust, 2005).

Sources of law

The most fundamental aspect of any legal system is in distinguishing between prescriptions and proscriptions that are legally binding and those that may only carry moral weight. Rules must exist for defining the process through which law is formed. In domestic legal systems, the creation of public law is often in the hands of legislative or administrative bodies. For example, when Parliaments pass legislation or ministries enact regulations, they are legally binding on the citizenry and other entities such as corporations. Many legal systems have clear and explicit "rules of recognition," or legal rules which in turn determine the norms that are legally binding and those that are not. The international legal operating system lacks an overall rule in this regard, leading Hart (1994) and others to say that international law is no more than a primitive legal system: "there is no basic rule providing general criteria of validity for the rules of international law" (Hart, 1994: 336). In our view, the operating system does provide some guidance as to what is legal and what is not, although there is no single unifying rule. The differences with municipal legal systems are several fold. First, there is no overarching rule in international law establishing the legal domain. Second, the rules that do exist are often less formal and decentralized and indeed subject to debate themselves. For example, there are some guidelines as to what constitutes customary law, but considerable disagreement, for instance, over whether unanimous resolutions of the United Nations constitute "instant custom" or not. Third, rules for change are less specific in international law than in municipal law, the latter of which often includes set processes for altering legal obligations.

Except for some organs of the European Union, the Inter-American system, and the Andean Court of Justice, international relations do not include a large set of formal lawmaking institutions. The sources of international law are largely positivist, emanating from the consent and actions of states. Thus, the operating system includes rules for treaty making and evolution (elucidated in the Vienna Convention on the Law of Treaties) as well as agreed-upon standards for the existence of customary law (e.g., use over time, acceptance of a legal obligation; see the classic *The Paquete Habana, The Lola*, 1900).[2] The operating system and its substrata also lay out how general principles, international organization resolutions, government documents, and judicial decisions figure into lawmaking.

The operating system also specifies a hierarchy of different legal sources. In national legal systems, written constitutional provisions trump national legislation or semi-autonomous regional entities can pass laws that supersede national standards. At present in international law, *jus cogens* (often referred to as "peremptory norms") is paramount, with no other source capable of modifying or superseding it and from which no derogation is permitted.[3] Thus, no international law permitting wars of aggression or slavery can be considered valid. Treaties generally fall next in the hierarchy above custom (although some exceptions exist in the case of obsolete treaties), and many other sources (e.g., national standards, guidelines, and court decisions) are not law themselves, but can serve to regulate international relations or provide supplemental sources as evidence of state behavior and custom.

Specifying where law comes from is the most fundamental component of the operating system, but once that is done, the next essential element is determining which actors have rights and obligations under those laws.

Actors/subjects

Another dimension of the operating system deals with actors, specifically determining which actors are eligible to have rights and obligations under the law. The operating system also determines how, and the degree to which, those actors may exercise those rights internationally. In many domestic legal systems, a variety of actors enjoy rights and obligations. Such actors include governments, corporations, individuals, groups, and other entities. In contrast, traditional international law has been largely

---

[2] United States Supreme Court, 1900, 175 US 677, 20 S. Ct. 290. Mr. Justice Gray: "By an ancient usage among civilized nations, beginning centuries ago, and gradually ripening into a rule of international law, coast fishing vessels, pursuing their vocation of catching and bringing in fresh fish, have been recognized as exempt, with their cargoes and crews, from capture as prize of war."

[3] Article 53 of the Vienna Convention on the Law of Treaties defines a peremptory norm of international law as one which is "accepted and recognized by the international community of States as a whole as a norm from which no derogation is permitted and which can be modified only by a subsequent norm of general international law having the same character." See Vienna Convention on the Law of Treaties, 23 May 1969, UNTS vol. 1155, p. 331.

confined to states. Historically, states had the exclusive right to create international law – both public and private. Furthermore, most of international law dealt with interactions between these states, and thus "subjects" of international law were narrowly drawn as well. As noted below, however, this has changed significantly over time.

Individuals in international law and foreign corporations enjoyed certain international legal protections, but those rights could only be asserted in international forums by their home states. For example, an alien person or a company incorporated in another state was entitled to protection by a host government. Yet if violations occurred, individuals and corporations would have to appeal to their home states before a diplomatic claim or international court proceeding could be launched on their behalf. Home states also have the legal right to settle claims on behalf of their nationals. For example, Libya received immunity from lawsuits in US courts filed by victims of the Pan Am 103 bombing as part of a settlement negotiated between the US and Libyan governments and subsequent act of Congress. In most domestic legal venues, foreign individuals and corporations have little or no standing to initiate claims and file legal suits directly absent any recognized legal status within that country. States can create obligations or rules that tie the hands of individuals, groups, and corporations holding the nationality of that state. For example, treaty provisions can become binding on multinational corporations through the doctrine of incorporation in most legal systems or via executing national legislation designed to give domestic effect to international legal obligations.

Thus, any legal operating system must specify its users. Those actors in the system are assigned roles in how the law is made, what rights are accorded to those actors, what obligations exist, and finally how, when, and by whom those rights and obligations can be exercised. A well-developed example of such actor specification can be found in the law of state responsibility. The centrality and complexity of this part of international law is perhaps reflected in the more than forty years (1955 to 2001) it took for the International Law Commission to complete the Draft Articles on Responsibility of States for Internationally Wrongful Acts (see UN GAOR, 1/55/10 (2001)). The Draft Articles cover such topics as identifying the elements of an internationally wrongful act, attribution of conduct, defining breach, discussing reparation for injury, and countermeasures. Although the Draft Articles do not cover the responsibility of international organizations and individuals, they reflect contemporary developments in international law by "mov[ing] away from a purely bilateral conception of responsibility to accommodate categories of general public interest (human rights, the environment, etc.)" (frontispiece, Crawford, 2002).

Jurisdiction

Any legal operating system must also have rules that define the rights of actors and institutions to deal with legal disputes and violations. This is conventionally covered under the topic of jurisdiction. Legal systems in a hierarchical arrangement (e.g., a federal system) will necessarily have to determine which legal issues and disputes are to be decided at which level of governance. With respect to international law, an important element is defining what problems or situations will be handled through national legal systems as opposed to international forums. Of course, there must be legal structures at both levels (see next section) to handle any assignment of disputes or concerns. Still, when such structures exist at multiple levels, the operating system can specify which takes precedence or which has the right to act first. For example, the jurisdiction of the International Criminal Court (ICC) is complementary to that exercised by national authorities (see Article 17, UN Doc. A/CONF.183/9).

The operating system also plays a role in sorting out disputes in which multiple states have jurisdiction over particular actions. Traditional international law has assigned great weight to the territorial and nationality principles. The former refers to the right of states to regulate actions within their territorial boundaries. Thus, most criminal and tort activity is regulated by national laws that assert jurisdiction based on the location of the offense. Jurisdiction could also be asserted based on the nationality of the alleged offender. States assert jurisdiction over their own nationals for certain violations even if the behavior occurred outside the borders of those states; treason is a notable example (see, for example, *Joyce* v. *Director of Public Prosecution* 1946). Both the nationality and territorial jurisdiction principles are consistent with "hard shell" views of state sovereignty. Extraterritorial jurisdiction, based on principles other than nationality, was rarely recognized in international law; most often this was granted on an *ad hoc* basis, for example through a status of forces agreement (SOFA) between a host state and a foreign state stationing troops on the host's soil. Recently, states have allowed national courts to handle claims involving terrorism, even if such acts occurred in other countries and were perpetrated by nationals of other states.

Historically, international law has permitted some issues to fall under the purview of all states, most often international crimes. For example, the Convention against Torture and Other Cruel, Inhuman or Degrading Treatment or Punishment (hereafter the Torture Convention) (1984) allows states to prosecute perpetrators in their custody, regardless of the location of the offense and the nationality of the perpetrator or victim, affirming the concept of "universal jurisdiction."

The specification of jurisdiction in the operating system serves several purposes. First, it reflects, and in turn reinforces, some broader elements of order in the international system, most traditionally the principle of state sovereignty. Second, and equally important, it provides regular procedures and predictability for actors in the system, who then know when and where legal disputes will be handled. The absence of such order would lead some violations never to be punished while others would be subject to multiple and perhaps conflicting actions by different states and venues. It also helps to ensure that remedies will be provided where harm or injury has occurred (see Shelton, 2006). Smooth operation or efficiency is thus served by specifying the domains of responsibility in international law.

Courts and compliance institutions

Once operating systems specify the sources of law, the players in the system, and the rules on jurisdiction over those actors and laws, there must be institutions and processes under which legal disputes might be heard or decisions might be enforced. In domestic legal systems and with respect to court systems, there is often an array of judicial institutions of which parties can avail themselves, and it is usually compulsory to do so once one party has appealed to a court for relief. In the international arena, permanent adjudicatory structures have historically been under-developed. Still, the Statute of the International Court of Justice provides for the creation of the institution, sets general rules of decision making, identifies the processes and scope under which cases are heard, specifies the composition of the court, and details decision-making procedures (to name but a few elements). There are also a variety of regional legal forums as well as those specific to a particular issue area, such as the Dispute Settlement Body associated with the World Trade Organization. The international legal operating system has also accommodated arbitration panels and *ad hoc* claims tribunals, such as the Iran–US Claims Tribunal created in 1981.

Beyond providing forums for dispute resolution, a legal operating system must provide mechanisms for ensuring compliance with the rulings from institutions and indeed the law in general. In domestic legal systems, there is a variety of direct (e.g., police authorities) and indirect (e.g., socialization) mechanisms associated with enforcement and compliance. The international legal operating system has tradition-ally been weak with respect to formal, enforcement mechanisms; no international police force or higher government authority is available, as at best the UN Security Council may authorize certain enforcement actions in limited areas such as illegal invasions. The operating system provides more extensive, but still limited, methods for monitoring com-pliance, but these can be narrowly drawn, such as the inspection activities carried out by the International Atomic Energy Agency in the area of nuclear non-proliferation (see www.iaea.org).

The international legal operating system has instead relied extensively on informal instruments such as self-interest, reciprocity, habit, and reputational concerns (Henkin, 1968) to induce compliance. That is, actors receive benefits from following the law, such as increased safety from following rules on nuclear waste disposal. They also comply with laws because the operating system allows victims of violations to with-draw from treaties or otherwise not comply themselves, imposing poten-tial costs on the original violator; for example, both sides may be worse off when there are reciprocal violations of trade treaties that reduce tariffs. International law compliance also becomes habitual when provi-sions become embedded in national practice, as in the case of customary law requirements for running lights on ships (see Convention on the International Regulations for Preventing Collisions at Sea (1972)). Finally, states are also concerned with their reputation (what has been called "diffuse reciprocity" – Keohane, 1986) and violations may affect the ability of that nation to conclude future agreements with other parties, who refrain from cooperation because of the unreliability of the violating state. Such informal mechanisms are as much a part of system operations as more formal institutions.

Comparisons with related ideas

Our conception of an operating system clearly overlaps with some prior formulations, but differs in some fundamental ways. Regime theory (Krasner, 1983; Hasenclever, Mayer, and Rittberger, 1997) refers to decision-making procedures as practices for making and implementing collective choice, similar to "regulative norms" (Barnett, 1995), which lessen transaction costs of collective action. Although these may be encompassed by the international law operating system, our conception of the latter is broader. The operating system is not necessarily issue specific (some elements are, others are not), but may deal equally well (or poorly) with multiple issues – note that the International Court of Justice may adjudicate disputes involving airspace as well as war crimes. Regime decision-making procedures are usually conceptualized as issue specific (e.g., on international whaling) and are also thought to reflect norms, rules, and principles without much independent standing.

Ellickson (1991) identified a series of "rules" that govern social interaction and included among them are a number that fall under the rubric of our operating system. These include *procedural* rules that provide the framework for interaction between actors as well as *remedial* rules that deal with how disputes might be resolved. Nevertheless, Ellickson was largely concerned with rules outside the context of law (hence the title of his book *Order Without Law*), and there are a number of differences between purely social norms and those that are endowed with a legal character (see also how Sandholtz and Sweet's 2004 definition of institutions as rules fails to make this distinction). Guzman (2008) refers to the *form* of agreements, which includes enforcement mechanisms; yet he also includes in this category other elements outside of our operating system conception, such as the degree to which states have pledged to comply.

Perhaps most famously, Hart (1994 – originally published in 1961) developed the notion of "secondary rules" to refer to the ways in which primary rules might be "conclusively ascertained, introduced, eliminated, varied, and the fact of their violation conclusively determined" (1994: 94). This comports in many ways with our conception of an international legal operating system. Yet Hart views secondary rules (his choice of the term "secondary" is illuminating) as "parasitic" (1994: 81) to the primary ones. This suggests that secondary rules follow in time the development of primary rules, especially in primitive legal systems (to which international law is sometimes compared). Furthermore, secondary rules are believed to service normative ones, solving the problems of "uncertainty," "stasis," and "inefficiency" inherently found with normative rules.

Most relevant for our purposes is the chapter-long discussion Hart (1994) gives to international law, concluding that although international law had some characteristics of municipal law, it was principally a form of social rule. He notes that international law (1) lacks a legislative component to make law, (2) operates in a system in which courts require the consent of participants, and (3) lacks a central effective system of sanctions for violators. His principal objection to international law as a legal system was that the "general character" of the rules in international law is not clear, specifically that it lacks a rule of recognition. Hart accepted the possibility that international law could evolve to the point where "[a] basic rule of recognition could then be formulated which would represent an actual feature of the system and would be more than an empty restatement of the fact that a set of rules are in fact observed by states" (1994: 231).

Our conception of an international legal operating system is somewhat different. For us, the operating system is often independent of any one norm or regime, and therefore is greater than the sum of any parts derived from individual norms and regimes. The operating system in many cases, past its origin point, may precede the development of parts of the normative system, rather than merely reacting to it. In this conception, the operating system is not merely a maid servant to the normative system, but the former can actually shape the development of the latter; this is consistent with classic international relations theory in which the structure or rules of the international system can affect behavioral interactions and outcomes (Bull, 1977; Waltz, 1979). For example, established rules on jurisdiction may restrict the development of new normative rules on what kinds of behaviors might be labeled as international crimes (see Chapter 5).

Neither is the operating system as reflective of the normative system as Hart implies it is. The operating system will develop some of its configurations autonomously from specific norms, thereby serving political as well as legal needs (e.g., the creation of an international organization that also performs monitoring functions). In the relatively anarchic world of international relations, we argue that this is more likely than in the domestic legal systems on which Hart primarily based his analysis. Indeed, this could explain why in many cases the operating system for international law is far more developed than its normative counterpart; for example, we have extensive rules and agreements on treaties, but relatively few dealing with the use of force. As discussed above, that international law lacks a unifying rule of recognition only means that it is not identical with municipal systems. The international law operating system includes many rules for identifying law, albeit more diffuse and imprecise than in national legal systems.

The expansion of the operating system

The development of the operating system in all of the areas enumerated above has been towards expansion – in the number of actors, in the forms of decision making, and in the forums and modes of implementation. Although international law remains principally a body of rules and practices to regulate state behavior in the conduct of interstate relations, much of international law now also regulates the conduct of governments and the behavior of individuals within states and addresses issues that require ongoing transnational cooperation. As a result, participants in the international legal process today include over 190 states and governments, international institutions created by states, and elements of the private sector – multinational corporations and financial institutions, networks of individuals, and non-governmental organizations. Not all participants carry the same level of authority in the legal process, but are recognized either in fact or in practice as playing a role in identifying and promoting particular values (Higgins, 1994). The partnership struck between non-governmental organizations and the government of Canada to promote a convention that bans the use of anti-personnel landmines is an example of the collaboration that various actors have undertaken in the international legal process, thereby giving new actors a role in the lawmaking and subsequent implementation process (Price, 1998).

Perhaps the greatest change in the expansion of actors in lawmaking is associated with the work of international organizations through their regular program of meetings, recognized structures, and experienced staff. The United Nations system, for example, has become a major generator of norms because of its experience in multilateral treaty-making and in the tremendous expertise built up in its Secretariat staff. With hindsight, it seems natural that the UN would have such influence, but the potential of norm-generation through regulation or administrative practice was perhaps not as well understood at the time of the UN's founding (see Slaughter, 1993). If the germ of such practice was present in the formation of the "technical unions" in the early twentieth century, advances in technology and the rapid increase in the number of issues requiring global solutions in the late twentieth century created both the need and the conditions for the UN to respond, and to do so in an increasingly legal way (see Goldstein, Kahler, Keohane, and Slaughter, 2000). The United Nations Charter provided the organization with a lawmaking function in Article 13 through the International Law Commission (ILC) that was set up for the codification and progressive development of international law. Although the ILC has certainly contributed to both the codification and progressive development of international law, in many respects, the lawmaking functions of other organs or agencies in the UN system have been the more significant. Notable developments have occurred in the internal law of international organizations, their work interpreting treaties and reports, issuing guidelines, and in providing the structural and institutional capacities to support multilateral discussions and negotiations to the point where one can assert process-based legitimacy (see Alvarez, 2005; Franck, 1990; Charney, 1993; and Claude, 1966).

A variety of actors have acquired legal personality under the operating system. Much of this is as subjects of international regulation. The elucidation and expansion of war crimes, for example, has assigned legal obligations to individuals (see Article 6, Charter of the International Military Tribunal, 1945). The same might be said for obligations assigned to multinational corporations, such as employment practices, worker safety, anti-corruption practices, environmental protection, and food safety, although the enforcement of such regulations might still be in the hands of host states or states of incorporation. The United States, for example, extends labor and other standards to corporate operations outside the US (Westfield, 2001–2).

Actors beyond states have also acquired new rights. For example, indigenous groups under the UN Declaration on the Rights of Indigenous Peoples are granted some international protections. The most notable expansions have been in the area of individual rights. Human rights law is an example of the normative system regulating behavior within states. Such human rights law, however, configures elements of the operating system in that the human rights protections granted convey legal personality on individuals, thereby rendering them capable of holding or exercising legal rights. Activities such as the follow-up conferences to the Helsinki Accords or the periodic meetings of the parties to the Framework Convention on Climate Change are specific examples in which operating system structures and processes have created opportunities for participation by non-state actors and individuals.

As actors have acquired additional rights under law, so too has there been an expansion of their abilities to exercise those rights in international forums independent of their home states. In selected areas, and often regionally specified, actors may press claims in international arenas. For example, individuals may bring complaints against their home governments in the Inter-American Human Rights Commission for such violations. In the European Union system, both individuals and corporations have legal standing before the European Court of Justice. Still, states retain most of the authority to press claims and assert rights, even if the subjects are individuals or groups within their borders.

There has also been an expansion in the forms of law. This has led to thinking about international rules as a continuum "ranging from the traditional international legal forms to 'soft law' instruments" (Chinkin, 1989; see also Weil, 1983), the latter of which function in ways similar to conventional international rules. This continuum includes resolutions of the United Nations General Assembly, standards of private organizations such as the International Standards Organization, as well as codes of conduct developed in international organizations (Charney, 1993). An example is the adoption in 1985 by the Food and Agriculture Organization of the Codex Alimentarius, a code of conduct on the distribution and use of pesticides. The concept of a continuum is useful because these modes are likely not to operate in isolation, but rather to interact with and build on each other (see Shelton, 2000). This is the case even within more traditional forms of international lawmaking in which customary practice and conventions work in tandem to regulate state behavior. The law applicable to the continental shelf is an example of this as customary practice became codified in a subsequent convention (see Part VI of the Third Convention on the Law of the Sea).

Custom was once the most common source of international law, but its lengthy developmental process led treaties to assume the primary role in positive international law. Yet the operating system rules have evolved substantially from standard requirements laid out in *The Paquete Habana, The Lola* (1900), specifically with respect to time. Whereas traditional custom required extensive practice over many years (the exact time varied according to the practice), now custom might develop more quickly and merely with the consensus of states rather than actual practice (Roberts, 2001). The consequence is that customary law has undergone a slight revival even as treaty making remains on center stage. In part, this is because of the expansion in the number of states and areas requiring international coordination, but the operating system has also expanded to encompass multilateral negotiation forums, often under the auspices of international organizations, to facilitate the development of law. The several UN Conferences on the Law of the Sea (1956, 1960, and 1973) are among the more prominent examples.

The forums and modes for implementation have also expanded. International law has developed vigorously beyond the concept of *dédoublement fonctionnel* (Scelle, 1932). With no separate institutions available to implement international law, this was a reasonable approach. Although international law still relies on domestic legal and political structures for implementation (see Chapter 4), the international community has also created new international institutions and recognized transnational legal processes that have over time become recognized forums in which to engage in decision making, interpretation, and recently even the prosecution of individuals on the basis of violations of international law (see Ku and Borgen, 2000).

Not only do representatives of states continue to meet to make law, but they also meet routinely in international settings to ensure its implementation and compliance (e.g., meetings of United Nations organs or the CSCE follow-up meetings after the Helsinki Accords in 1975). After World War II, states met periodically in GATT (General Agreement on Tariffs and Trade) "rounds" in which large numbers of states worked to construct economic agreements. These have become regularized under the World Trade Organization.[4] Another well-known example of ongoing meeting and agreement is the 1992 United Nations Framework Convention on Climate Change that provides for an annual meeting of the Conference of the Parties (COP).[5]

There has also been an expansion in the number of international tribunals (see Charney, 1999). In the early twentieth century, states had few choices beyond the Permanent Court of International Justice and the Permanent Court of Arbitration. Now, there are many other institutions available, most notably at the regional level; the European Court of Justice and the Inter-American Court of Human Rights are examples. Although these courts have different state memberships and jurisdictions, many provide states (and other actors) with an opportunity to press a claim and to seek remedy outside of an exclusively national jurisdiction. In addition, more formal *ad hoc* institutions have been created for specific purposes, such as the US–Iran Tribunal, created in 1981 to sort out competing claims following the Iranian Revolution in 1979 and still in existence as of this writing.[6] Various, and narrowly drawn, war crimes tribunals (e.g. for the former Yugoslavia and Rwanda to name two) are part of this trend as well. The successful efforts to set up a permanent international criminal court (International Criminal Court – ICC) was a major change in this process by adding a new, permanent institution to the operating system in order to address new problem areas for international law – the international legal and political accountability of individuals whose actions constitute international crimes and national legal systems failing to prosecute them.

The jurisdiction elements of the operating system have involved more of a reconfiguration of responsibilities than an expansion *per se*, largely because of the uniqueness of this component. More aspects of behavior have fallen under international purview, with torture and genocide now

---

[4] See www.wto.org for general information on issues covered by the negotiating rounds since 1947.
[5] See unfccc.int/meetings/.   [6] See www.iusct.org.

joining traditional crimes such as slavery and piracy under universal jurisdiction provisions. Still, this dimension of the operating system has perhaps been less elastic than others. Even with more behavior under international scrutiny, especially in the human rights area, international courts and bodies often have jurisdiction in a secondary fashion, following the unwillingness or deferral of national authorities to exercise jurisdiction. For example, the International Criminal Court has only complementary jurisdiction, being unable to take on a case if national authorities are investigating or have taken legal action against a defendant.

At the turn of the twentieth century, the international legal operating system was highly state-centric with little formal apparatus with which to monitor compliance and resolve disputes. In this sense, the operating system was heavily dependent on the diplomatic processes of major states. A century later, the operating system is more diffuse in the powers it allocates to actors, and there has been a quantum increase in the forums and institutions that support it. This expansion has been driven by a number of factors, including greater formalization in international law and the increase in the multiplicity of actors and states involved. Yet one might also refer to a similar expansion in the normative system, which, as we note later, is a source for some of the new rules for the operating system.

The normative system

The second system of international law is the normative one. We choose the word normative to describe the directive aspects of international law because this area of law functions to create norms out of particular values or policies. Using a different set of analogies, we could imagine *normative* processes as quasi-legislative in character by mandating particular values and directing specific changes in state and other actors' behaviors. We use the term norms to be largely synonymous with binding rules and law in the rest of this book. These are the specific prescriptions (e.g., "due diligence" in international environmental law) and proscriptions (e.g., ban on civilian targets during war) that are most associated with international law.

In defining the normative system, the participants in the international legal process engage in a political and legislative exercise that defines the substance and scope of the law. Normative change may occur with evolution of customary practices, a traditional source of international law. Yet in recent historical periods, normative change has been precipitated by new treaties (e.g., the Nuclear Non-Proliferation Treaty) or by a series of actions by international organizations (e.g., UNSCOM activities in Iraq).[7] Nevertheless, the establishment of international legal norms still is less precise and structured than in domestic legal systems where formal deliberative bodies enact legislation. Legal norms in the domestic arena are almost always written and the product of a clear lawmaking process. Nevertheless, the results are equally binding across systems.

In contrast to the general terms associated with topics of the operating system (e.g., jurisdiction or actors), the topics of the normative system are issue specific, and many components of the system refer to sub-topics within issue areas (e.g., status of women within the broader topic area of human rights). Thus, the international system has a series of rules on the release of environmentally harmful gases (see Kyoto Protocol), the treatment of prisoners of war (see the various Geneva Conventions), the breadth of territorial waters (see the Law of the Sea Convention), and even on such mundane topics as space debris (see Convention on International Liability for Damage Caused by Space Debris). In domestic legal systems, the configuration of issue areas and specific norms would look quite different. Most systems have specific rules on taxes, health care, and individual freedoms as well as less important topics such as speed limits for automobiles and designated animals as national symbols.

In summary, the normative system of international law defines the acceptable standards for behavior in the international system. These are issue-specific prescriptions and proscriptions. Although we speak of the normative system as a whole, it is empirically more atomized with different issue areas exhibiting stronger or weaker regulation of international behavior, and the development of law in a given issue area often proceeds largely independent of other areas.

Comparison with related ideas

References to the term "norms" abound in the study of international relations, and it is not always clear what is conveyed by a particular construction. In the regimes literature (Krasner, 1983), norms and principles (e.g., orthodox versus embedded liberalism in trade) are broader philosophies of how states and other actors should behave. Although they tend to be issue specific (e.g., trade, human rights), regime norms

[7] We do, of course, recognize that even with the trend toward treaties as the primary source of new international law, many treaties in the last several decades have largely codified existing customary practice (e.g., significant portions of the Law of the Sea Conventions).

are not generally defined at the micro-level (e.g., precise changes in rules governing certain human rights violations). In this sense, they are similar to what Barnett (1995) refers to as "constitutive norms." Our conception of norms is, on the one hand, narrower and more precise. We focus on normative elements that have a legally binding character, analogous to the idea of rules in the regime literature. Because we are interested in the international legal system, our conception of the normative system does not include acts of "comity" or so-called "soft law," which might be appropriate subjects for a broader inquiry into international norms. Indeed, many scholarly analyses, especially those with a constructivist orientation, are unclear about what distinguishes the legal realm from social norms (Reus-Smit, 2004). On the other hand, we have a deeper conception of norms that goes beyond broad general principles to include specific elements about behavior. That is, our normative system is concerned with particular prescriptions and proscriptions, such as limitations on child labor (see chapters 2–11 of Sandholtz and Stiles, 2009 for extended discussions of ten other examples).

Our conception of a normative system is similar to what Hart (1994) defines as primary rules that impose duties on actors to perform or abstain from actions (see also Ellickson, 1991 on *substantive rules* and Guzman, 2008 on *substance*), but there is an important difference. Hart sees primary rules as the basic building blocks of a legal system, logically and naturally coming before the development of what we define as the operating system components. For Hart, a primitive legal system can be one with developed rules, but without substantial structures to interpret or enforce those rules. We see a more developed international legal system in which norms may exist without specific reference to the operating system, but yet cannot function without using the operating system's functions and capacities. Nevertheless, the normative system may remain somewhat autonomous from the operating system and may even lag behind in its development.

The evolution of the normative system

The normative system of international law has undergone explosive growth, in scope and specificity, over the past half-century, although it remains underdeveloped relative to its domestic counterparts. The most obvious indicator of such growth is in the number of treaties, most of which primarily contain normative provisions. Starting from 1500 to 1900, there were fewer than 500 multilateral treaties and supplementary instruments. In the twentieth century alone, there were over 5,000 such agreements, with the majority appearing since 1960 (Gamble, 2006).

Even though there has been an explosion of new rules in the normative system, there are tremendous differences across individual issue areas. Such differences are not a function of the length of time that a given issue has been on the international agenda, as normative rule making does not develop in a linear progression.

Many issue areas have long been on the international law agenda. Proscriptions on the use of military force have their roots in natural law and early Christian teachings on just war. Yet there has been comparatively little expansion in this area relative to others. The norm of self-defense finds its roots in natural law and is of long-standing import, now reflected in the UN Charter. Attempts to modify it to include preemptive action, in the form of the so-called Bush doctrine of preemption, have failed to find consensus and have served only to reaffirm the principles laid out in *The Caroline Incident* (1837)[8] almost two centuries ago (see Reisman and Armstrong, 2006 and Taft and Buchwald, 2003). In the area of use of force, *jus in bello* (regulating the conduct of war) remains far more developed than *jus ad bellum* (regulating the decision to use military force). Even so, the latter still relies extensively on rules drawn up early in the twentieth century and immediately following World War II.

The law of the sea has also long been a part of the international normative system. Many normative rules concerning the law of the sea (e.g., right of innocent passage) also have long pedigrees in customary practice. Many of the elements of the Third Law of the Sea Convention (UNCLOS III), which entered into force in 1994, reflect traditional concerns, such as the breadth of territorial waters and fishing rights, and thereby reflect no expansion in scope even as they include changes in specific regulations. Yet, that agreement also expands the normative reach of the legal system by creating rules on new subjects (e.g., seabed mining) or problems not envisioned or recognized earlier. UNCLOS III also is indicative of greater depth in the normative system, as the level of specificity in the law has increased dramatically even when the purview of the subject matter has not.

Some current issue areas of international legal concern, most notably with respect to human rights and environmental protection, have developed

---

[8] This classic formulation provided by US Secretary of State Daniel Webster noted that self-defense was legitimate when there was "a necessity of self-defense, instant, overwhelming, leaving no choice of means, and no moment for deliberation." Furthermore, the response could not be excessive or unreasonable (see Jennings, 1938).

almost exclusively over the past sixty years. This is part of a broader trend of the normative system carving out new areas for regulation of behavior. In the international environmental area, legal norms have sought to regulate a wider range of behaviors. Early international law on the environment focused on the straightforward concerns of riparian states. More recently, normative rules have been drafted on such concerns as ozone depletion, water pollution, endangered species, and other problems.

There has been perhaps no greater expansion in the normative system than with respect to human rights. A century ago, this would not have been a recognized subfield of international law, and indeed human rights law was limited in legal contexts. Yet the international community has codified or developed new standards of behavior for states and others vis-à-vis individuals and groups as subjects of international law. These include protections for women, children, indigenous peoples, and laborers to name but a few. Yet, the normative content of human rights is unsettled with respect to many components (see, for example, Henkin and Hargrove, 1994). The United States, for example, promotes items included in the International Covenant on Civil and Political Rights, but eschews involvement with the International Covenant on Economic and Social Rights. The place of democracy in the panoply of rights is not automatically accepted, with many differences across regions in particular. (For example, this norm is accepted in the Western Hemisphere and in Europe (see Inter-American Democratic Charter, 2001 and the Warsaw Declaration Towards a Community of Democracies, 2000), but not in the Middle East. Debates surrounding the universal versus culture-based character of human rights are another indication that the normative content of international human rights law is still under development.

Some notes on issue-specific and regional subsystems

In the above discussion, we have implicitly assumed that there are single operating and normative systems applying to all states. In reality, this needs some qualification. First, some elements of the operating system are highly issue specific, such that they are applicable only to particular elements of the normative system. For example, provisions for the inspection of nuclear facilities by the International Atomic Energy Agency (IAEA) relate only to nuclear proliferation. Similarly, WTO dispute resolution mechanisms are unique to trade, although they cover a broad scope of concerns in the trade area. Nevertheless, it would be a mistake to classify these subsystems as independent of the broader operating system. In most cases, there are general operating system provisions that exist for that same normative area, and thus the system is not characterized by islands of specific operating system elements. One has to look at the system as a whole to see the interconnected webs of the specific and the general to understand the operating system components. In addition, what may start out as issue-specific operating system provisions may expand as the same procedures are used for new or different problems (Guzman, 2008), within or outside the given normative area; this is called "conversion" in the comparative study of national institutions (see Thelen, 2006). Furthermore, similar procedures are adopted in other normative areas, based on the precedents established in the original issue area. With respect to the latter, it is not surprising that actors look to successful procedures in creating new pieces of the operating system. The wide use of consensus as a decision-making mechanism in international negotiations is such an example.

In the last several decades, elements of coherent legal systems on a regional level have developed, especially in Europe. For example, the European Union has its own laws (directives) superseding the national laws of member states, covering a wide range of normative areas (e.g., agriculture, transportation) as well as incorporating certain elements of its own operating system, such as the European Parliament to make laws and the European Court of Justice to adjudicate disputes. Other regions are less developed than Europe, although they may have certain structures and norms unique to the region, especially as part of trade agreements.

How do these "subsystems" interact with the global systems described above? In our conception, such subunits share many of the characteristics of the operating and normative systems at the international level. In most cases, they perform many of the same functions, albeit at different levels. Thus, they are best considered as additional layers of legal operating and normative systems rather than something *sui generis*. As with the issue-specific elements of the legal system, regional components supplement and interact with operating and normative elements at the global level. A full consideration of these linkages is beyond the scope of this study. We do, however, make occasional reference to regional system components when they provide good illustrations of the arguments that we advance in subsequent chapters.

The specification of the operating and normative systems of international law provides a conceptual basis for analyzing international law. Yet at this stage, we have only provided a descriptive or classification scheme for elements of international law. Although our approach is an advance over previous conceptions, it alone does not provide a theoretical basis for understanding the dynamics of international law. For that, we need to provide a theory that incorporates the normative and operating systems, but also specifies how they interact and the conditions for change therein. In the next sections, we offer such a formulation.

Systems theory

We have used the terms operating and normative *systems* and we take that descriptor seriously in modeling how these systems interact. The study of systems dominated much of international relations during the 1950s and 1960s (e.g., Kaplan, 1957). Most of that and subsequent work concerned the stability of different systems (for example, the debate over bipolarity versus multipolarity: Waltz, 1964; Deutsch and Singer, 1964) or how the international system constrained the actors or agents in it (e.g., the so-called agent–structure debate; see Dessler, 1989). There was also an interdisciplinary movement toward the development of general systems theory (e.g., Lazlo, 1983), in which it was thought similar processes could be identified across physical, biological, and social systems. Most of these efforts have atrophied, and system-level analysis has focused increasingly on international norms (those of a non-legal character) or movements (e.g., democratization). Nevertheless, there are a number of useful insights from those literatures that help us understand the central questions in this book.

Our focus here is not on the international system writ large, often defined in terms of power relationships. Rather, we are concerned with the international legal system, a segment of the international political system as a whole. Specifically, we are interested in the interactive elements of the two subsystems – operating and normative – that compose the legal system as a whole. In this sense, we are more concerned with subsystem interaction (interaction within a broader system) than we are about a single international system exerting influence on its agents.

In noting this relationship, we begin with a general overview of system types and some of their processes that are postulated to operate within the international legal systems.

Some general system types

There are a number of system types (for a taxonomy, see Boulding, 1985) that might be applied to a wide variety of social, biological, political, communication, and economic processes. International law is frequently described as a primitive system, and accordingly many of the conceptions of it tend to be at the lower end of the complexity scale. Indeed, a legal system might need to limit its complexity in order to ensure predictability (Miller and Page, 2007), an essential feature for legal relationships between actors.

To the extent that authors even think in these terms, international law is described largely as a mechanistic system. Such systems have relatively low complexity and are guided by simple parameters (Boulding, 1985). Effects are generally unchanging and unidirectional. In international law schema, this is the way that the intersection of the operating and normative systems is often described. The mechanistic element is evident from the way that the operating system is supposed to function. In various conceptions, the operating system of international law provides the signals and commands that make multiple functions and modes possible, and when functioning often requires little conscious effort. Higgins (1994) describes this as "humdrum stuff": "The role of law is to provide an operational system for securing values that we all desire – security, freedom, the provision of sufficient material goods" (Higgins, 1994: 1). In this view, the operating system is merely composed of the hidden cogs that allow the normative system to run.

Hart (1994) has similar ideas about the two systems. As noted above, he divides legal systems into two components, "primary" and "secondary" rules, roughly corresponding to our normative and operating systems respectively. The creation of primary rules is largely exogenous in his conception. The mechanistic aspects are contained in the way that secondary rules are created in response to primary rules. Secondary rules, operating system components in our nomenclature, are largely uninteresting from Hart's perspective. They always follow sequentially from primary rules, and primary rules have a causal influence on them. That is, secondary rules merely service primary rules and therefore exercise no independent influence.

Hart (1994) and similar notions of legal systems share several ideas or implicit assumptions. First, they effectively assume that the operating system is not independent of the normative system. All aspects of the operating system are said to be tied to specific aspects of the normative system in order to give the latter effect. Second, the causal relationship between the two systems is unidirectional; the normative system always leads to the accompanying changes in the operating system. The reverse is not conceivable under their framework. Third, in a mechanistic fashion, changes in the normative system always produce accompanying alterations in the operating system.

We find that these conceptions do not fully capture how the two systems interact and offer a different formulation. First, we recognize a separate and interactive relationship between the normative and operating systems. Indeed, the following chapters are dedicated to exploring and explaining such interaction. Yet we also carve out space for at least the partial autonomy of the two systems. That is, normative system provisions can exist without accompanying operating system provisions. For example, the international community might create human rights provisions, such as expanding the rights of women or children, without the accompanying mechanisms to monitor or enforce them. Similarly, operating system components can be generic and therefore not specific to normative provisions. Indeed, aspects of the operating system exist (e.g., arbitration provisions) that are underutilized (see the discussion below on balance). Within our framework then, questions about *when* and *how* the two systems interact to prompt changes in one another (questions addressed in Chapters 3 and 5) might be posed. Such questions are largely uninteresting if one assumes a mechanistic position on the international legal system; changes in the operating system flow directly and automatically from the normative system. We also take issue with the assumption that the normative system drives the operating system. Our conception assumes a two-way causal relationship, although not necessarily one of symmetrical strength.

Clearly, the operating system is influenced by the normative system and the relationship is positive. This is consistent with mechanistic conceptions. Yet, as we note, below, the causal relationship is neither automatic nor does it produce optimal outcomes. In addition, even when system change does occur, it may produce unintended consequences (Jervis, 1997). Consistent with that, and more unconventional, is the notion that the operating system can influence the normative system. Reversing the causal arrow, we do not expect to find similarly strong relationships. Generally, the specific content of treaties, especially their normative prescriptions and proscriptions, will not be a function of the operating system provisions, but rather a series of other factors such as power and national interests. Furthermore, we recognize that such interests and other factors may be responsible for determining *both* the operating and normative systems. Nevertheless, provisions of the two systems are usually created separately and at different times and to that extent the operating system may still have lagged and indirect effects (Jervis, 1997) on the normative system even as interests and other factors have changed over time.

Most other types of systems do not fit the international legal system well. This is largely because the complexity of such systems is well beyond the limited character of the international legal system (see Miller and Page, 2007). At the same time, aspects of complex adaptive systems that examine the aggregated outcomes of actor interactions or emergent properties from those actions might be relevant for understanding the capacity generated by interactions between international law's operating and normative systems. Our conception of the operating and normative systems does not view components as solely derivative of actor interactions, and systems in our conception have autonomy and some independent influence on agent behavior.

In population or demographic systems (Boulding, 1985), system change is largely a function of extant system properties, giving such systems their own internal dynamic. International law is clearly not a system that is exclusively conditioned by, or responds to, only its current components. Similarly, international law does not fit well with the conception of law as an autopoietic system (Teubner, 1988; 1993; Luhmann, 2004). Such a system produces and reproduces its own elements by the interaction of those elements, with rules of recognition at the core (Teubner, 1988). Although autopoietic approaches acknowledge that legal systems are open to the environment and may intersect with other systems, they place much more emphasis on internal processes and system autonomy than is warranted for international law. Indeed, it is not surprising that the major works on autopoietic legal systems make no reference to international law.

International law as interconnected evolutionary systems

Rather than a mechanistic system in which the operating system follows from the normative one, we see international law as an evolutionary system (see Rottleuthner, 1988 on the use of biological metaphors in the study of law). In international legal terms, this means that the system does not automatically change through immutable rules or processes (as may be the case with certain laws of physics), but rather is subject to change in its parameters. Evolutionary systems have a tendency toward greater complexity (Boulding, 1985) over time, and this fits with the above descriptions of the expansion over time in the operating and normative systems. Evolutionary systems, especially ecological ones, involve interacting subunits whose cooperation allows each subunit to flourish (Boulding, 1985); this conception maps well on to our conception that the operating and normative systems can have a mutually reinforcing impact on one another.

Merely stating that international law is an evolutionary system does not fully describe its operation as there are a number of components or dimensions that vary within evolutionary systems. Below we discuss a number of these characteristics and apply them to international law and our two subsystems.

Boundaries

In analyses of legal systems, a great deal of attention is often devoted to the boundaries of the system, with specific attention to what is legal and what is not. As we discussed above, this is more ambiguous in international law in that it lacks a single, unifying rule of recognition. Still, our conceptions of the operating and normative systems are substrata of an international legal system that is defined by what constitutes hard law, namely rights and obligations that are accepted as legally binding by actors in the system.

Yet the boundaries of international law are not as simple as might be implied above. With respect to universally accepted treaties, there is little doubt about what legal elements exist (even if there is some disagreement over their application). In other cases, treaties with a limited number of parties or customary law with some ambiguities with respect to obligations provide less clear cases. In this way, the international legal system might be better understood as a "fuzzy set" (Klir and Yuan, 1995; Zimmermann, 2001), in which elements (individual rules) may be less than 100 percent members of the set or some components are not fully law. This stands in contrast to the traditional dichotomous distinction between legal/not legal (e.g., Luhmann, 1988). Thus, the boundaries of the international legal system are not as defined as in other legal systems. Still, there are clear distinctions between what aspects fall at least partially within the international legal system set and a variety of elements that are entirely outside that realm; the latter include prescriptions that are merely comity, shared norms without legal obligations, and most other actions or standards that actors regard as falling within their rights to follow or not. Thus, "soft law" and the like are considered outside the international legal system, although as noted in Chapter 4, such elements may be helpful in facilitating compliance with international legal norms.

Soft law and other non-legal aspects are relevant for the international legal system because other political and social systems exist alongside the international legal one and the latter is a permeable, not a closed, system. International law exists along with other systems, specifically those constituting the international political and social environment. Yet the legal one does not exist in isolation; the boundaries of the international legal system are open to other systems. Those contexts influence the direction and application of international legal standards. Indeed, below and in the next chapter, we note that several of the most important factors precipitating change in the international legal system are exogenous.

Special mention is deserved for the relationship of domestic legal systems and their international counterpart. In the era of globalization, the distinctions between these systems have often been blurred. In our view, the relationship of national legal provisions to the international legal system takes several forms, often varying by issue area, but also by the national legal system involved. In some instances, the two are wholly separate, concerned with different matters (local versus international matters) as in the case of primary education versus normative provisions on the law of the sea. In other cases, domestic law is complementary to the international legal system as it serves to fill in gaps left by the global system; some of these roles (e.g., domestic legal processes) are discussed in Chapter 4. In still other cases, domestic and international law are synonymous as the international norms are embedded in national legal systems because of the monist character of the domestic legal system or because national legislation with those international norms has been enacted, as is the case with some human rights provisions. Finally, international and domestic legal systems intersect and overlap by agreement in certain areas, such as the specification of concurrent or consecutive jurisdiction for certain crimes; in these cases, provisions concerning domestic legal systems are part of the international legal operating system.

Balance

Among the key concepts in the analysis of any system is balance or equilibrium in the non-game theoretic sense. Although it means different things in different contexts, generally it refers to the existence of stability and/or symmetry in the system. We address aspects of stability below, but in the present section we address the issue of balance. In our domain, balance refers to the degree to which the operating and normative systems are aligned. That is, does the operating system provide all the necessary elements in order to give effect to the rules in the normative system? This is what we refer to below as the optimal arrangement: the operating system is well designed to fulfill the behavioral aspirations of the normative system. An imbalance would signify that some prescriptions or proscriptions exist without the means to create necessary ancillary rules, monitor behavior, ensure compliance, and/or adjudicate disputes. Such an imbalance would have critical consequences for the ability of international law to influence behavior. Less critical, but still indicative of imbalance, is when operating system procedures are above and beyond what is needed for the normative system. That is, operating system mechanisms exist in international law, but are not necessary or no longer correspond to the needs of the normative system.

Traditional approaches to international law view the two systems in general equilibrium. Changes in norms automatically produce necessary alterations in the operating system. In this way, the mechanistic system has cybernetic (Boulding, 1985; Steinbrunner, 1974) qualities. When a new norm or rule is created, information flows to other parts of the system and adjustments are made to the operating system in order to restore balance. The notion that the operating system could be "over-developed" does not fit into this framework; it is inconceivable that the operating system would be created independently of the normative system. Similarly, causal ideas about operating system change producing normative change are also antithetical to these theoretical formulations.

In our conception of the international legal system, balance between the operating and normative systems is neither necessary nor even likely. Indeed, as Guzman (2005: 589) notes with respect to one aspect of the operating system, "no commentator argues that enforcement measures in international law are sufficient to secure optimal levels of compliance." As noted below, changes in either system are far from automatic, but the product of deliberative choice by the agents (usually states) authorized to make such decisions. As with many systems, there is some inherent pressure for restoring balance when it is out of kilter; one might assume that actors will desire to make sure that the operating system is effective enough to implement a new, shared norm or there is a bureaucratic push to utilize parts of the operating system (e.g., rights of certain actors to participate in lawmaking) even when the extant norms make little use of them. Nevertheless, there are circumstances in which states agree to new norms, but could be less than enthusiastic about certain provisions being effectively enforced or wish to retain control over such enforcement (e.g., by retaining national jurisdiction primarily or exclusively). For such situations, actors actually work to retain imbalance by blocking operating system change or by deliberately placing the operating system at suboptimal levels. Thus, there is nothing routine about changes in the two systems.

Normative treaties include provisions that provide for operating system institutions and processes in the same agreement; thus, changes in the two systems are simultaneous with the entry of the agreement into force. For example, the Patent Cooperation Treaty (1970 and amended in 2001) includes provisions for the creation of an Assembly and an International Bureau that are charged with, among other duties, amending regulations and implementing treaty provisions respectively. More often than not, however, normative provisions are adopted and there are no accompanying operational provisions (Guzman, 2005), and indeed the extant operating system might not accommodate the new rules well. For example, the Convention for Elimination of the Worst Forms of Child Labor (1999) contains no provisions for enforcement at the international level, relying almost entirely on national enforcement mechanisms. Furthermore, we also posit that there will be some operating system changes that are made largely independent, or in advance, of normative changes. For example, the Convention for the Establishment of the Inter-American Tropical Tuna Commission (1949) specifically provides that the Commission make recommendations on actions required to preserve the tuna stocks in the eastern Pacific. The Commission's recommendations could lead to new fisheries law in the future. Furthermore, granting NGOs some role in lawmaking can be a precursor to normative change, not a consequence. Yet such expansion of lawmaking rules may just as easily *not* lead to any normative change, especially in the human rights area.

Imbalances are likely to vary by issue area and agreement type, although little research has examined such patterns. Perhaps the only research that has addressed this problem concerns the compliance elements of the operating system vis-à-vis norms. Within treaties, dispute resolution and monitoring provisions are often unspecified, but they are more likely in multilateral agreements rather than bilateral ones. Such mechanisms, especially dispute resolution institutions, are less likely in high stakes areas, but paradoxically more likely when higher compliance might be expected (see Guzman, 2005 for an explanation). Still, one finds more dispute resolution provisions in human rights and trade treaties; monitoring mechanisms are more common in environmental accords (Guzman, 2005).

Operating–normative system configurations

When a new or modified norm emerges in the international legal system, there are several possible reactions from the operating system (or vice versa), and therefore several joint configurations between the two systems. The first possibility is that the systems remain in balance because no changes are necessary. That is, the operating system is already equipped to handle the new norm. For example, most new trade agreements will fit snuggly into the current configuration of the operating system with WTO rules and procedures at the center. In Chapter 5, we argue that actors may adopt certain norms precisely because the operating system mechanisms are already in place.

A second possibility is that operating system change is simultaneous with the normative change. Most commonly, this would involve a treaty that not only creates a new norm but also includes provisions for the operating system mechanisms needed to give the norms effect; such provisions might include the creation of a new international organization or the assignment of certain monitoring tasks to an extant organization. For example, the Inter-American Tropical Tuna Commission was established by treaty specifically to pass measures that would manage the tuna stock in the eastern Pacific. Another example is the creation of the International Seabed Authority in UNCLOS III to govern the seabed area that was beyond national jurisdiction.[9]

A third configuration exists when operating system change follows normative modifications, but does so in a lagged fashion. That is, it may take months, years, or decades before the requisite operating system change is made in order to bring it into equilibrium with the normative system. In the interim, the two legal systems are in a state of imbalance. Consider, for example, the adoption of the Genocide Convention in 1948, but the establishment of an International Criminal Court to prosecute such crimes only in 2002. This might occur for a variety of reasons (see Chapter 3), but the point is that imbalance persists in the interim. We also may not know *a priori* if such an imbalance is temporary or permanent. The conditions that led to an imbalance can persist for many years or the system may adjust more quickly. The idea that change is inevitable is not falsifiable (the absence of change is not evidence that future change might not happen) and indeed may border on wishful thinking.

---

[9] Divisions between the developing and developed world occurred with regard to the seabed. To avoid the creation of competing regimes, an agreement was struck in 1994 that took into account the concerns of many of the developed states with regard to the Authority's functions and activities. The International Seabed Authority came into operation in 1996.

A fourth configuration is one of "permanent" imbalance between the two systems. This may be indistinguishable from the imbalance that is only temporary, as indicated in the previous configuration; it may be impossible to know at any given time whether the imbalance is fleeting or likely to persist in the long run. Imbalance can come about from three scenarios. One is where operating system changes are made that actually *undermine* the normative system; thus, operating system change is in the direction of creating or accentuating imbalance. Although this represents an interesting case in which actors seek to dilute new rules, it is not common.

More likely is the case that no changes are made to the operating system even when such alterations are needed with the advent of a new norm. This is the case of the adoption of the Universal Declaration of Human Rights with little apparatus or process for monitoring the protection of these rights. Yet a third scenario is conceivable as well. That is, operating system change occurs following normative change, but the former is inadequate or less than what is necessary to ensure balance. Again, drawing from human rights, one might think of the period prior to the coming into force of the International Covenant on Civil and Political Rights (ICCPR) (1976) and the work of the Human Rights Committee as an example of when human rights was given official stature within the UN system (1945), but the Human Rights Commission was not adequate to address any violations. Similarly, the Permanent Court of Arbitration was created over a century ago but at least until 1990 was dramatically underutilized in settling disputes between parties. Given the increasingly complex and numerous elements of international law, it is unlikely that there are many points in time, if any, in which the two operating and normative systems are perfectly aligned.

The impact(s) of imbalance

What is the net effect of a lack of equilibrium between the two systems? A tilt in favor of a developed normative system with an underdeveloped operating system has several consequences. Most notably, the effectiveness of the normative system (defined as having the proper behavior followed by actors in the system) depends largely on the operating system, the mechanisms and processes that are designed to ensure orderly processes and compliance with those norms. The normative system could facilitate compliance in isolation from the operating system by "compliance pull" (Franck, 1990). Compliance pull is induced through legitimacy, which is powered by the quality of the rule and/or the rule-making institution. Still, "primary rules, if they lack adherence to a system of validating secondary rules, are mere *ad hoc* reciprocal arrangements" (Franck, 1990: 184). Compliance pull may exist under such circumstances, but it will be considerably weaker than if the operating system is well developed. Thus, limits on monitoring and enforcement will precipitate more violations of norms.

A weak operating system will also make the prosecution of violators or dispute resolution in general more difficult. Unclear rules on jurisdiction can create some gaps in the system that could be exploited by violators. A reliance on national or territorial jurisdiction, for example, in torture cases provides for inefficiency in that governments are left responsible for perpetrators, which are most likely to be their own high officials. The net result is a lack of enforcement and thereby perverse incentives to violate the norms themselves. Similarly, an operating system of extradition that is built upon an incomplete patchwork of bilateral agreements will be inefficient in ensuring that criminals are caught and punished. The protection of human rights provides another example where "[t]he prominence of the state-centric paradigm has inhibited the development of alternative models for the protection of human rights. As a result, only limited efforts have been made to establish fora that recognize the rights and duties of individuals and that allow individuals to enforce these rules in an effective manner" (Aceves, 2000: 131).

An inefficient operating system can also have ripple effects on the creation of norms. Historically, custom was the primary source of international law. As a result, however, the collective preferences for new rules on trade, the environment, and other issues could not be enacted quickly or in response to changing needs. Until treaties became a more prominent part of the international legal system and multilateral negotiating forums became institutionalized, the development of the normative system was crippled. Such mechanisms are but one instance in which the transaction costs of law creation are reduced by an efficient operating system.

An underdeveloped system is not necessarily fatal to the international legal system; such imbalances may be temporary, but systems can continue to operate indefinitely even if the imbalance persists indefinitely. The case of enforcement and monitoring mechanisms is illustrative. Failure to ensure compliance because of inadequacies in the operating system could be tolerable provided that deviance is confined to "acceptable limits" (Chayes and Chayes, 1993), which is above a level that would threaten the norm involved or the whole system. Even a fully functioning system will have some slippage. Enforcement might not even be necessary for an effective operation of a regime; Gilligan (2006) argues that even though the ICC does not have the power to apprehend criminals, this might not be necessary to deter crimes and prosecute guilty parties.

An overdeveloped operating system has implications as well, although not as deleterious as the reverse. Excess capacity means that provisions go unused. This seems most costly when formal institutions are involved. If adjudicatory bodies are functioning, but have a limited scope because of the limited range of normative rules, then a suboptimality of a different kind arises. The International Court of Justice has historically been underutilized, ruling on fewer than three contentious cases or advisory opinions per year (see Satzer, 2007 for a discussion).

Our conception of international law as an evolutionary system allows for the possibility of change, but unlike mechanistic systems, that change is not automatic. Accordingly, the operating and normative systems exist in various states of imbalance over time. Why do the leading actors in the system (most often states) tolerate suboptimality? Such a decision may be purposive as actors don't want the system to be in balance and therefore run efficiently. States may desire the freedom of action that suboptimality provides (Cook, 2004) or the freedom to resolve conflicts with self-help mechanisms or negotiation (Rovine, 1976); the fear of losing in an adjudicatory body is a reason not to create such a tribunal or allow it wide-ranging jurisdiction (Rovine, 1976). States may also be willing to tolerate some normative violations because there is not the zero-sum game (what violators lose, victims win) associated with domestic contract claims, and therefore little incentive for states to create procedures from which they could only be hurt and not benefit (Guzman, 2005). Of course, in pursuing their interests, states could discover a tradeoff between normative and operating system provisions in an agreement (Guzman, 2008), with some imbalance a necessary result. Finally, it might also be the case that suboptimality was not envisioned, but practice reveals problems in the execution and the system cannot be quickly or easily reengineered because of stickiness or path dependency (see below).

Change in the system

Our primary concern in this book is with changes in the operating and normative systems, and in particular with how changes in one system affect the prospects and configuration for change in the other system. Thus, a centerpiece of our framework for the international legal system must be some precepts about the conditions for change, even though, as we noted above, such change is far from inevitable.

Noting broadly that the international legal system is an evolutionary one does not automatically lead one to posit a particular process of change. Any model of international system change must specify several elements (Zinnes, 1980). The first is whether the process of change is deterministic or more stochastic. We have already indicated that the latter is a better characterization of international legal change. Second, a specification must indicate whether the factors driving the change are endogenous or exogenous; we discuss this below and specify broadly the key factors. Finally, the pace of change must be indicated, whether there is dramatic or gradualist transformation, a concern to which we now turn.

In the field of evolutionary biology, there are essentially two competing models of change. The traditional "gradualist" model views changes in an evolutionary way as slow and roughly at a constant rate. That is, "species" evolve in a largely linear and incremental fashion, adapting over time to changes in the environment and to the needs of the organism. Changes in a gradualist system are also easily reversed (Baumgartner and Jones, 1993), and therefore don't leave much memory or positive feedback in the system. Applied to the international legal systems, this model suggests that the two would adapt solely to the needs of states and the global community as new problems, such as non-tariff barriers and environmental degradation, arise. Major changes in the system would be apparent only in retrospect as such alterations would build slowly and in a step-by-step fashion rather than dramatically. With respect to the interaction of the two systems, a gradualist view would seem to map well with the mechanistic processes described by some legal scholars. Slight changes in the normative system prompt adaptations in the operating system, albeit not always immediately. There is equilibrium over time, but perhaps some imbalance as the systems react to one another.

The gradualist view of evolution (see Gould, 1983 for a description) has come under significant criticism among evolutionary biologists, such that its validity is no longer widely accepted. The same critiques applied in that field might also be applied to its use in international law. Gradualist views of biological evolution lost supporters largely because the fossil record did not match the predicted changes in species. The creation and extinction of species were characterized more by sudden, rather than incremental, changes. There were also long periods of stasis or stability as opposed to continual adaptation.

International legal change no longer, if it ever did, fits a model of gradualist evolutionary change. When custom was the primary source of international law, it was clear that the law changed slowly and gradually as one of the requirements for new customary law was that practice occurs over an extended period of time. Still, custom did not undergo a continual process of change. Indeed, customary law more typically lasted for many decades or centuries without alteration. For example, the specification of the territorial sea as up to 3 miles from the coast dates its roots back hundreds of years (Kent, 1954) and survived all the way to the Territorial Seas Proclamation in 1988, when the limit was extended to 12 miles. Modern international law is characterized now primarily by treaty making, which does not produce a process in which law evolves gradually. More often, a single major treaty, such as the GATT agreements, represents a dramatic break from past practice. Furthermore, the creation of international institutions also does not come about gradually, but represents dramatic breaks with past practice. One caveat is in order. Such changes in international law could result from political processes and changing conceptions (e.g., notions of state sovereignty) that arise slowly and percolate through the international system. Still, the legal manifestations tend to be abrupt. For example, years of negotiations characterize many trade agreements, but the law itself breaks a period of settled law and practice and ushers in a new era of normative rules in a given subject area or in the operating system.

In evolutionary biology, the failure of gradualist theory to map with the fossil record led to a new theoretical formulation: punctuated equilibrium (Eldredge, 1985; 1995; Gould and Eldredge, 1993). The punctuated equilibrium model is predicated on the idea that change takes place suddenly and dramatically, rather than incrementally over time. Significant environmental changes (e.g., climatic shifts) are the triggering mechanism for such changes. Some species die out because of those changes; dinosaurs are perhaps the most famous and frequently cited examples. Other organisms adapt to the new circumstances by developing new capabilities or shedding old ones. In the punctuated equilibrium model, periods of rapid change are followed by long periods of stasis. Thus, rather than change being the predominant process, it is the *absence* of change over time that is the most common characteristic of evolutionary systems.

One might wonder how well evolutionary models and particularly the punctuated equilibrium model might be applied to political processes. In fact, such models have been prominent parts of the scholarly literatures on American public policymaking and international relations. Baumgartner and Jones (1993) examined policymaking in American political institutions. Instead of incremental policy adoption, they identified processes of rapid change, specifically positive feedback from "escalatory bandwagons," "slippery slopes," and "waves." They also noted that the political system was never in equilibrium, but did have points of stability. Changes in stability sometimes came suddenly. Their description of legislative lawmaking fits well with the punctuated equilibrium model.

In the field of international relations, discussion of system change is filled with metaphors about "jumps" (Jervis, 1997), "critical junctures" (Capoccia and Keleman, 2007), and "step-functions" (Genco, 1980), all suggesting periodic and dramatic change. The punctuated equilibrium model, in particular, has been applied most notably to enduring international rivalries, long-standing militarized competitions between the same pairs of states, such as India and Pakistan (Cioffi-Revilla, 1998; Diehl and Goertz, 2000; see also Durant and Diehl, 1989). Such models are frequently contrasted with gradualist perspectives on such rivalries. Punctuated equilibrium models of rivalries posit that the beginnings and ends of rivalries come about suddenly and often following a significant political shock (Colaresi, 2001; Diehl and Goertz, 2000); such dramatic environmental changes can come from international-level events such as world wars or substantial shifts in the power distribution as well as from more micro-level shocks, such as a regime change in one of the rivals. These are seen as necessary, but not sufficient, conditions for changes in the relationships between two states. The dynamics of rivalries, in the form of conflict frequency and other patterns of behavior, are said to be established early in the rivalry. That is, there is a short "lock-in" period in which rivalry patterns are established. Those remain until they are displaced by the termination of the rivalry. This stands in contrast to gradualist conceptions in which rivalry dynamics are not fixed, but change slightly over time in response to rival interactions and environmental factors. The punctuated equilibrium view of rivalries has received significant empirical support (Cioffi-Revilla, 1998; Diehl and Goertz, 2000; Colaresi, 2001; Goertz, Jones, and Diehl, 2005).

More directly relevant to our concerns is the application of the punctuated equilibrium model to international norms by Goertz (2003). He does not make a distinction between norms, regimes, institutions, and other elements, and thus there are no direct analogues to the normative and operating systems here. Nevertheless, he explicitly adopts the punctuated equilibrium model as it applies to international change. Most relevant is his model of the creation of international institutions. Assuming that a new problem (e.g., airline hijackings in the 1960s) has arisen requiring some international action, a series of conditions or factors determine whether institutions are created to address that problem. One is an exogenous shock or crisis, such as a world war. This is obviously consistent with the punctuated equilibrium model derived from evolutionary biology; a significant environmental change is necessary to dislodge existing practices. The other conditions are less tied to the punctuated equilibrium model, but nonetheless thought to be critical for institutional creation. The actions of leading states (hegemons) and the input of various other, non-state actors (e.g., international organizations, NGOs, epistemic communities) are part of the creation process. Each of the three conditions is necessary for institutional change; jointly, they are sufficient for new institutions.

The implications of Goertz's model for international change are clear. Although the three conditions may be frequently present individually, the presence of all three simultaneously might be assumed to be less common. Yet that concatenation is necessary for change to occur. First, this means that some problems will not be addressed because one or more of the conditions is lacking. Disaggregating the international legal system into our two component parts, it suggests for our purposes that the operating and normative systems will not always be in harmony even if they "should be" in some sense. Second, because the presence of the three conditions is necessary for change, such evolution will likely be infrequent rather than continuous. Again, this is consistent with the punctuated equilibrium framework.

Although the punctuated equilibrium approach has multiple and deep roots in the analysis of public policy and international relations, there are some dissenting scholarly voices, particularly in the field of comparative institutional analysis. Early work there (Krasner, 1984) outlined a process of institutional change that emphasized rapid speciation. Yet, more recently, this characterization has come under strong criticism, with more gradualist models of change offered as alternatives. Yet such critiques and reformulations, whatever their value with respect to institutions in advanced capitalist economies, seem less applicable to international law. Thelen (2004) notes that institutions survive shocks, but this is not a fatal indictment of the punctuated equilibrium approach here and in international relations more broadly; such shocks are only necessary conditions and one might expect legal rules to survive many shocks. Still, she (Streeck and Thelen, 2005) acknowledges that institutional change in the first half of the twentieth century was driven by what we would term as shocks such as wars. Indeed, it is these events that change the benefits that actors get from institutions (Hall and Thelen, 2006). Thelen (2004; 2006) argues that institutional change happens through cumulative, incremental adaptation rather than breakdown and replacement of extant institutions. This might be the case of well-developed national government institutions, but the international legal operating system has far fewer structures and doesn't seem to be characterized by the institutional breakdown that German institutions (the subject of Thelen's study) do. The processes of layering (creating new institutions alongside similar old ones) and conversion (using old institutions for new purposes) are much less common in international law for the same reason, although we do note a few instances in subsequent chapters. In sum, gradualist views of institutional change exist, but they seem best applied to political systems that are far more developed and exist at the national level, rather than the operating and normative systems that we have described here.

A punctuated equilibrium theory of international law

In this section, we adapt the punctuated equilibrium approach into a framework that can be used to analyze international law. In doing so, we discuss broadly how international legal systems change, persist, and how the two systems influence one another.

Stasis in the system

One of the characteristics of a punctuated equilibrium process of evolution is that most of the time a system stays the same, with change occurring only infrequently. With respect to international law, this signifies that the operating and normative systems (formal, legal elements) are not in constant flux, but are stable from one time point to the next, with some significant exceptions. One of the traditional assumptions of international law's value was that it provided order and stability to the international system, and therefore periods of stasis were generally regarded positively. The shortcoming, however, was that such stasis could also be seen as (and actually creates) the ineffectiveness of the international legal system to carry out its normative aspirations. Indeed, international law's ability to effect change may be limited (Moore, 1973), suggesting that the operating system may never be perfected.

An astute reader might immediately point out that new treaties are signed and ratified every day in the world and that this is suggestive of a gradual evolutionary process rather than one in which change is more sporadic. There is no denying that some normative treaties are adopted frequently, but such agreements tend to be more narrowly drawn (bilateral treaties are the most common). For example, the US–Canada Income Tax Convention (1980) regulates citizens or residents of one country who may be liable for taxes in the other country. We are interested in alterations in the operating and normative systems that have global impact and represent significant modifications of existing practice. *Major* changes in the normative and operating systems do not occur frequently, and once implemented tend to set the tone for legal relations for many years to come. These represent "critical junctures" (Capoccia and Keleman, 2007) in the system whose legacies may be "distant," that is whose consequences will persist for a long period of time. For example, major GATT and WTO multilateral agreements have only occurred once every decade or more on average. In most cases, we argue, international legal change in a given sector or with respect to a particular problem is characterized only by infrequent and substantial alterations in the rules of the game. Some agreements are not necessarily indicative of change, but rather of stasis. For example, treaties might reflect long-standing customary practice and make essentially no changes to existing law; the Geneva Conventions on the Law of the Sea in 1958 are illustrative of the mere codification, and therefore continuation, of legal rules. In other cases, treaties are renewed. The Nuclear Non-Proliferation Treaty was negotiated to last twenty-five years and then was extended indefinitely and without modification in 1995.

Key parts of the operating system also harden quickly and last for extended periods. The International Court of Justice, created as part of the UN Charter in 1945, is largely unchanged structurally from its inception. Thus, although some modifications to the systems occur in isolated fashion in continuous time, dramatic alterations and those with long-term implications are the exceptions. Most often, the international legal system is stable. One only has to examine international law textbooks to see that even though content is added, the basic principles and components of the normative and operating systems remain the same one edition after another, with revisions to the framework of international law tending to be major and infrequent.

Why are the operating and normative systems stable and resistant to incremental change? There are a number of non-mutually exclusive explanations. Historically, custom was a long-term process of change, and it shared some characteristics of gradualism. Yet even custom stayed largely the same for many years – witness the rules for diplomatic immunity. Change would only take place after practice became established for many years and only then could it be said that a legal obligation existed. Treaties have replaced customary law as the primary method for creating new international norms and operating system procedures. The character of treaty making dictates that major changes evident with new treaties will be infrequent. The process of treaty making involves significant transaction costs. Important agreements usually take many years to negotiate, especially those in multilateral forums. Then it may be several years before a treaty enters into force as well, given that there are often a minimum number of ratifications needed before the treaty takes effect. Accordingly, states devote extensive time and diplomatic efforts to making treaties. There could also be domestic political costs in securing ratification. Under these conditions, the processes are inherently long and states do not wish to renegotiate immediately after an agreement is implemented because of the costs.

The tendency toward stasis is also reinforced by the "stickiness" and path dependency (Pierson, 2004; Page, 2006) properties of legal change. When new norms or operating system rules are adopted, they become embedded in national government policy and international interactions. In effect, they become standard operating procedures that are resistant to change. If new environmental standards are adopted for example, these precipitate changes in national law, which subsequently alter industrial processes in countries. Many of these changes involve the adoption of expensive technologies. States will be reluctant to have their industries adopt such changes, only to impose on them further in a short period of time. Thus, environmental standards in the form of treaties will be negotiated with target dates in the distant future; for example, the Kyoto Protocol was opened for adoption in 1997, but does not expire until 2012. The implementation of standards might be gradual, but the law itself, once established, is designed to be in place for an extended period. International institutions are particularly resistant to change; many persist for years, in largely the same forms, even as their original purposes no longer address current needs (Shanks, Jacobson, and Kaplan, 1996; Pevehouse, Nordstrom, and Warnke, 2004).

International legal rules also become embedded in government practice. Government bureaucracies plan for and adopt rules of their own according to the prevailing normative and operating systems. This includes designing policies that meet present normative requirements. For example, national militaries write rules and procedures in their manuals and train their personnel so as to conform to international humanitarian law, including the interrogation of prisoners of war. Foreign and economic ministries plan strategies and prepare actions based on existing procedures in the WTO dispute resolution forum. In addition, as actors comply with international standards and processes, psychologically they become attached to the status quo and create other routines that support current practice.

We know from extensive studies of bureaucracies that they are resistant to change and provide a brake on dramatic changes in government policy (March and Simon, 1958; Halperin, 1974). Thus, once international rules are set, there is a path dependency and positive feedback (Jervis, 1997) created in which associated processes lock in those rules and serve to reinforce them through national governments.

The processes of change

As in biological systems and international systems broadly (Jervis, 1997), the two international legal systems change in fits and spurts rather than evolving gradually. Sassen's (2006: 419) description of legal change is particularly illustrative: "[old] capabilities can jump tracks and become part of new organizing logics." She further notes that some of these activities seem to burst onto the scene out of nowhere. Thus, the timing of system mutation should be associated with major environmental changes, a view consistent with those that see change in legal systems coming exogenously. In biological systems, such changes are dramatic shocks such as dramatic climate shifts or other weather-related phenomena such as drought or famine.

What are the political equivalents of such shocks? Such political shocks come in a variety of forms, each of which changes the international environment. These include wars, major technological changes, and major political changes (Sandholtz and Stiles, 2009; see also Diehl and Goertz, 2000 for an application to enduring rivalries). Some of these are single events in a narrow time frame that trigger potentially system-changing actions, such as the 9/11 attacks on the World Trade Center in New York, dramatic acts of genocide in Bosnia or Rwanda, or even economic crises (Widmaier, Blyth, and Seabrooke, 2007). Others could be more extended events such as world wars; wars are frequently cited as instigators of system change, but only those of great magnitude are likely to have this effect (Siverson, 1980). Still others may be processes that extend over a period of time, such as the global waves of democratization (Huntington, 1991) that occurred in 1970s and 1980s or the amassing of scientific evidence on global warming. These are accumulating effects (and one could also envision combined effects of different types) that occur gradually, but which do not take place concurrently, but only after a certain threshold or tipping point and then with great magnitude.

Whatever the kinds of shocks, they share a number of characteristics. First, shocks are significant events and processes, and thereby they are distinguished from day-to-day international political interactions. Second, their impact is felt among a large portion of the globe and among many states, rather than affecting only a few. For example, a civil war has dramatic effects for a given state and its neighbors, but little impact on other states in the international system. Third, the shocks must have the effect of dramatically altering existing political arrangements and perceptions. That is, the normal course of conducting international politics must be rearranged as a result of a shock. Clearly, world wars disrupt the power distribution among leading states in the global system and the post-war system includes new alliances and relationships, usually quite different than what occurred before the conflict. Yet, a dramatic alteration in perceptions can be just as important as actual shifts in relationships. Increasing democratization modifies the values that states prize most, and more democratic governments will alter the configuration of trading relationships, alliances, and a series of other interactions (Mitchell, 2002). As with climate change, there is the opportunity for a reordering of the processes that characterize the system. Finally, triggering shocks can push change in certain directions (Sandholtz and Stiles, 2009), focused either on certain issue areas (e.g., human rights) or kinds of operating system change (e.g., the development of international courts).

Political shocks to the international legal system do not automatically produce changes in the operating and normative legal systems. They function only as *necessary* conditions for such change, but the capacity for change must also be present for any change to occur. That is, political shocks are not monocausal explanations for the adoption of new rules and institutions. Various other conditions are necessary – some are broader requirements such as those concerning major power states described below. Thus, the absence of change following a political shock is not evidence for the falsification of the punctuated equilibrium theory. Some shocks will be peculiar to the particular issue area or sector involved in the change. Thus, not all political shocks will produce changes or not all the changes will be coterminous with the shock; with respect to the latter, there may be a significant lag between the shock and the dramatic change in the international legal system. The presence of several necessary conditions is also a reason for why legal change is infrequent; individual favorable conditions might be present at various times, but the proper concatenation of conditions may only occur at certain "ripe" (Zartman, 2000) moments.

Some political shocks have far-reaching consequences, with effects across a range of operating system components and normative issue areas. For example, World War II led to the creation of new norms on prisoners of war and human rights as well as reconfigured operating system institutions in the area of international finance and trade. Other political shocks have narrower, sectoral effects. The aforementioned 9/11 attacks seem to be influencing international legal rules on terrorism, but do not have any impact on environmental or law of sea rules, to name but two.

A second component in the process of international legal change is the role of leading states in facilitating that change. Historically, leading states have played a central role in the creation and modification of international law. When custom was the leading source of law, it was the major powers in the international system that had the capacity to establish such practices. For examples, rules on the law of the sea came from practice and major power states were often the only ones with navies, or at least certainly the ones who engaged in naval warfare and commerce most often, and therefore were in a position to shape maritime law.

Major states also possess the tools of power to persuade and coerce other actors to make, or resist, changes in the operating and normative systems (for the role of power, see Sandholtz and Stiles, 2009). Thus, we anticipate that such states will act as instigators of changes in numerous instances. Yet single states alone are unlikely to precipitate change. Once again, major power influence is only a necessary, not a sufficient, condition for legal change. Furthermore, it is rare that one state can dictate all of international law for the whole system; it usually takes the consent of all or most of the leading states to effect such changes. Leading states might be defined globally as well as sectorally.

We posit rapid and infrequent change in the international legal system, but many systems also experience entropy, or the inevitable and steady deterioration of some system elements. This is inherently a gradualist process. We don't deny that some entropy exists, but it is less than what existed historically and the entropic process is not a significant part of legal change. When international law was based primarily on custom, there was a natural process of decay during legal change as norms evolved to encompass new behaviors. Now, with treaties the predominant source of law, these generally do not wither away, but are stable over time and replaced abruptly with new agreements. Unlike custom, treaties do not necessarily need ongoing reinforcement to retain their obligatory character, best evidenced by boundary delimitation agreements. There are still instances of old and obsolete treaties fading away as states ignore them, but these instances are not common.

System interaction

The focus of this book is the interaction of the normative and operating systems, and the changes in those systems. Clearly the same external forces that generate change in one system can produce alterations in the other. These may occur simultaneously or sequentially. Yet the international legal system is an adaptive one and, therefore, pressures for change in one system might be said to come from pressures in another.

As noted above, a change in the normative system does not automatically produce changes in the operating system. Yet the original change does produce some impetus for change in the other system. That is, we can't merely assume that both systems are solely the product of exogenous forces such as political shocks and major power interests. There is a self-regulating tendency in the interaction of the two systems toward equilibrium or balance. The short-term result could be stasis or equilibrium, but interactions between the two systems can generate the capacity needed to respond to a systemic shock. The establishment of the United Nations provides an example where its founders were in a far better position to build on the experience of the League of Nations than were the founders of the League of Nations who pioneered the concept of such an institution. Yet, as we discussed, we reject the automatic regulation and restoration of equilibrium that some posit. Thus, in predicting change in one system from change in another, we need to model both external influences and those internal (endogenous) to the system itself. The processes that we outline in Chapters 3 and 5 reflect this combination of influences.

Many models of system regulation assume a closed system, in which the processes are all internal to the system. Yet international law is hardly impervious to the broader international political system. Actors in that broader system have interests in ensuring (or not) that the legal system functions effectively. Accordingly, we argue that some of the regulation of the two legal systems, especially in redressing imbalances, will come from outside the international legal system. For example, deficiencies in the operating system, such that the normative system's prescriptions are not effective, might prompt extra-systemic adaptations. Such responses might not make the legal system run perfectly, but they can redress some of the imbalance problems that occur. In Chapter 4, we examine some of these mechanisms with respect to the operating system.

On legal and computer systems

In the previous sections, we outlined the basic components of the operating and normative systems, and provided a general framework for how they interacted. These two legal systems as we have defined them share some similarities with computer systems. Discussing our legal systems in terms of computer systems will hopefully elucidate their features and interactions.

Our choice of the term "operating system" is far from coincidental in that the corresponding computer system plays many of the same roles as the legal one. A computer operating system generally consists of the hardware on which the computer functions. One element of the computer system is its basic capacity for running programs. This includes its RAM, hard disk space, and CPU speed. Another component is the basic platform, now most commonly Windows or Linux. Those platforms configure the computer and determine how any action by the computer will take place. Computers also have various peripherals, including scanners, printers, and speakers, which allow the user to perform a series of additional functions. None of these elements constitutes computing activities *per se*, but no such activities can be carried out without one or more of these systems.

The legal operating system has some similar components. Its institutions and processes constitute hardware that is available for use. Yet such hardware has inherent carrying capacity; for example, most international courts can handle a limited number of cases per year and international negotiating forums generally only deal with a subset of relevant issues at a time. NGOs and other actors/mechanisms (covered in Chapter 4) might serve as plug-ins or updates, filling in for the inadequacies of the operating system and providing necessary information and functions. The speed of these decision-making processes is also conditioned by their rules and procedures, roughly comparable to computer speeds.

Start-up protocols on computers also define the legitimate users of the systems and their rights to read, access, and modify files (e.g., administrator rights). This is analogous to the specification of actors and their rights in the legal operating system.

The normative system is analogous to the various software programs that run on a computer. Such software (browsers, word processing programs, games) have little or no interface with one another. They occupy separate spaces on the hard disk or computer slots, and most serve very different purposes from one another. Similarly, many legal rules in different issue areas (e.g., trade, human rights) exist independently of one another. Despite these differences, they use most of the same components of the operating system in order to run properly. Some games, however, need special elements unique to the game or the genre (certain flash players) and these can be installed for such purposes. Similarly, certain parts of the normative system have their own unique structures and procedures, even as they share some general operating system components along with other sets of normative rules.

As might be evident, the software and operating systems must be minimally compatible for the former to run. Insufficient memory or hard disk space can cripple a software program at the outset. Even if software runs on a computer, it might be very slow or unable to perform certain functions if the operating system's capacity is insufficient. Normative rules in international law can have effect only when they are compatible with the operating system. A proscription on a given subject is meaningless in international law if it does not meet the standards for being a law (as opposed to merely being a good idea) and was presented by an unauthorized user (an actor without the power to make law). Some norms are prohibited by the operating system, such as those that violate *jus cogens*, which acts as a spam or virus filter does on all potential laws.

Changes in computing systems are also similar to those in our two legal systems, at least with respect to speed, magnitude, and the interaction of the systems. Generally, neither computer hardware nor software systems change in a gradual fashion from the perspective of one's personal computer. Rather, they tend to come in spurts with the appearance of new products on the market. Typically, an individual buys a computer with given components, with the idea of running particular software in mind. As the user acquires new software, it might not be necessary to upgrade a computer; the computer hardware could already be compatible with the new software and indeed the user might purchase software based on that compatibility. Similarly, the normative system need not prompt changes in the legal operating system on all occasions (see the discussion of necessity in Chapter 3) and norms might be adopted because they fit into preexisting structures and processes (see Chapter 5). Shifts to new software and hardware tend to occur simultaneously although not necessarily; many users continue with old versions of MS Office even as they acquire newer versions of Windows.

There are some differences, however, between computer and legal change. The assumption is generally that computer change is desirable, and hence the use of the term "upgrades" to signify improvements in processing capacity and task performance. That is not necessarily the case with international law as changes in international law might not serve the values of all the users or the international community as a whole. In addition, there is an assumption that computer systems become simpler in the sense of being user friendly over time. In contrast, international legal change is more likely to make the system have greater complexity and navigating that complexity could be more difficult with expanding rules, institutions, and processes.

With respect to the intersection of the international and domestic legal systems, one might make an analogy to peer-to-peer computer networks. The two computers (international and domestic) share communication paths and there is some coordination of tasks across the two networks. In other cases, one computer is given priority or exclusivity in some tasks (e.g., jurisdiction rules, sovereignty restrictions). This is quite similar to heating/cooling and electric systems in modern buildings; multiple systems exist and the task might be separated by floors, with some areas serviced by two separate, but integrated, systems.

In the next three chapters, we explore the interaction of the two systems, beginning with how changes in the normative system condition changes in the operating system; this is equivalent to understanding how new software requirements prompt users to upgrade or modify hardware. Chapter 4 deals with the equivalent of "patches" or adaptations in which system incompatibilities are dealt with outside the framework of the basic operating system. The following analysis, Chapter 5, explores how hardware capacity influences decisions to acquire and to run software (norms).

3

The influence of normative change on the operating system

In the previous chapter, we outlined the basic components and interactions of the normative and operating systems respectively. What happens when there is a change in the normative system? The framework and discussion in Chapter 2 indicated that changes in the normative system do not always lead to commensurate transformations in the operating system as are implied in other treatments. Such alterations might not be needed, but it could also be the case that even desirable shifts in the operating system lag behind or do not occur at all, leaving the two systems in a state of imbalance. What our framework did not provide at that point, however, was a specific model that gave a causal explanation for when and why operating system changes occur (or not). In this chapter, we provide such a model, consistent with the tenets of our theoretical framework.

Normative change comes most commonly in the form of a treaty that creates new rules in a substantive area such as patent rights or the treatment of diplomatic personnel. For example, the UN Convention to Combat Desertification (1994) obligates states to mitigate the effects of drought, among other responsibilities. Less common would be changes from alterations in international customary law or law crafted in international bodies (e.g., UN Security Council) empowered to authorize legally binding decisions. For example, the imposition of sanctions on Libya following the Lockerbie bombing in 1988 is an instance of changing rules, albeit very narrow and potentially time bound. Another example may be UNSC resolution 1368 (2001) which recognized an act of terrorism as a threat to international peace and security following the attacks of September 11, 2001. UNSC resolution 1371 (2001) went on to state the need to combat such threats by all means permissible under the Charter. Thus, understanding when important operating system changes are made (or not) and determining how malleable the associated conditions are will be critical for effective policymaking.

A model of operating system change

In this section, we take the theoretical framework laid out in the previous chapter and seek to account for the different configurations of balance laid out there. Not surprisingly, we will be emphasizing factors that would account for stasis, accompanied by infrequent, but rapid change in operating system components. Our model specifies several necessary conditions for normative change to produce operating system change, with other factors essentially operating as limiting conditions or veto points.

There are some assumptions and caveats underlying our analysis below. We focus on operating system changes that succeed or occur simultaneously with normative change in this chapter. This is not to say that the reverse is not possible or that the process is not recursive; indeed the previous chapter notes that this is likely. We want to isolate and examine the "norms produce structural changes" process as a first step in understanding the complex interaction. Thus, because we take norms as a given, their genesis (including the influences of structure) is outside the scope of this analysis. We return to the process of normative change in Chapter 5 when the causal arrow is reversed.

In summary, there are several components to our model, which we address serially below. First, there must be some *necessity* for change in the operating system in order to give the new or modified norm legal effect. Yet pure necessity is not enough for operating system change; some type of political shock or change in the international environment must provide the impetus for change to occur. Even in the presence of necessity and political shocks, however, change is still not guaranteed. Two conditions, opposition by leading states as well as domestic political and legal constraints, might prevent or limit the scope of the operating system change.

The necessity of necessity

In the punctuated equilibrium framework, we expect that the operating system is usually static and somewhat resistant to change. That is, the operating system is not in constant flux. Because it is purposive, however, the operating system does respond to environmental changes. Consistent with the idea of stasis or stability, we posit that the operating system for international law only changes in response to necessity. That is, we might anticipate operating system alterations only when the status quo system cannot handle the requirements placed upon it by the adoption of new normative standards. Necessity does not generally derive from institutional breakdown (as discussed in the comparative institutions literature; see Krasner, 1984, and Thelen and Steinmo, 1992). International legal institutions are not well developed, and even when in existence they do not necessarily collapse or find themselves outdated. As noted below, necessity comes from several other sources. There is also the assumption, of course, that states actually want to implement normative provisions, rather than let them linger with largely symbolic effects. We also put aside the possibility that the operating system might change independently of the normative system and therefore for reasons other than necessity because our concern in this chapter is only with the dynamic interaction of the two systems.

Some of the logic underlying the necessity requirement is related to the contractualist model of international regime formation (Keohane, 1984). In this model, states cooperate and build institutions in order to lessen the "transaction costs" associated with the negotiation, monitoring, and enforcement of agreements. In particular, regimes are designed to mitigate the sanctioning problems that arise at the international level when seeking to assure that states follow certain prescriptions. Thus, such approaches to regime formation focus on the efficiency of new structural arrangements. In other cases, cooperation is necessary in order to meet "global public goods" objectives such as the eradication and prevention of disease, environmental protection, and arms control (Barrett, 2007). In these areas, the actions of a few may benefit all, but the failure to act would potentially be harmful to all.

Necessity goes beyond simple efficiency, however, and stresses that the operating system must change in order to give effect to new standards. Thus, necessity assumes that some actions must be completed (an inherent increase in efficiency), but it does not presuppose that the operating system change will necessarily be the *most* efficient arrangement, and therefore may fall short of rationalist expectations. The contractualist approach to regimes recognizes that institution creation is not done in a vacuum, but rather in the context of past efforts and institutional experiences. Thus, the status quo becomes an important reference point for potential regime alterations. With respect to our concern with the international law operating system, extant system arrangements vis-à-vis new norms become critical. Accordingly, there seem to be three separate elements of necessity, any one of which may precipitate changes in the operating system: insufficiency, incompatibility, and ineffectiveness.

When legal norms are completely *de novo*, and therefore dissimilar to existing norms, it is likely that the legal operating system does not possess relevant provisions to deal with those new rules. This is less common in highly developed political and legal systems, but for most of its history, international law and its operating system have been very limited. When the operating system is therefore *insufficient* to give effect or regulate relations surrounding the new norm, it might be expected that changes occur in that operating system to accommodate the new rules. An example of such change would include the construction of a committee for regulating the observance of a new environmental law, similar to how the United Nations Commission on Sustainable Development was created following the Conference on Environment and Development in 1992.

In some cases, actors immediately recognize that new norms find no analogue structures in the operating system. Thus, it is not surprising that some treaties include provisions for new legal structures or processes. For example, the Third United Nations Convention on the Law of the Sea (UNCLOS III) includes the International Seabed Authority, which administers resources in the areas beyond the national territorial seas and exclusive economic zones (EEZs), and this institution arises out of new norms for seabed mining in international waters.

Related to the insufficiency of current operating arrangements is their *incompatibility* vis-à-vis alterations in legal prescriptions. The extant operating system in international law might not simply be inadequate to deal with new norms; it may be contrary to them. At that point, some reconciliation is necessary. For example, holding national leaders responsible for torture or other crimes (Torture Convention) creates new norms, but is incompatible with notions of sovereign immunity; the Spanish case against General Pinochet is indicative of this tension (see *R. v. Bow Street Metropolitan Stipendiary Magistrate, ex parte Pinochet Ugarte* (No. 3) 2 All ER 97) as is the case of *Congo v. Belgium* (ICJ Reports, 2002). The International Court of Justice concluded in *Congo v. Belgium* that the immunity of officials from the jurisdiction of foreign courts was absolute and included charges of war crimes or crimes against humanity. Immunity, however, would not extend to any actions taken in a private capacity even during the period the individual held office. Exceptions to foreign sovereign immunity need to be created in order for the operating system to be consonant with these new agreements and the legal norms embedded in them and/or national systems need to be strengthened to prosecute such crimes (see Bianchi, 1999).

Once again, actors recognize the problem of incompatibility, and new structures and processes are created accordingly. Much European Union law was predicated on the legal standing of individuals and other state actors in judicial settings, but this was contrary to most international arrangements and had to be altered. Still, not all the incompatibility problems are evident during negotiations for new norms or even at the time of ratification. It may take several years before actors learn of the conflicting aspects of the normative and operating systems (see Burley (Slaughter) and Mattli, 1993).

A third variation of the necessity condition concerns *ineffectiveness*. Unlike insufficiency, which presupposes the complete absence of relevant operating arrangements, the ineffectiveness variation finds operating mechanisms present, but not well designed to meet the particular challenges presented by the new or modified norm. Thus, some specific changes in the operating system are needed that reflect the new norm. For example, compliance mechanisms based on reciprocity might be largely ineffective with respect to emerging norms in areas such as human rights. There, the violation of legal standards by one state has little commensurate effect on the probability that other states will also violate the law (and thereby impose costs on the original violator). Indeed, reciprocity concerns sometimes undermine compliance as states implicitly cooperate *not* to sanction one another for such violations. This is illustrated by UN member countries' refusal to denounce human rights atrocities committed by their neighbors or vote for resolutions against them in the UN Human Rights Council. Another example is the inadequacy of *ad hoc* rules of evidence in international criminal tribunals, which often allow judges to admit any evidence with probative value; adopting some basic rules of evidence could shorten and simplify trials (Murphy, 2008).

As indicated above, there are instances in which the current operating system can easily handle new or modified norms. Indeed, actors may be drawn to adopt such norms, *ceteris paribus*, given that the transaction costs are lower because new operating rules don't have to be created and actors have less uncertainty with the operations of current institutions, based on prior experiences.

Although we argue that some necessity is required for operating system change, we leave the question of exactly what proposed changes appear on the international agenda and which actors press for those changes as exogenous (see Thelen, 2004, and Sandholtz and Stiles, 2009 for some discussion on which factors determine the kinds of institutional change adopted). At this stage, we believe that proposals for change are always available in the marketplace of ideas. This is consistent with public policy analyses that postulate that there are always "solutions" present in the system, but these must wait for the right conditions before they are seriously considered or adopted (Cohen, March, and Olsen, 1972; Kingdon, 1995; see also Sassen, 2006 on capabilities). Many of those proposals will arise and be promoted by a concatenation of actors in the international policy process. These would most prominently include states with a direct interest in facilitating operating system change (e.g., coastal states seeking compliance with pollution rules), epistemic communities, and other policy entrepreneurs (e.g., international lawyers), as well as international governmental and non-governmental organizations. The key point in this section, however, is that the efforts of these actors to propose or champion operating system change will fail unless necessity considerations prevail.

The impetus of political shocks

Necessity is required for operating system change to occur, but our punctuated equilibrium theory posited that strong forces in the system resist change. Accordingly, we argued that some significant impetus must be present before the operating system adjusts to the normative change. That impetus must come from a significant *political shock*. As noted in Chapter 2, political shocks can be discrete events, such as world wars, acts of terrorism, or horrific human rights abuses. Shocks might also appear as significant processes, such as global democratization, that extend over a period of time. All political shocks, however, represent dramatic changes in the international political environment, which in turn facilitate modifications in the international legal operating system.

There are roughly two types of effects from political shocks. First are political shocks whose impact is largely sectoral, that is they affect only segments of the operating or normative system. For example, a shift away from the gold standard might be expected to affect international economic law rather than human rights law, as well as the accompanying operating system components. Second are political shocks whose breadth is so great as to impact multiple issue areas as well as the operating system components that cut across issue areas. For example, the world wars rearranged state relations broadly and opened the opportunity for significant legal change in a variety of areas, as did decolonization.

Political shocks can have a number of effects on international relations, and thereby facilitate operating system change. First, they can radically reorder relations between states, such that previous impediments to cooperation are removed. In particular, alterations in the international political environment change the distribution of benefits from certain policies. Previous animosities or divisions sometimes give way to alliances between former enemies. Not surprisingly then, the growth of international organizations is greatest immediately following the end of major wars (Singer and Wallace, 1970). Operating system change might not have been possible previously because of disputes between states or restrictions imposed by the international environment. A change in that environment breaks down the barriers to the adoption of new policies, here new legal structures or provisions. Second, political shocks may place issues or policies on the global agenda, and thereby prompt the community of states to take action upon them. For example, some human rights concerns only become salient issues following catastrophic violations. Thus, even though operating system change is needed, there might be no action until the issue becomes salient. We know from numerous studies of public policy that while a multitude of problems exist, only a subset receives government action, often as a result of dramatic events or changes in the political environment (e.g., a new government).

Political shocks can have the effect of changing the normative and operating systems either simultaneously or sequentially. That is, an initial political shock prompts a normative change (e.g., restrictions on the use of military force after World War I), and this almost immediately includes corresponding changes in the operating system (e.g., the creation of the League of Nations and its provisions for dealing with aggression). One might speculate that the magnitude of the change affects the likelihood of this scenario; that is, the greater the shock, the more likely it is to have consequences for both the normative and operating system simultaneously (Siverson, 1980). Still, there are other factors at play and it is quite likely that change is not simultaneous.

In another scenario, the operating system change does not result from the same shock as that which prompted the initial normative change; it takes another shock, potentially many years later, for the operating system to be altered. Thus, our model recognizes that normative and operating change might not be coterminous. This will lead to cases in which there is a lagged and possibly suboptimal adjustment in the operating system, leading to imbalance. The inability of the UN security system to respond with force in cases of gross violations of human rights such as in Rwanda, the former Yugoslavia, and Darfur showed the difficulty UN members had in agreeing to a formula or mechanism for providing forceful UN-sanctioned international responses to these cases. Even at this writing, provisions for humanitarian intervention and "responsibility to protect" are not fully accepted, nor are any institutions or other operating rules designed to implement them.

As conceptualized, political shocks are necessary conditions for operating system change, but not sufficient ones. That is, not every political shock will produce an operating system change; some shocks will occur with few or no after-effects. This fits well with the notions of stasis and infrequent rapid change. As necessary conditions, political shocks will be more common than their effects on the legal system as the latter require other conditions to be manifest (for more on necessary conditions, see Goertz and Starr, 2002). The League of Nations experiment might be seen as an example where the shock of World War I created an initial willingness to consider a collective approach to matters of war and peace. Yet, it took another war for states to undertake the kind of structural change to make such a collective system work. Furthermore, as we have seen in the discussion about humanitarian intervention, the UN system itself remains in need of further change.

Although we see operating system change flowing from requirements of necessity and spurred on by political shocks, two factors may limit or stifle operating system change even under those conditions: (1) the opposition of leading states; and (2) domestic political and legal factors.

The role of leading states

Among the most prominent theoretical schools in international relations is hegemonic stability theory (see Kindleberger, 1973; Keohane, 1980). According to this approach, typically applied to international economics, a system leader and its preferences define and shape the interactions that occur within the international system. The hegemon also subsidizes the provision of public goods in order to enhance the stability of the system. The leading state must have the capacity and the willingness to produce the resources or infrastructure necessary for the smooth operation of the system. The United States since 1945, and in some conceptions Great Britain prior to that, fulfilled that role.

If one were to adopt some hegemonic version of operating system change, then such change would only occur when it was in the self-interest of the hegemon and when that state took the lead in facilitating the change. This would mean providing the public goods necessary for norm compliance. A related claim is made by Goldsmith and Posner (2005) who argue that international legal rules are a reflection of the interests of the leading states in the system. Many of these arguments are only a short distance removed from realist conceptions of international law as epiphenomenal and merely a product of states' interests.

We are hesitant to adopt the extreme view of the role of leading states espoused by the hegemonic stability model and related approaches as an explanation for international legal change. The model has come under intense criticism (see Pahre, 1999) and even one of those who helped formulate it acknowledges the limited empirical support it has received (Keohane, 1984). Furthermore, Keohane (1984) also admits that a hegemon is neither necessary nor sufficient for cooperation, and by implication therefore for operating system change. Some scholars (Hawkins, 2004) go so far as to contend that international institutions generally don't develop from the impetus of major powers or at very least hegemons can't impose international legal change (Sandholtz and Stiles, 2009).

Despite these limitations, there is good reason to consider revised and more modest elements of the hegemonic stability idea as relevant for international legal change. That hegemonic stability theory is inadequate or incorrect does not mean that the behavior of leading states is unimportant (see Goertz's 2003 discussion of leading states and institutional change). Whether in creating law, institutions, or in developing general standards of behavior (i.e., custom), the history of international law has predominantly been written by Western states, and in particular, the major powers. For example, traditional requirements for "prompt, effective, and adequate" compensation in the event of nationalization or expropriation of property serve the interests of powerful states with foreign investments more than weaker, host states that are the recipients of such investment.

In arguing that leading states can arrest or inhibit operating system change, however, we break from hegemonic stability models in several ways. First, we do not confine ourselves to the influence of one leading state, but instead focus on several powerful states. No one state has been able to impose its will on the international legal system. Furthermore, the identity of leading states has often varied by issue area; for example, leading naval powers historically exercised a disproportionate share of the power in shaping the law of the sea. Such advantages were institutionalized in trade negotiations via the "major interests" norm in which states with the greatest interests in a given area had the most influence on treaty provisions (Finlayson and Zacher, 1981).

Second, we differ in our emphasis on the operating system, rather than hegemonic stability's preoccupation with norm development. Some scholars (Ikenberry and Kupchan, 1990) have argued that normative change can only arise with the active support of the hegemon. Our concern here is not with the origins of normative change, but rather its consequences for the operating system. Yet a hegemonic view of norm origination seems to suggest that operating system change would automatically follow from the original normative change. Thus, normative and operating changes stem from the same cause. Nevertheless, we deviate from this perspective. We can conceive of circumstances in which norms arise outside the purview of leading states in the world. As Sikkink (1998) notes, hegemonic models have great difficulty accounting for the rise of human rights and other norms. Moreover, interpretive (Klotz, 1995) and other approaches (Keck and Sikkink, 1998) make compelling cases for the role of non-state actors in norm formation. Yet, it may be the case that norms can arise without the support, or even with active opposition, from leading states in the system. Indeed, some changes in the operating system with respect to the sources of law and actors have facilitated this, points addressed in Chapter 5.

Still, leading states can be the key actors that determine whether norms are reflected in the actors, jurisdictional requirements, and institutions that make up the operating system. Even if we accept that norm origination requires the consent of the leading states in the system, it is conceivable that such states could still choose to block operating system changes. Support for normative change can largely be for symbolic reasons (e.g., the adoption of the Universal Declaration of Human Rights), but without substantive impact. Leading states might support human rights norms, for example, while also opposing individual standing before international bodies and other operating changes that would facilitate the observance of the norm (see the discussion in the previous chapter on why states may choose suboptimality). If leading states benefit from the status quo, they are worse off under an operating system change and move to prevent that change; this circumstance can be true for many states, but leading states have the power to protect their interests.

Third and most critically, we see the power of leading states as lying in their ability to block operating system change rather than impose such modifications (see Tsebelis, 2002 on veto players). In this way, leading states can act much as the "Big Five" do in the UN Security Council: a veto can prevent action, but no single state can compel the adoption of a particular policy. The enforcement of normative rules largely depends on the willingness of leading states to bear the costs of enforcement (Goldstein, Kahler, Keohane, and Slaughter, 2000). Yet strong states have incentives to resist delegating authority to new institutions, one component of the operating system. Strong states bear greater sovereignty costs associated with such delegation (Abbott and Snidal, 2000). Furthermore, such leading states have to bear disproportionate burdens in providing the public goods associated with operating system change; the prevalence of free riding and the unwillingness of leading actors to bear those costs are barriers to policy change (Alston, 2000). Where appropriate, this makes localized or embedded solutions potentially more attractive to leading powers (Dubinsky, 2005).

Thus, assessing the preferences of leading states is vital to determining whether, and to what extent, operating system change occurs. Key considerations are how such operating system change affects the strategic and economic interests of those states. Equally important are the costs of such change borne by the leading states vis-à-vis the private benefits accrued to those actors. An example of this might come from the use of reserve currencies in which the country whose currency is serving as the reserve has a far greater access to credit than other countries. At the same time, serving as a reserve currency imposes special burdens of monetary and fiscal policy that might clash with domestic economic interests. This conflict stems from long-term policy considerations in the interests of the reserve currency, but shorter-term considerations for domestic economic needs. Thus, in the case of the US dollar, Americans could (and some would say should) have to face tighter credit in order to maintain the strength of the dollar as a viable reserve currency (see Heldring, 1988). We argue that change will likely *not* occur in the operating system when such an alteration threatens the self-interest of the dominant states and/or is actively opposed by one or more of those states. Change, however, could still prove to be sufficiently minimal and ineffective so as not to challenge the interests of the dominant states at least in the short term. The necessity of consent from the dominant state(s) can, therefore, be seen as an obstacle that needs to be overcome prior to any effective operating system change taking place.

Several caveats are in order. First, if a major power state is not a party to the normative component, it may lose its ability to influence any operating system configuration designed to support such rules. Thus, there is some risk to rejecting a treaty such as the Kyoto Protocol or the Rome Statute establishing the International Criminal Court as it may limit the ability of the state to influence how it is implemented or monitored. Even if a major power state ratifies or accedes to the agreement later, the opportunity to influence the surrounding operating system could be lost. Second, a major power state might choose a unilateral strategy to mold the operating system vis-à-vis its own rights and obligations rather than writ large. If the monitoring and enforcement provisions of a given agreement are separable by individual party, then a major state could decide to limit the operating system's effect on its interests, even as a stronger system exists for all parties. Below, we note that the United States has withdrawn from ICJ jurisdiction with respect to the Genocide Convention, even as many other parties are still subject to that institution. Later, we also discuss efforts by the United States to limit the exposure of its soldiers to the International Criminal Court.

Domestic political and legal influences

Domestic political concerns can act as intervening factors that affect the outcomes of operating system change. In addition, some operating system changes require that domestic legal systems also be altered. For example, norms against political torture or child marriage necessitate appropriate changes in the domestic legal systems of treaty signatory states. Indeed, any non-self-executing agreement requires some type of domestic political action to give it effect. Furthermore, national constitutions differ in the degree to which they incorporate customary law as well (Ginsburg, 2006). This goes beyond the ratification process, which may be essential to norm creation. Rather, it involves making changes to domestic laws and standards in order to accommodate the new international norm – this might involve providing remedies for norms within domestic legal institutions, altering jurisdictional rules, or changing the legal standing of individuals or groups to bring claims. In the *LaGrand Case (Germany* v. *United States)*, for example, the International Court of Justice referred to the obligation of the United States "to review" cases of conviction and death sentences imposed on foreign nationals in violation of the individual's rights under the Vienna Convention on Consular Relations (ICJ Reports, 2001, para. 317) even though these cases fell under the criminal jurisdiction of individual political units within the United States.

In creating and implementing new norms, state leaders are placed in the position of conducting "two-level" games (Evans, Jacobson, and Putnam, 1993), one with international adversaries and the other with domestic constituencies. Domestic constituencies offer a potential veto point at which operating system change can be stifled. Even a sincere leader might not be able to deliver on promises to enact domestic legal reforms. Depending on the processes in the given political system, a leader's agreement to a norm might only be a small step to its internal implementation. Such norms could require additional legislation or need to survive constitutional challenge.

In other instances, domestic jurisdiction requirements negate any protections guaranteed by the new norm. For example, were the United States to agree to abolish capital punishment, the national government would have difficulty implementing this on the state level given federalist structures and constitutional guarantees of individual states' rights. The US Supreme Court ruled in 2008 (*Medellin* v. *Texas*) that the US national government could not force the state of Texas to follow provisions of the Vienna Convention on Consular Relations without executing legislation. A leader could have executive authority to commit her/his country to the international norm, but lack the political power domestically to implement it. An example is a president or prime minister who leads a minority or coalition government whose members do not support the norm or who attach the equivalent of post-ratification reservations to its implementation. The US, for example, ratified the Climate Change Convention in 1992. Nevertheless, the Kyoto Protocol met with resistance even though the US under the Clinton Administration had played an active role in negotiating the protocol. Concern about the protocol generated a unanimous resolution in the US Senate opposing it. President Clinton nevertheless signed the protocol in 1998 with the "stipulation that he would not recommend ratification unless the protocol was adjusted to address US concerns" (Brunnée, 2004: 623).

An insincere leader could actually support the creation of an international norm, but move to block the necessary changes in the national legal system for domestic political purposes. Such action permits a principled stance abroad, and a politically popular or necessary position at home. For example, the People's Republic of China adopted the International Covenant on Civil and Political Rights, but has given little indication that it will incorporate many of the treaty's protections into its domestic laws. Beyond leadership incentives, domestic interest groups might seek to block national implementation of international normative changes. This occurs when their political or economic interests are harmed by such implementation. For example, labor and manufacturing groups in the United States have sought to weaken the adoption of domestic regulatory mechanisms that give effect to international environmental agreements. State leaders may also sign and ratify agreements establishing certain norms knowing that the government lacks the capacity to enforce or implement them (Avdeyera, 2007).

Thus, international legal changes with a domestic component will be less likely to be adopted than those without this characteristic. One might also presume that operating system changes requiring domestic action will take longer than those without this restriction, if only because domestic legislative processes are an additional hurdle to operating system change. Operating system change with a domestic political component might also be incomplete or inefficient, given that such changes must be adopted by over 190 different states in large, multilateral agreements; it might be expected that not all of them will adopt such changes or at least will do so in different ways and to different degrees. As a means to overcome these barriers, multilateral environmental agreements have moved towards using framework conventions in order to build global consensus on the need for collective action, to provide focus on certain priority issues, and to allow evolutionary and organic growth of a regime thereby giving domestic systems time to adapt and to adjust (Brunnée, 2004). This technique though could pose particular challenges for major powers since "[i]n these ongoing multilateral processes, it is more difficult for individual parties to determine agendas, to resist regime development, and to extricate themselves from regime dynamics" (Brunnée, 2004: 637). This, in turn, creates more strident opposition to international agreements at the domestic level in major powers.

The model above provides some clues on when operating system change might occur. It does not, however, specify the form that such change might take. Indeed, this raises a fundamentally different question than the ones addressed above and is beyond the scope of our present inquiry. Nevertheless, we might speculate that in many cases, the form of the operational system change (for example, actor rights) will be directly related to the form of necessity. When multiple changes are possible and those changes are at least partly substitutable for each other (e.g., changes in jurisdiction versus creation of supranational institutions), we expect that several factors come into play. Because of inertia in the system, the least dramatic change will be privileged. Furthermore, the preferences of leading states and the influences of domestic political processes will proscribe certain options. What remains will be the set from which operating system change may be adopted, providing the right conditions are present. Some of these concerns are evident in our discussion of the genocide norm in the following section.

Illustrating the interaction between the operating and the normative systems: the case of the genocide norm

The previous sections provide extensive, and somewhat abstract, theorizing about the two international legal systems and their interrelationship. In this section, we illustrate these ideas by reference to international legal change in one issue area – genocide. This is not intended to be a full test of the theoretical framework above. Indeed, this is beyond the scope of any one study, although in cumulative fashion a series of studies across many components of the normative system would serve to be a test of our expectation that international law works dynamically and interactively on multiple levels, for multiple purposes, and frequently by linking several topic areas. Rather, here we have more limited ambitions to demonstrate the systems we postulate and the processes of change that we describe.

Genocide is selected as the issue area for illustration in large part because of the breadth of acceptance for the norm in the world community. There is less controversy over the idea that genocide is wrong as compared with human rights norms concerning economic well-being for example. We, of course, recognize that there is some controversy over the specific provisions of the genocide norm, as reflected in some states' initial reluctance to sign the Genocide Convention or the reservations that they attached to their acceptance. Still, genocide provides us with an opportunity to view operating system change for a norm in which consensus appears broad and strong, among the purest cases for analysis. In contrast, norms on the use of force have historically been more controversial.

Another key consideration in selecting genocide is it that deals with behavior on both the international and domestic levels. Genocide law is primarily focused on the treatment of individuals within state borders, but changes in statutory limitations and jurisdictional rights for prosecuting crimes such as genocide have had an equally important impact on the international level in enforcing human rights norms. Although some may argue that the genocide norm has distant roots in natural law, its development and accompanying operating system changes are almost exclusively post-World War II phenomenon. Thus, genocide provides us with a case of norm adoption, much like those in international environmental law, which developed in the modern era and represents the new wave of international lawmaking. This allows us to examine more closely a narrow time period, a more manageable task than perusing an expansive period such as that covering the development of the law of the sea.

We explore genocide by first identifying key normative and operating system changes in the period under study. Yet we do not consider only actual operating system changes. Rather, we also consider instances in which operating system change did *not* occur in some areas and/or was merely proposed in the wake of a normative change. Specifically, how does the timing of subsequent operating system change (if such change occurs at all) correspond to our expectations? What conditions surround the operating system change and how do those comport with the conditions proposed above? What patterns of operating system change are evident? In all cases, this involves properly identifying the normative and operating system changes, specifying their causal sequence, and searching for the key factors suggested by the approach (George, 1979; George and McKeown, 1985). Although there are a number of changes in this issue area, for illustration purposes we describe only three, comprising some of the central components of the operating system: jurisdiction, institutions, and actors.

The genocide norm

That the systematic killing of national, ethnic, racial, or religious groups – genocide – was against international law was perhaps established prior to World War II; indeed some international and national court cases (e.g., *Reservations to the Convention on the Prevention and Punishment of Genocide*, 1951) explicitly make this argument. Nevertheless, the genocide norm was solidified and extended (the prohibition of genocide is no longer confined to wartime) in 1946 with the adoption of UN General Assembly resolution 96 and codified in the Convention on the Prevention and Punishment of the Crime of Genocide (1948). The convention elucidates a definition of those groups who might fall under the purview of the genocide definition as well as acts (e.g., forcible removal of children) that would constitute violations.

Prior to this time, there were few legal structures with which to deal with genocide. States had to rely on diplomatic protest or armed intervention (something not recognized under international law at the time) as mechanisms to punish those who committed genocide. These were rarely, if ever, exercised, as evidenced by the Turkish massacre of Armenians during World War I and the lack of retribution from that incident. Since World War II, genocide has clearly been recognized as contrary to international law. Yet most of the debate surrounding the adoption of the Genocide Convention, and throughout the 1950s, concentrated on refining the definition of genocide and the groups that might be subsumed under the definition (Kader, 1991). That is, prospective changes in international law dealt more with the normative system than the operating one.

The Genocide Convention has now passed its sixtieth birthday and is generally regarded as a triumph of international human rights consensus in a world of cultural and political diversity. Yet it is equally regarded as a failure in its ability to prevent genocide or to punish those responsible, as mass killings and their aftermath in Cambodia, Bosnia, and Rwanda illustrate. A review of the international law of genocide over the last six decades reveals a mixed bag of operating system changes designed to give the treaty effect and many missed opportunities to revise the operating system toward that same end. Clearly, most analysts have regarded the operating system for genocide as weak and largely ineffective (see Lippman, 1998 and ASIL, 1998 for a historical retrospective on genocide law over its first fifty years). The genocide in Darfur in the early twenty-first century and the limited international response have only served to emphasize the inadequacy of the system even though some improvements have been made.

Jurisdiction

Article VI of the Genocide Convention lays out the jurisdictional limits for prosecuting individuals suspected of genocide. The primary basis of jurisdiction is the territorial principle, whereby criminals are prosecuted according to where the offenses allegedly took place. Territorial jurisdiction is not necessarily exclusive as criminals might also be prosecuted under the nationality or passive personality principles depending on national laws; the nationality principle permits prosecution according to the citizenship of the alleged perpetrators whereas the passive personality principle is based on the nationality of the victim. Article VI recognizes the jurisdiction of an international penal tribunal, assuming one has been created and accepted by the relevant states. Most notable is the absence of provisions for universal jurisdiction (part of what Van

Schaack, 1997 calls the Convention's "blind spot"), whereby any state having the defendant(s) in custody could conduct a genocide trial. Of course, universal jurisdiction may effectively exist in practice, as demonstrated by national court cases to punish acts of genocide. *Attorney General of Israel* v. *Eichmann*, 1961, is a particularly dramatic example of this where Adolf Eichmann was kidnapped by Israeli operatives from Argentina and brought to Israel for trial and subsequent execution. In the United States, as an alternative to universal jurisdiction, the response was to deny entry into the country or to remove. In the case of individuals like John Demjanjuk who became naturalized US citizens after World War II, their citizenship was revoked and sixty-six other former Nazi officials were denaturalized as part of the US Department of Justice Office of Special Investigations effort to locate any remaining individuals in the US who took part in the Nazi atrocities during World War II.[1] Many states have taken this position, although it is far from certain that this is widely accepted. Indeed, war criminals past and present have been granted safe haven and/or protection in other states, largely on political grounds.

Over the past sixty years, there has not been much change in jurisdiction provisions for genocide. The war crimes tribunals for the former Yugoslavia and Rwanda both include provisions for concurrent jurisdiction between national courts and the tribunals, but international courts were given primacy. The International Criminal Court defers prosecution to states that have jurisdiction, but allows the ICC to take action only when such states are "unwilling or unable genuinely to carry out the investigation or prosecution" (Article 17(1)a of the Rome Statute).

Part of establishing territorial jurisdiction involved creating domestic legislation that makes genocide a crime (as provided in Article V of the Genocide Convention). Yet, very few states have undertaken to incorporate the necessary provisions in their own legal codes. Largely, the operating system for criminal acts has undergone little dramatic change with the adoption of the Genocide Convention. What best explains these circumstances?

---

[1] "A federal court in Cleveland ... stripped John Demjanjuk of his US citizenship, ruling that federal prosecutors proved [during] a two-week trial in May and June 2001 that he served the Nazi regime during World War II as a 'willing' guard at Nazi camps for more than two years." The court found that Demjanjuk served at four such camps, including the notorious Sobibor extermination camp, where he participated in "the process by which thousands of Jews were murdered by asphyxiation with carbon monoxide." From the US Department of Justice Press Release, "Federal Court Finds John Demjanjuk Assisted in Murder of Jews as Nazi Guard and Revokes his US Citizenship," February 21, 2002.

jurisdiction rules. Overall, the expectations of the model are fulfilled. The basic conditions for international legal change were present, but such change was arrested by opposition of leading states as well as domestic political conditions not conducive to the change.

There were some favorable conditions for the move to universal jurisdiction in the 1990s, but those same conditions were more conducive to other operating system changes, ones that rendered the need for universal jurisdiction largely moot. These were the creation of *ad hoc* war crimes tribunals and a permanent international criminal court (ICC). This illustrates how change on one dimension of the operating system can sometimes compensate for inadequacies on other dimensions.

Institutions

As much of the contemporary debate over genocide has focused on compliance mechanisms, it is perhaps not surprising that the most profound changes, proposed and actually implemented, center on institutions designed to ascertain and punish violations. It is in this part of the operating system that the most changes have been contemplated, although the number and scope of those implemented are considerably less than what has been proposed.

At the birth of the Genocide Convention, extant institutions were assumed to bear the primary burden for monitoring compliance with the norm and dealing with violations. In part, this may be a function of the available institutions for these purposes, but there was also significant opposition to proposed new structures. The Genocide Convention itself contains provision (Article VIII) that "Any Contracting Party may call upon the competent organs of the United Nations to take such action under the Charter of the United Nations as they consider appropriate for the prevention and suppression of acts of genocide . . . " The United Nations was just beginning to create the operating mechanisms to deal with human rights violations. The Commission on Human Rights (UNCHR) was the logical UN organ to deal with the problem of genocide and certainly other organs, such as subcommittees dealing with the treatment of minorities, would also be appropriate. Of course, threats to international peace and security stemming from and involving genocide could be handled by the Security Council. Article IX of the Convention also provided for referral of disputes to the ICJ.

Although genocide was to be handled within the institutions of the United Nations, there were various proposals for a permanent international criminal court. Indeed, such ideas date back to the earlier years of the twentieth century, but opposition from some key states killed those proposals, a result consistent with the expectations of our model. Although there were already the precedents for *ad hoc* tribunals (Nuremberg and Tokyo) stemming from World War II, support in the international community was not strong enough to create a permanent court.

It soon became obvious that UN human rights mechanisms were inadequate to deal with human rights violations in general, and with respect to genocide in particular. The UNCHR was historically a weak institution, with limited powers and torn by political and ideological disagreements among its members. Some states that were among the worst violators of human rights were elected to membership on the UNCHR. Indicative of this, Sudan was chosen as a member in 2004 in the midst of genocidal acts in Darfur. The UNCHR was so ineffective and held in such disrepute that it was replaced by the UN Human Rights Council in 2006. Yet this body was only incrementally changed from the UNCHR and modifications in its powers and composition were considerably less than envisioned in various reform proposals.

In the decades following the adoption of the Genocide Convention, various proposals for special committees or courts dealing with genocide were suggested, although never adopted. Seemingly recognizing the futility of pursuing these ideas, the international community began to create alternatives both within and outside the international legal system. The failure to make changes within the operating system has led some scholars and diplomats to suggest the normative system be altered in ways that enhance enforcement. For example, there has been an attempt to expand the norm of humanitarian intervention with the responsibility to protect so that states could militarily intervene in the affairs of other states for the purposes of redressing human rights violations or humanitarian emergencies. Although its validity is not universally accepted (see discussion in Joyner, 2007 and Weiss, 2007), this provides a mechanism to deal with genocidal acts, one that is only appropriate if supranational mechanisms are lacking. Many other proposals and efforts have sought to improve genocide enforcement, but have done so outside of the framework of international law. There have been various ideas for early warning systems for genocide and various committees to monitor compliance (e.g., Deehr, 1991). Non-governmental organizations (NGOs), such as International Alert, have also been created to work on compliance concerns. This suggests that adaptation to the failure of the operating system may occur extra-systemically (that is, outside of the international law operating system), the subject matter of the next chapter.

The 1990s saw renewed activity in terms of institutional changes in the operating system. Clearly, the United Nations system has been more intimately involved in genocide issues as the Security Council, ICJ, and other organs have dealt with the political shocks occasioned by the conflicts in Rwanda and the former Yugoslavia. Yet this level of activity is still perhaps below what might have been envisioned or hoped for at the time the Genocide Convention was adopted. More significant has been the creation of specific institutions to deal with genocide. The United Nations created a war crimes tribunal in 1993 to address the conflict in Bosnia and surrounding territories, and then adopted a similar tribunal a year later in response to the Rwandan civil war. The UN has also backed a special war crimes tribunal for Sierra Leone. Yet these courts were *ad hoc*, with their scopes limited to particular incidents.

Only in 1998 did the proposal for a permanent ICC finally receive support from a broad cross-section of states, and the court became operational in 2002. The ICC is a dramatic change in the international legal operating system. That body was granted international legal personality and was given powers to investigate and prosecute a set of international crimes, including genocide.

The key questions here are (1) why was the international community not more successful in creating institutions to deal with genocide, and (2) what accounts for the flurry of activity in this issue area during the 1990s, culminating in the creation of the ICC? Although it is clear that the theoretical operation of UN institutions remained compatible with the genocide norm, it soon became evident that such institutions proved inadequate and ineffective in practice. By the 1950s, it was obvious that UN agencies would not be able to meet the requirements for norm compliance for a range of human rights, not the least of which was genocide. At that point, the push for an operating system change would be renewed or in some cases begin. Yet, it was over four decades before such necessity was addressed. In large part, it was the political shocks of the 1990s that brought the international criminal court back to the international agenda.

The movement toward *ad hoc*, and now permanent, courts to handle genocide and other concerns lies in the political shocks of the last decade. Indeed, policymakers explicitly cite such shocks as prerequisites for such occurrences. The United Nations saw the genocidal acts in the former

Yugoslavia and Rwanda as the triggering events while others cited the end of the cold war as the facilitating condition (see Buergenthal, 2006; Kirsch, 2007). In any case, it did appear that a dramatic change in the political environment was necessary for a revival of the international criminal court idea. Either a rearrangement of political coalitions or a shock to the conscience of civilized nations (or perhaps both) provided the necessary impetus.

Of course, previous acts of genocide in Cambodia did not spur new action. There are several possible reasons for this lack of effect. As a necessary condition, political shocks may not always produce operating system change, even in the presence of other conditions. It may also be the case that the magnitude of the Cambodian shock was not enough to prompt action, given the lower levels of international publicity accorded that event and that details of the atrocities were not fully revealed until years later. Yet, the Cambodian genocide took place prior to another key shock, the end of the cold war, which proved crucial in the development of international institutions. This suggests the *combination* of political shocks was crucial to operation system change, at least in this case.

The conditions were then ripe for an operating system change in the form of new institutions, just as they were for moving toward universal jurisdiction. Yet the international legal system adapted in the direction of the former, rather than the latter, largely because the behavior of the leading states and the domestic political factors did not loom as large as impediments to change.

The United States initially opposed the creation of an international criminal court. Other important states, such as Britain, were also reluctant to support such an initiative. Consequently, while the idea of such a court persisted, it did not start on the road to becoming a reality until near the end of the twentieth century. This, together with the absence of political shocks, helps explain why few institutional changes were evident in the operating system over an extended period. Although the United States did not lead the charge for an international criminal court, it did not actively oppose the creation prior to the Bush Administration; indeed, the Clinton Administration had supported the general concept of the ICC.[2] US opposition has related more to certain provisions for the court, and the US has sought changes in the ICC treaty before becoming a

---

[2] President Clinton signed the treaty before leaving office, but ratification prospects were uncertain given significant opposition in the United States Senate. President George W. Bush then took the unusual step of "unsigning" the treaty in 2002.

party. Thus, this position is not equivalent to active and unequivocal opposition. Indeed, the US has also been a leader in pushing for the *ad hoc* war crimes tribunals that might be considered predecessors to the permanent court. In addition, only seven states opposed the Rome Conference resolution supporting the court and virtually all of Western Europe as well as Russia voted in favor. Furthermore, except for some opposition among Republican representatives in the US Congress and segments of the US military, the creation of such a supranational institution does not necessarily raise issues of domestic legal changes that might block or dilute its implementation.[3]

Many US concerns focused on the possibility that US military personnel serving abroad could be dragged before the ICC. Even though the Rome Statute that created the ICC contained a provision against reservations, the US has found ways to address its concerns without becoming a party, but also without blocking this new component of the operating system. The US has persuaded the UN Security Council and other recipients of US peacekeeping or military forces to grant immunity to those personnel against arrest, detention, or prosecution; this insulates US citizens in these capacities from ICC prosecution. In contrast, there would be few such assurances that personnel would be sheltered from foreign courts under a system that permitted universal jurisdiction. It has been through this process, albeit including a lengthy time-lag from the adoption of normative change, that operating system change in the form of *ad hoc* tribunals and the ICC has come about. Leading states such as the US would also be unwilling to enhance the power of the UNCHR or its successor, given that those bodies would largely be under the control of coalitions of states opposed to Western interests. In addition, many other states did not support an enhancement of those institutions, even as they gave at least verbal support to the human rights norms that those bodies were supposed to protect.

Clearly, necessity indicated that viable institutions needed to be created in order to give effect to the genocide norm. Yet political shocks to give such institutions impetus were sporadic over the coming decades and the opposition of leading states stifled several initiatives. The ICC comes about with new political shocks in the form of large-scale mass killings in the early 1990s. Only the US among key states stood in

---

[3] Except perhaps with respect to extradition; the lack of agreements with some neighboring states on handing over suspects to the war crimes tribunal for the former Yugoslavia has created some "safe havens" for war crimes suspects.

opposition, but the Clinton Administration did not attempt to prevent the creation of the institution, only change some of its provisions. Subsequently, the US has taken some actions that limit the reach of the ICC, making it suboptimal, but the court is now functional. It is too early at this writing to assess its efficacy.

Subjects/actors in international law

Identifying the actors who have rights and responsibilities is a key element of the international law operating system. Traditionally, public international law has assigned most of these elements to states, although the status of individuals, groups, and organizations was enhanced in the 1980s and 1990s (Arzt and Lukashuk, 1995). The Genocide Convention holds individuals directly responsible for genocidal acts (Article IV), with no ability to hide behind the veil of the state, consistent with the Nuremberg precedent. The ICC has similar provisions. Other than piracy and a few other concerns, such international crimes are unusual when the norm is to hold states responsible. Yet the Genocide Convention has few provisions for state responsibility, even though one might expect many acts of genocide to be committed by individuals acting on orders from state authorities. Article IX provides for referral of disputes over interpretation, application, or fulfillment of the Convention to the International Court of Justice. Yet this avenue has rarely been pursued. Despite efforts of some NGOs, signatory states were unwilling to press a case concerning Khmer Rouge killings in Cambodia and a case involving Pakistan and India was withdrawn after a negotiated agreement between the two states. Only the case brought by Bosnia-Herzegovina against Yugoslavia (*Bosnia and Herzegovina* v. *Yugoslavia, Serbia, and Montenegro*) has directly fallen under this provision of the treaty. The International Court of Justice issued its judgment in this long and complicated case in February 2007,[4] finding that Serbia had failed to prevent the genocide of more than 7,000 Bosnian Muslims at Srebrenica in July 1995; Serbia had further failed to cooperate with the International Criminal Tribunal for the Former Yugoslavia (ICTY) to apprehend and bring to trial key individuals (Ratko Mladic, former commander of the army of the Republika Srpska (VRS) and Radovan Karadzic, former president of the Republika Srpska) responsible for this genocide (see *Bosnia and Herzegovina* v. *Serbia*, 2007). The complex background of this case was to take into account the work of the

---

[4] The case was initially filed by Bosnia in March 1993.

ICTY and the International Court of Justice's reliance on ICTY decisions to evaluate the intent of the actions to determine whether genocide had occurred (see *Bosnia-Herzegovina* v. *Serbia*, 2007: paragraphs 245–376). Another genocide case (*Croatia* v. *Serbia*) remains on the court's docket. This was filed in 1999, but has not progressed since 2002 and may not do so on jurisdictional grounds. The upshot of this record may be that state-to-state suits in the ICJ on the basis of Article IX will remain rare with the establishment of the International Criminal Court, which is now available to hold individuals accountable for acts of genocide, particularly in light of such convictions at the ICTY and the International Criminal Tribunal for Rwanda (ICTR). This could even be more likely because there was no penalty against Serbia beyond the declaration in the ICJ's judgment that it had failed to prevent the specific act of genocide in Srebrenica and that it should take steps to deliver individuals responsible for these acts to the ICTY.

The major question is why the operating system, at least with respect to genocide, concentrated on individual responsibility to the neglect of state responsibility. The inertia of the extant system provides some explanation. Individual responsibility for genocidal acts could fit quite comfortably with the prevailing territorial and nationality jurisdiction principles, prevalent in the international legal system for criminal behavior and reiterated in Article VI. To rely exclusively on state responsibility would have been inconsistent with extant operating system practice. State responsibility is usually handled on the diplomatic level and through claims commissions (note the agreement between the United States and Germany on compensation to Holocaust victims and their families) or international courts. Imputing individual responsibility only makes sense if there are proper legal mechanisms for trying individuals suspected of genocide; yet the operating system is still deficient with respect to evidentiary standards and extradition to make this process efficient (Ratner and Abrams, 1997; Murphy, 2008). Yet this is wildly unrealistic in that many of the perpetrators would be committing genocide at the behest of the state. Holding states *and* individuals responsible would seem to be necessary. The provision for ICJ intervention in state disputes over genocide proved to be inadequate in the long run, given that many states accepted the Genocide Convention only with reservations that lessened the likelihood that Article IX on ICJ referral would ever be operative. ICJ jurisdiction would be problematic in any event when genocide was committed by a state against its own citizens, leaving no other state with standing to bring a case before that body.

The shock of World War II and the Holocaust shaped not only the normative system changes that were to occur, but also the operating system changes. The experience at Nuremberg probably led drafters of the Convention to emphasize individual responsibility given the frequent claims of Nazi officers that they were only following orders and the absence of any real state to hold responsible – note that both Germany and Japan had occupation governments. Yet, subsequent acts of genocide in Cambodia and elsewhere, shocks in and of themselves, did not produce any further operating system changes with respect to state responsibility. More recent experiences with respect to Sudan indicate great deference to that state's government in dealing with the conflict in Darfur and a reluctance to undertake any kind of legal action against it, even as the ICC had indicted its president. Thus, political shocks do provide some purchase in understanding operating system change, although they are suggestive of more change than actually occurred in recent times.

The focus on individual responsibility may be partly accounted for by reference to US policy, as well as that of its allies and some other leading states. After World War I, the United States opposed individual responsibility for war crimes, but switched positions at the time of the Genocide Convention, thus removing an obstacle to system change. Still, the United States resisted new powers to hold states accountable for actions. It was feared that the United States could be hauled before the courts of another country, representing a potential threat to the idea of sovereign immunity. This is a fear shared by many other states, including China. The United States did not ratify the Convention, even with its narrow focus, until the late 1980s, again indicating that it was reluctant to grant sweeping powers under the Convention. Indeed, US reservations with respect to the compulsory jurisdiction of the International Court of Justice led to the dismissal of Yugoslavian claims against it for NATO actions in Kosovo; US allies also sought to exclude ICJ action based on jurisdiction grounds. Accordingly, there is opposition among leading states to redressing the inadequacies of ICJ supervision of state behavior and indeed those states have relied on that inadequacy. Domestic political opposition, especially in the United States, has prevented any further expansion of legal powers to act against states accused of genocide. The Security Council remains the primary multilateral mechanism to punish state perpetrators of genocide (and other threats to international peace and security); the Security Council is also the organ empowered to give effect to ICJ judgments. The major power veto and the general limitations of that organization prevent it from playing a major role. With respect to genocide, states have been reluctant to implement national legislation to bring other sovereign states before their own courts, fearing reciprocal problems for their own actions.

Conclusion

This chapter has focused on where and how imbalances exist between the normative and operating systems. It identifies the conditions required to prompt change to correct the imbalance. But it recognizes that even if change occurs, it may not be adequate to correct fully the imbalance. There may be several reasons for this: inability to see a workable solution, the opposition of leading states or powers, or a lack of capacity to operate the needed change. Therefore, we can expect a considerable time-lag between the establishment of a norm and the correcting of any imbalance it may have with the existing operating system. This observation could prompt greater interest in formulating the structure and process for carrying out a norm at the same time that a norm is created. The danger with this approach is that of creating competing regimes that cut into the effectiveness of a system-wide or universal regime and produce differing legal pronouncements on similar or identical issues. This is not unlike the conflicts any federal system faces where its constituent parts may have differing practices and/or regimes.

Our analysis in this chapter provides insight into the development of the operating system where changes are generally prompted by a keenly felt and recognized need by enough elements of the international lawmaking community to carry out the change. The next requirement is to overcome the tendency towards the status quo. This is where a shock or strong external impetus can be effective in building broad support for an operating system change. Having crossed the basic threshold of recognizing a need and of generating the will to change, identifying the actual solution and ensuring the capacity to carry out that solution are important, but not as critical as the first two conditions. Changes to the operating system made to respond to needs in a specific normative area can serve as models or actual vehicles for other normative developments. We will explore this further in Chapter 5. Thus, while norms add to the normative content of the international legal system, operating system changes add to the governing and regulatory capacity of the international legal system.

4

Extra-systemic adaptations to systemic imbalance

From the analysis in the last chapter, it is evident that changes in the normative system do not always, and indeed often do not, immediately produce commensurate changes in the operating system. That could leave the two systems temporarily, or perhaps permanently, in imbalance. The result is that actors might not comply fully with rules, the rights of other actors could be unprotected, and remedies for violations of norms might not be available or are precluded.

Is the international legal system doomed to suboptimality? In a *closed* system, all interactions are endogenous and any regulation must come from the interactions inside the system. Such systems often have little adaptive ability, at least in the short term, because they cannot draw upon external resources or mechanisms when things go wrong. For example, computer software and platforms without the capacity for data sharing have largely atrophied in favor of more permeable systems. As we indicated in Chapter 2, however, the international legal system and its component parts are embedded in the broader international relations system. Accordingly, this *open* system is subject to influence from external forces; indeed, the political shocks necessary to systemic change are just one example of how external factors influence international law. Just as those influences can prompt change in the operating and normative systems, so too might external factors affect the implementation of the normative proscriptions and prescriptions and, by doing so, provide the international legal system with added adaptive capacity. Indeed, when the international legal system cannot regulate itself, the solutions are likely to be exogenous as Luhmann (1988: 22) indicates: "in legal operations, the interrelationships of these two spheres [Hart's primary and secondary rules] can only be recognized and only be practiced if the same norm quality is involved in both spheres. Otherwise, compensation for the inadequacies of law would lie outside the law."

Because the international legal system is not perfectly self-regulating and imbalances between the operating and normative systems occur, various actors may undertake actions that are outside the formal legal operating system, but nevertheless fill some of the gaps left by the suboptimal operating arrangements. In this chapter, we delineate the motivations of these strategic actors and then discuss the four processes or ways that such actors work to redress the imbalances created by the absence of a fully self-sufficient international legal system.

Opportunities and impetuses for adaptation

Before describing the forms of extra-systemic adaptations, it is worth briefly discussing the context under which they occur. Unlike biological systems, which may be inherently adaptive, the international legal system requires some agency to achieve change. Actors outside or inside of the legal operating system must observe the imbalance and have incentives to redress it. Even those actors (e.g., states) who are central to the international legal system might operate outside its confines in providing action to deal with the imbalance of the two systems; the actions occur outside the operating system because the actor has a special reason for going outside that system or the actor has failed to achieve change within the system. A variety of actors can be involved in these extra-systemic changes, ranging from states to international organizations (intergovern-mental and non-governmental), private enterprises, and in limited cases even individuals.

Most often, these parties are the ones who are willing *and* able to supply the mechanisms needed to ensure norm compliance. There could be a variety of actors who have strong preferences for the norm involved, but do not have the capacity to provide the needed mechanisms to redress the deficiencies of the operating system. In other cases, actors have the necessary resources and the desire to see norm compliance, but choose not to provide them for a variety of reasons: efficiency, other priorities, and the like.

The ability of actors to supply adaptations is not equal across the different components of the operating system. Outside of the system, there is probably little that actors can do directly to affect the rights of parties to make international law or to confer legal personality on those actors; these are endogenous. This is not to say that the subjects of law cannot be expanded in national legal systems, but there is little that can be done to change the *international* subjects of *international* law external to the system. This is why it remains important to undertake changes in some parts of the operating system even as extra-systemic adaptations compensate for deficiencies in others.

Agents could expand the rights and obligations of actors in national legal systems vis-à-vis international law. One can find such an example in the adoption of international human rights standards as part of some national constitutions (see Buergenthal, 2006). This has the effect of giving individuals legal standing in domestic courts to protect rights given to them by international instruments. It is an example of grafting the international obligation onto a national system for implementation. Similarly, actors can't change what constitutes international law through external mechanisms, but they can pursue alternative mechanisms (see discussion of soft law below) that achieve many of the same objectives as international treaties and custom.

The greatest opportunities for extra-systemic adaptations seem to lie in the broad area of implementation, specifically providing additional resources, institutional venues, and monitoring mechanisms to ensure that any norms adopted are followed in practice by the relevant parties. National legal action may be the primary mechanism used by states. This can involve changes in the rules of national courts, but it might also mean adaptations in terms of jurisdiction rules. Many of the basic jurisdiction principles (e.g., territorial, protective) lie in the hands of national governments anyway, and alterations in these could deal with broader problems than jurisdiction, although individual national actions can only deal with pieces of what might be a global problem. For example, a state may expand protective (to protect the state) or passive personality jurisdiction (based on the identity of the victim) in order to encompass some crimes, such as terrorist acts, if the international operating system is too diffuse to detect effectively, investigate, and prosecute such crimes.

Motivations

There are several broad reasons why agents seek to provide solutions to the operating–normative system imbalance. First, some agents act for largely altruistic reasons. They believe that their efforts are superior to extant operating system procedures or they feel compelled to act in order that certain values in the international political system are protected or enhanced. As operating system change is infrequent and often only partial, such actors can't afford, or are unwilling, to wait for the essential changes in the system that only come decades later or not at all. This is most evident in the human rights area in which private organizations, such as Human Rights Watch, carve out roles for themselves in reporting on human rights violations to promote more vigorous monitoring and action by the public bodies charged with overseeing human rights obligations.

Second, actors decide to take action for largely self-interested motivations. This can come in several forms. One is that organizational actors want to enhance their roles – task expansion behavior characterizes organizations of all varieties. Particularly in the case of NGOs, their *raison d'être* could require that they assume gap-filling roles and ultimately expand them in order to sustain the organization and its broad purposes. An example is the transformation of the Lawyers Committee for Human Rights into Human Rights First. The latter's president Michael Posner discussed the organization's "continued evolution into an even more visible, publicly engaged, results-driven organization which in turn reflects the new environment in which we conduct our work" (Posner, 2005/6: 4). In doing so, he referenced the organization's roots in using "legal expertise to engage in impact litigation, to provide quality legal representation to asylum seekers and to offer expert legal commentary and analysis on issues of the day" (Posner, 2005/6: 4). Yet his vision for the future was to add "targeted public advocacy campaigns" to their traditional litigation and policy analysis work. One such campaign was the End Torture Now campaign started in 2004 to end coercive interrogation practices and the secret detention of prisoners. Thus, from the work of experts in litigation and policy analysis, the new Human Rights First now also organizes broad-based public campaigns to support its policy objectives. The End Torture Now campaign, for example, recruited more than 75,000 e-activists throughout the US and around the world to support US legislation to end these practices.

Self-interested actors also benefit from private goods that attend to ensuring that international norms, even those with a public-goods component, are observed. For example, commitments to disarmament or other forms of arms control lead actors to share intelligence information (e.g., satellite images) with others about violations, including institutions within the international legal operating system. The immediate benefit is enhanced national security, especially for a state that is a neighbor to the alleged violator.

Third, the intervention of other actors could be to ensure that some issues not automatically part of the existing structures and processes are included. Actors might desire that issues concerning indigenous peoples, for example, be included as part of the monitoring of environmental accords. Note, for example, that the Arctic Council includes permanent participants from six groups of indigenous peoples: the Aleut International Association (AIA), the Arctic Athabaskan Council (AAC), the Gwich'in Council International (GCI), the Inuit Circumpolar Council (ICC), the Saami Council, and the Russian Arctic Indigenous Peoples of the North (RAIPON).[1] Extra-legal mechanisms ensure that such concerns are reflected in the implementation of the norm, something that would not occur under present operating system mechanisms.

Finally, actors, especially individual states, could desire greater control over the implementation of norms. Accordingly, they create structures and processes outside of the international legal operating system, perhaps even blocking efforts at operating system change. In these cases, the regulation of norms is left to domestic legal systems or powerful actors, who then retain some discretion (and national sovereignty) over the norm as it affects those actors. This is important in that it shows that actors are not always motivated by achieving greater compliance with specific international norms when they create mechanisms to supplement or replace international legal procedures. This also serves as a means to lower the level of perceived risk for states to accept such obligations, thereby enabling more states to participate and to create a broader base of parties even if it means allowing states greater discretion as to how they discharge those obligations.

The Statute of the International Criminal Court provides an example of this where states parties to the Statute share jurisdiction with the ICC. In the opinion of some, a shared international criminal responsibility is the most effective in holding individuals responsible for international crimes where "[n]ational courts form the front line of a system of enforcement. Supranational tribunals act as a backstop where national courts are unwilling or unable to adjudicate" (Burke-White, 2002: 3).

Below, we identify four different processes by which the operating–normative system imbalance is redressed. We should note that the outcomes of all these processes are not necessarily a fully functioning and effective system of norm implementation. Extra-legal adaptations still leave holes in the operating system unfilled and even when gaps are addressed, the adaptations could be inefficient or ineffective. Still, most adaptations have the effect of improving norm implementation and the effect of the normative system.

---

[1] See http://arctic-council.org/section/permanent_participants.

Extra-legal mechanisms for adaptation

NGOs and transnational networks

Among the most well-positioned actors to supplement or substitute for the international legal operating system are private groups or networks whose activities cross national boundaries. Most obvious are non-governmental organizations (NGOs), whose numbers have increased dramatically since 1990, swelling to over 30,000 (Kegley, 2008). In addition are transnational networks and "epistemic communities" (Haas, 1992), sets of individuals, often sharing particular expertise in an issue area, who coordinate actions and policy advice to promote normative goals. Processes involving these actors can be important gap fillers in addressing problems in the operating system.

Traditionally, NGOs were involved only in the process of norm creation. Most notably, they raised the salience of global problems, and helped mold treaty language, albeit usually working through national delegations. The prominence of women's issues on the international agenda today and the adoption of treaties such as the Convention on the Prohibition of the Use, Stockpiling, Production, and Transfer of Anti-Personnel Mines and on Their Destruction (or Ottawa Treaty) and the Statute for an International Criminal Court are examples of strategic NGO–state alliances that resulted from highly effective political lobbying (Ku and Gamble, 2000) – see more on this in the next chapter. Increasingly, however, NGOs are also assisting with elements of the operating system, particularly with the monitoring and implementation of legal instruments (Cohen, 1990; Charnovitz, 2006). This is not an entirely new phenomenon as the International Committee of the Red Cross has performed such monitoring and review functions in the area of international humanitarian law since 1863.[2] The difference is that today many more organizations are performing such functions in a larger number of issue areas that reach more deeply into a state's life. As treaties increasingly provide frameworks rather than static statements of norms, NGOs now also have a wider range of opportunities to influence the development of both the normative and operating systems. Root noted this phenomenon in the early twentieth century and wrote that: "Most of them [international societies for specific purposes] are not consciously

---

[2] The International Committee of the Red Cross describes itself as "an independent, neutral organization ensuring humanitarian protection and assistance for victims of war and armed violence." See www.icrc.org/eng.

endeavoring to develop international law, but they are building up customs of private international action. They are establishing precedents formulating rules for their own guidance, many of them pressing for uniformity of national legislation and many of them urging treaties and conventions for the furtherance of their common purposes" (Root, 1911: 583). Haas explains the opportunity provided to private expert or "epistemic communities" by the political and institutional process as they provide information to decision makers: "To the extent to which an epistemic community consolidates bureaucratic power within national administrations and international secretariats, it stands to institutionalize its influence and insinuate its views into broader international politics" (Haas, 1992: 4).

Contemporary circumstances have created further opportunities for NGOs to play more roles as a supplement to, or substitute for, the international law operating system (Charnovitz, 2006). This stems, in part, from international law's shift in focus from concerns of the state to those of the individual. This puts potential victims in a position to report violations, particularly when assisted by NGOs, that are able to reach broad transnational and international audiences. The technical character of many issues now facing policymakers continues to make them, as they have been for decades, receptive to expert information. "New technology and the increasingly complex and technical nature of issues of global concern not only increase decision makers' uncertainty about their policy environment but also contribute to the diffusion of power, information, and values among states, thereby creating a hospitable environment for epistemic communities" (Adler and Haas, 1992: 387). Greater complexity also increases the number of potential operating system gaps to fill, and thereby provides greater roles for experts and NGOs (Alter and Meunier, 2009).

Technology has also "broken governments' monopoly on the collection and management of large amounts of information" (Mathews, 1997: 50). Technical experts, such as climatologists with respect to environmental agreements, can thus offer professional evaluation on meeting treaty standards as well as assist in designing new mechanisms for compliance in order to avoid future problems (Ku, 2007). Events leading up to the signing of the Ottawa Treaty provided an example of the new power that individuals linked by technology, organized into a political network, and working in alliance with governments can wield (Green, 1997; see also Price, 1998). This influence can be particularly strong if the group is allied with states that are important either to the creation or the implementation of a particular norm. For example, private groups such as cetologists, whaling managers, and environmentalists promoted their views and positions with regard to the killing of whales through sympathetic government representatives (Peterson, 1992). In this way, private experts did not directly influence policy outcomes, but were present enough in the process to set limits that prevented the International Whaling Commission from swinging either toward no consumption or more consumption of whales. Thus, some NGOs are well positioned to assume roles in the implementation of norms, especially in those areas in which effective compliance requires specialized expertise or knowledge. Furthermore, NGOs have to remain flexible to survive because they rely on the voluntary contributions and commitment of individuals and their perceived influence toward meeting a particular commonly shared objective (see Charnovitz, 2006).

Beyond expertise, NGOs have been directly called up to perform operating system functions heretofore carried out by other actors. Intergovernmental organizations (IGOs) have specifically contributed to the prominence of NGOs as they have sought to circumvent governments. As governments seem less able or willing to meet the financial needs of norm monitoring and compliance, IGOs have tapped the vast private wealth available through the intermediation of NGOs. Thus, as national governments have been less willing to carry out the duties of the operating system or support international institutions that will perform those functions, NGOs have been called up to fill the gap, often as "subcontractors" to broader IGO efforts (Weiss and Shaw, 1998).

NGOs can also supplement government and IGO capacity in helping to keep abreast of specific issue areas and to assist in ensuring that certain obligations are met. Again, the work of the World Health Organization provides an example. WHO Legal Counsel Gian Luca Burci reports that "[m]ost relevant information comes to WHO from third parties, be they international agencies, NGOs or even individuals in the countries concerned" (Burci, 2005: 442). WHO then contacts the government of the affected country to seek confirmation. This is important when even the most well-staffed government agencies may not be able to monitor compliance or respond quickly to changing circumstances. Dai (2007) also argues that individuals reporting violations provide low-cost and "on the ground" monitoring of violations of human rights and other such obligations that pit individuals against the state. Many of these victims align with NGOs to give their message and plight broader reach. Some NGOs also have far greater resources than their governmental counterparts. For example, the International Union for the Conservation of Nature and Natural Resources (IUCN) has a large annual budget and a staff of hundreds (as reported in Dai, 2007).

NGOs have been especially instrumental in filling operating system gaps in human rights and the environment, issue areas in which political support and capacity on the ground is needed. These are also areas in which there is incentive for the victims to report non-compliance and in which states are likely to ignore individual complaints absent political pressure from the inside, the outside, or both. Their abilities to organize movements and to target particular issues make NGOs an important ally for victims to tell their stories to the world. Private organizations have an advantage in pursuing these activities within countries that neither foreign governments nor international institutions could. Furthermore, the political power and experience gained in promoting various norms continues beyond the enactment of specific obligations to monitoring their ongoing development and implementation. Given their familiarity with the issues and the players, NGOs or other private entities might, in fact, be more expert at monitoring and be better placed to implement norms than the formal governmental organizations created to do so. Indeed, the International Law Association Committee on Cultural Heritage recognized "the role of NGOs . . . both in defining the larger process of regulation and in implementing the harder law forged by intergovernmental agreement and custom" (ILA, 1998: 220). The report specifically noted the work of several categories of NGOs considered to be important in the work of protecting cultural heritage: private dealers, auction houses, collectors, museums and art galleries, anthropologists and archaeologists, indigenous and ethnic groups, artists, historic preservationists including archivists and art historians.[3] Keohane and Nye (2000) observed that in addition to the formal governance provided by states and the intergovernmental organizations that they created, governance now also takes place through networks of agents that can be both public and private and that derive credibility from their flexibility and dynamism to address new issues with fewer start-up costs (see also Sikkink, 1993).

In addition to NGOs, we see that voluntary, transnational networks have demonstrated their power to contribute to the operating system, especially to influence states in the monitoring of state conduct in the treatment of their own citizens. "Principled issue networks," as agents for

[3] See List of Current Committees at www.ila-hq.org.

change in state behavior and even in international standards, have emerged from the increased level of private transnational activity. As Ku (2007: 5) recognizes, "ad hoc partnerships have been formed to perform functions that centralized, formal public institutions seemed unable to address either effectively or adequately on their own."

Made possible through resources provided by foundations, spurred on by the commitment of individuals, and held together by new technologies, these transnationally linked organizations have had some notable achievements, particularly in the protection of human rights (Sikkink, 1993). Even decades ago, the kind of "people power" generated by Helsinki Watch, Charter 77, Solidarity, and other groups eventually created the channels for political activism that brought pressure for human rights and, ultimately, an end to the cold war from within the Warsaw Pact countries themselves. Yet, while it seems clear that the public sector can no longer function effectively without the cooperation and participation of the private sector and the involvement of individual citizens, it remains true that the private sector cannot solve all problems without the infrastructure and coordination that states and international institutions provide.

Another example may be drawn from the anti-capitalist or anti-globalization movements that shadowed the summits of the world's leading economic powers starting in the late 1990s to protest the perceived economic inequalities and injustices created by the liberalizing trade environment. This movement spawned major demonstrations in 1999 during a meeting of the World Trade Organization in Seattle, at the World Bank Board of Governors meeting in Washington, DC in 1999, and at the Genoa Group of Eight Summit in 2001. The violence that caused the death of a protester in Genoa may have served as a turning point after which the International Monetary Fund and the World Bank agreed to a dialogue with the protesters. These protests and the press coverage that they invited managed to raise public awareness of the potential injustices created by the globalizing economy (see Kaldor, 2003).

The importance of NGOs and private transnational networks functioning as part of civil society caused UN Secretary-General Kofi Annan to note that: "We must also adapt international institutions, through which states govern together, to the realities of the new era. We must form coalitions for change, often with partners well beyond the precincts of officialdom" (Annan, 2000: 7). As Kaldor (2003) argues, the elements of civil society – voluntary associations, movements, parties, and unions for example – enable individuals "to act publicly." In today's globalized world, these elements are also enabled to act transnationally.

We note that some transnational networks are not exclusively built between private actors, but some are actually bridges connecting officials in different governments. Such official, albeit informal, networks can play key roles in ensuring the effectiveness of international standards. A prominent current example is in the global effort to fight terrorism. Slaughter (2004: 1–2) explains:

> Public attention focused on military cooperation, but the networks of financial regulators working to identify and freeze terrorist assets, of law enforcement officials sharing vital information on terrorist suspects, and of intelligence operatives working to preempt the next attack have been equally important. Indeed, the leading expert in the "new security" of borders and container bombs insists that the domestic agencies responsible for customs, food safety, and regulation of all kinds must extend their reach abroad, through reorganization and much closer cooperation with their foreign counterparts . . . Networked threats require a networked response.

Yet there are concerns about whether the international legal operating system can rely on these informal arrangements. First, the *ad hoc* and selective character of these partnerships has caused concern about the effectiveness and reliability of such arrangements as durable pillars of global governance. Second, there is an exaggerated perception of the ability of NGOs and transnational networks to carry out a wide range of operating system activities. The potential fragmentation in information, resources, and decision making could, in the long run, be a threat to the order and authority that are requisite to civil society (see more on this problem in Chapter 6).

Despite these concerns, most scholars acknowledge the positive influence that NGOs and transnational networks have had on contemporary international law in areas such as the well-being of individuals, human rights, gender and race equality, environmental protection, sustainable development, indigenous rights, nonviolent conflict resolution, participatory democracy, social diversity, and social and economic justice (Charnovitz, 2006; Otto, 1996). In the broadest sense, we might be moving toward the point where effective and sustained attention to these issues requires the political and financial mobilization of resources at all levels from local to global. This is where the voluntary, local, and issue-specific character of NGOs and transnational networks makes them a useful link between the subnational community and national and international communities and institutions. By providing a link, NGOs and transnational networks supplement the human and financial resources of governments, intergovernmental organizations, and other elements of the legal operating system.

Legal internalization

Traditional conceptions of the international legal operating system rely on international institutions and processes to supervise norms. Yet, one of the adaptations to inadequacies in this system is to rely on *domestic* legal mechanisms to pick up the slack. These are quite distinct from executing legislation required of treaty obligations or other mechanisms that are part of the operating system. This is described well by the third component of Koh's (1997: 2649) view of transnational legal process, internalization:

> Legal internalization occurs when an international norm is incorporated into the domestic legal system through executive action, judicial interpretation, legislative action, or some combination of the three . . . Judicial internalization can occur when domestic litigation provokes judicial incorporation of human rights norms either implicitly, by construing existing statutes consistently with international human rights norms, or explicitly, through what I have elsewhere called "transnational public law litigation."

Legal internalization redresses problems with implementation or enforcement in which some states are unwilling to follow the international norm. The problem could take place for a variety of legal, political, social, or economic reasons. For example, states might prefer to deal with sensitive international norms through domestic processes, which are more malleable or reflective of national cultural practices. National legal systems could also demand national enforcement of international precepts. In Canada, depending on the subject matter, implementation of a treaty obligation could require separate actions not only of the Federal Parliament, but also of individual provincial legislatures because of the division of legislative power provided by Canada's Constitution.[4] Legal internalization can also take place when domestic lobbying embeds international law norms into binding domestic legislation or even constitutional law that officials of a non-complying government must then obey as part of the domestic legal fabric. Local actors then attain standing to press claims and seek redress in domestic courts.

---

[4] See Government of Canada, International Treaties: Canadian Practice at http://dsp-psd. pwgsc.gc.ca/Collection-R/LoPBdP/BP/prb0004-e.htm.

The 2004 ruling by the Oklahoma Court of Criminal Appeals in *Osbaldo Torres* v. *State of Oklahoma* provides an example of how domestic legal institutions are involved in giving effect to the decisions of the International Court of Justice (specifically the case of *Avena and other Mexican Nationals (Mexico* v. *United States of America)*, No. 128 (March 31, 2004)). The *Avena* case was brought on behalf of the government of Mexico before the International Court of Justice because of the failure of the United States to notify the Mexican government of the arrest and detention of more than fifty Mexican nationals in ten different states of the US. The Mexican nationals were subsequently tried and sentenced to death, but claimed relief for the failure of the United States to carry out its obligations under the Vienna Convention on Consular Relations to make available access by foreign nationals to appropriate consul.

In its decision, the International Court of Justice found that the United States had violated Article 36 of the Vienna Convention on Consular Relations and ruled that: "the appropriate reparation in this case consists in the obligation of the United States of America to provide by means of its own choosing, review and reconsideration of the convictions and sentences of the Mexican nationals . . . by taking account both of the violation of the rights set forth in Article 36 of the Convention . . ." (ICJ, *Avena*: 66, para. 143). The judgment went on to specify what it considered to be appropriate review and reconsideration and further noted that "the clemency process, as currently practiced within the United States criminal justice system, does not appear to meet the requirements [of providing access to consuls during the overall judicial proceedings]." (ICJ, *Avena*: 72, para. 152, subpara. 9). The Oklahoma Court of Criminal Appeals acknowledged that the US was bound by treaties, in this case, the Vienna Convention on Consular Relations, and that:

> [a]s this Court is bound by the treaty itself, we are bound to give full faith and credit to the *Avena* decision. I am not suggesting that the International Court of Justice has jurisdiction over this Court – far from it. However, in these unusual circumstances the issue of whether this Court must abide by the court's opinion in *Torres's* case is not ours to determine. The United States Senate and the President have made that decision for us.[5]

---

[5] Oklahoma Court of Criminal Appeals: *Osbaldo Torres* v. *State of Oklahoma* (No. PCD-04–442) (May 13, 2004). See also Damrosch, Brief of International Law Experts and Former Diplomats as *Amici Curiae* in Support of Petitioner, Appeal from the District Court of Oklahoma, County, State of Oklahoma Case No. CF-1993–4302 (April 30, 2004).

Nevertheless, the existence and degree of legal internalization is always subject to the limits imposed by the national law in question or, in the case of the United States, by the US Constitution as well as relevant federal and state laws and practices. For example, in a similar case to those noted above, the US Supreme Court in *Medellin* v. *Texas* held in 2008 that ICJ decisions were not binding federal law and that ICJ judgments could not be enforced over state rulings and procedures, at least in the death penalty and consular notification questions raised by the *Medellin* case. The US Congress could still pass legislation to give effect to the Vienna Convention on Consular Relations, but legal internalization is not automatic either with the adoption of the convention or with the ruling by the ICJ.

In the United States, there may be a trend toward an increase in adaptive behavior. The editors of the *American Journal of International Law* (Damrosch and Oxman, 2004: 42) observed in one year that:

> On the docket of the United States Supreme Court in 2004 is a substantial cluster of cases at the intersection of constitutional and international law. In the previous two Supreme Court Terms, the Court had adverted to sources of law and practice outside the United States, in its treatment of constitutional claims involving the death penalty and same-sex relationships. The apparent willingness of the Court to consider international and foreign authorities in reaching its conclusions on contested issues of international law has raised to new prominence the debate over the relationship between constitutional and international law. It is not yet clear whether the new (or newly rediscovered) interest of the Court in international sources presages a long-term trend towards a more cosmopolitan constitutional jurisprudence. On the assumption that this represents more than a passing fad, advocates before the Court . . . for example, in the cases involving the "enemy combatant" detainees at Guantanamo Bay – have vigorously pressed arguments concerning international and foreign law in connection with the constitutional issues at stake. The Court's acceptance of quite a few cases raising a mixture of international and constitutional questions for decision . . . may signal that the Court is preparing for a new era of engagement with legal developments external to the United States, or, alternatively, that it seeks to limit (or in any event to delimit) the relevance of such developments for the US legal system.

The European Union represents a special case and one in which internalization has gradually become a matter of routine. Burley (Slaughter) and Mattli (1993: 42) described this:

> Until 1963 the enforcement of the Rome treaty [the constituent treaty of the European Union], like that of any other international treaty,

depended entirely on action by the national legislatures of the member states of the community. By 1965, a citizen of a community country could ask a national court to invalidate any provision of domestic law found to conflict with certain directly applicable provisions of the treaty. By 1975, a citizen of an EC country could seek the invalidation of national law found to conflict with self-executing provisions of community secondary legislation, the "directives" to national governments passed by the EC Council of Ministers. And by 1990, community citizens could ask their national courts to interpret national legislation consistently with community legislation in the face of undue delay in passing directives on the part of national legislatures.

The pioneering work in the development of a regional human rights system that the jurisprudence of the European Court of Human Rights represents is a further important example of the interactions between supranational and national systems of law. One of the more sweeping recent examples is that of the British incorporation of the European Convention on Human Rights into its domestic law that "marks a dramatic shift in how individual rights are conceptualized under British law . . . The Human Rights Act, which puts courts and other public authorities under a positive duty to 'give effect' to the rights enumerated in the European Convention in their day-to-day activities, marks a shift in the perception of civil liberties from residual freedoms to positive rights" (Vick, 2002: 330).

The incorporation of international norms into domestic legal processes has several advantages. Among the most notable is that the monitoring and enforcement of the law is invested in national legal operating systems, all or most of which are more developed than the international system. This means that norms violations are more likely to be detected, and most importantly there are established mechanisms for dealing with such violations. Although there has been a significant increase over the last decade in the creation of international tribunals, the international court system is still quite weak and structurally limited when compared to its domestic counterparts. Indeed, one might argue that legal internalization is, in some cases, superior to international operating system equivalents.

Legal internalization, however, is not without its flaws or limitations. First, internalization is probably most effective in monist legal systems in which national and international law are part of the same system. In addition, the adaptation is strongest in systems in which international laws supersede national laws (e.g., Germany) as opposed to those in which the national and international laws are considered co-equals (e.g., United States).

Second, legal internalization as an adaptation to operating system inadequacy is likely to be incomplete when viewed from a global perspective. For internalization to be fully effective, it must take place in over 190 different states. This is unlikely, as some states will resist such actions and there is no assurance that such internalizations will be consistent with the objects and purposes of the international norms. Indeed, the capacity of individual states to internalize international standards varies widely and may result in providing international protection only to those living in the most advanced countries with the best developed domestic political processes and institutions.

Even if it were to occur universally, the lack of democratic processes and legal mechanisms in many states will prevent international norms from influencing the behavior of government officials. Authoritarian states are often characterized by a lack of independent interest groups to press for norm compliance or an ability of state officials to subvert the legal process in order to avoid being held accountable for norm violations. There are instances, however, of states allowing access to their national courts to hear claims based on actions that occurred outside the boundaries of that state. Belgium has enacted universal jurisdiction provisions that might allow it to prosecute former Israeli Prime Minister Ariel Sharon for actions during the 1982 invasion of Lebanon. Furthermore, foreign plaintiffs have relied on a US law from over 200 years ago, the Alien Tort Claims Act, to make claims for actions that did not occur in the United States and did not involve any US citizens (Slaughter and Bosco, 2002). Thus, there are even adaptations for other failed adaptations to inadequacies in the international operating system.

Third, legal internalization may be ill-suited or irrelevant for international norms that deal exclusively with the interactions between states, absent an internal component. Thus, although in some sense these adaptations are the ideal response to operating system failures, in practice they are likely to be only a partial solution.

Other domestic legal and political processes

Not all the national solutions to an inadequate operating system involve legal internalization. Other domestic legal and political processes may be called upon as well. One of the most serious inadequacies of the present international operating system is in the issue area concerning the use of force. Whether it has been providing the definitive interpretation of the concept of humanitarian intervention, interrogation of prisoners, or of preemptive action in the face of some other perceived threat, the UN Charter system dealing with the use of force has come under increasing stress since the end of the cold war in 1989 (Boutros-Ghali, 1995). Yet if the current structure of international institutions does not effectively address these questions, does this necessarily mean a return to a self-judging and unregulated international security system? Implicit in that question is the assumption that without international supervision by international institutions, state behavior is essentially unregulated. Such a conclusion would overlook the considerable number of national safeguards that can exist at the state level to protect against the wasting of lives and resources through military operations that do not serve a state's interests. This is relevant to international regulation because the international system also tries to eliminate the unregulated use of force in order to minimize destruction and loss of life and, as such, is consistent with the purposes of many national safeguards.

National safeguards are not a substitute for international regulation or legal internalization, but when the latter fail or prove inadequate, regulation can and does move to the national level. National safeguards further come in two forms – the formal and the informal. Formal safeguards are found in constitutions and national institutions such as legislatures, courts, and budgets. For example, in the United States, the power to wage war is vested in the Executive as the Commander in Chief. Nevertheless, waging war over the objections of a substantial portion of the population, and particularly if Congress has triggered a desire to involve the legislature more directly in decisions of war and peace, creates a tension. This contest came to a peak in the United States during the 1970s and the Vietnam War. Congress decided to assert its prerogatives by enacting the War Powers Resolution in 1973. Even though the resolution "affirms a congressional understanding of the original constitutional intent to require congressional participation in decisions 'to introduce United States Armed Forces into hostilities,'" US presidents from Richard Nixon to Bill Clinton regarded the resolution as unconstitutional. President George W. Bush acted in conformity with the resolution by seeking and obtaining specific authorization for the war on terrorism (September 2001) and for the war in Iraq (October 2002) (Damrosch, 2004: 134).

In Germany, the long-held view that the Basic Law of 1949 (*Grundgesetz*) only allowed the use of German armed forces in military activities in defense of the North Atlantic Treaty area was changed following the 1994 ruling by the Federal Constitutional Court in the

International Military Deployments Case. The Court articulated the following view of the German army, that the constitutional rules "seek to ensure that the Federal Army, instead of becoming a source of power solely for the use of the Executive, will be integrated as a 'parliamentary army' into a democratic constitutional system governed by the rule of law, in other words to preserve for Parliament a legally relevant influence on the establishment and use of the armed forces" (*International Military Deployment Case*, 1994: 348). In the United States, the budget is in the hands of the legislature so that Congress can assert power by cutting off funds to continue a conflict. Following the involvement in the former Yugoslavia, Canada and the Netherlands adopted more formal and regularized consultations with Parliament prior to the commitment of any troops to military operations. A survey of the new members of NATO showed that they "have had to pay attention to domestic constituencies and allow opportunities for transparent deliberation about decisions that could embroil those countries in military conflict" (Damrosch, 2004: 146). Even in the United Kingdom, parliamentary bodies in both the House of Lords and the House of Commons have been examining an appropriate role for Parliament in decisions regarding the commitment of British troops.[6] These institutions and their underlying processes provide disincentives or prohibitions against norm violation that are independent of international influences, but nevertheless effective. For example, if prohibitions against certain human rights violations were embedded in national law, then these might have been present even before the development of a concomitant international norm.

Informal safeguards operate through political culture and public opinion. For example, the press and the political process provide opportunities for skepticism to be voiced about a war and create the conditions to end the involvement in a conflict. The Vietnam War in the US was clearly a case in which the tide of public opinion slowly turned, making continuation of the war impossible (Mingst, 2003). The effectiveness of these safeguards varies widely depending on the strength of the domestic political system, including whether it is democratic and how open it is to public debate. To the extent that international norms are shared by domestic audiences and/or are encased in national cultures, there will be

---

[6] See House of Lords Select Committee on Constitution at www.publications.parliament. uk/pa/ld200506/ldselect/ldconstr/236/23607.htm; the UK Government Consultation Paper on War Powers, October 25, 2007.

informal, but powerful, constraints on government officials to adhere to those norms. This may occur even if national legal constraints are absent. The availability of email and other virtually instant modes of communication now make the hardships and excesses of war difficult to conceal or to ignore. One need only recall that the appalling conditions of the Abu Ghraib prison were revealed by a soldier who had photographed the practices with a cell phone. The rejection of leaders in Spain in 2004 and in Australia in 2007 after they had taken their countries to war further demonstrates the power of the ballot box to change policies that appear to be excessive and ineffective.

Domestic political processes further provide international institutions opportunities to influence government behavior because all governments have to respond in some way to domestic constituent demands (Dai, 2007). This is particularly true for weak international institutions that would otherwise have little means to reach beyond the officials of any state. Dai (2007) notes that the Long-Range Transboundary Air Pollution Convention facilitated the involvement of environmental activists in the compliance process, and indeed helped legitimize the environmental demands of pro-compliance activists.

Such informal, national mechanisms might be supplemented by a general trend toward multilateralism as a basis for foreign policy. Even when not institutionalized by international organizations, states can pressure other, recalcitrant states to adhere to international norms. The international community of states will also monitor the behavior of others, and seek conformity of behavior, usually in the favor of the international norm. Discussions about the unilateralist positions of the United States because of its reservations with regard to the Kyoto Protocol and the Rome Statute of the International Criminal Court are two examples in which there seemed little opportunity to express a contrary view that would not be regarded as fundamentally hostile to the protection of the environment or the prosecution of international crime. Thus, even in the absence of formal legal mechanisms, the international community can enforce its standards of behavior.

National political and legal processes can also take on more prominent roles in cases when international law appears inadequate to address particular circumstances. When existing international standards and structures are under stress, national debate and political process can help to fill the gap and set the criteria for action as well as the limits for such operations (Roberts, 1999). For example, the closer the use of military force gets to full-scale war, the more national systems play a role in the decision to take part in such operations and in overseeing them. This process, in turn, contributes to shaping both the practice and scope of international action. As the Panel on UN Peace Operations concluded in 2001: "[T]he United Nations does not wage war. Where enforcement action is required, it has consistently been entrusted to coalitions of willing States, with the authorization of the Security Council acting under Chapter VII of the Charter" (UN Report, 2001: para. 53).

The interactions of international and domestic decision-making processes have been well recognized by international organization scholars such as Cox and Jacobson (1973: 428), who concluded that the significance of international organizations is better judged "not as how independent they are of states, but how far they involve the effective policymaking process of governments." What debates in the United States and the United Kingdom over the 2003 war in Iraq now tell us is that involving the effective policymaking processes of national governments is no longer adequate in all cases. National decision-making processes require certain levels of legitimacy that may now include appropriate international authorization and standards. At the same time, international standards may require national political processes to implement and to maintain compliance (see Ku and Jacobson, 2003).

As with other adaptations to international operating system gaps, reliance on domestic political and legal processes is far from foolproof. Similar to internalization, there will be considerable variation across states with respect to national laws that serve to monitor and protect international norms. In addition, we recognize that domestic audiences and cultures are not always supportive of international norms; note the divergence between international norms on the status of women and cultural views on female genital mutilation. Furthermore, government officials could choose to ignore or circumvent domestic law or public opinion in foreign policy. The rule of national law and the ability of domestic audiences to sanction violators (for example, at election time) is much greater in democracies than in states that lack an independent judiciary and mechanisms for public input into policy formulation. Yet domestic economic concerns often trump foreign policy concerns in elections, and thus this is an imperfect process to support international norm compliance.

Despite its limitations, relying on domestic legal and political processes as substitutes for the international operating system has some very attractive features. Most notable is that if international norms are already protected in national legal systems and well ensconced in national culture and attitudes, international law can be almost self-enforcing. One might think of the widespread acceptance of diplomatic immunity and the need for national systems to pass the requisite laws and set up appropriate systems in order to ensure protection and immunity of diplomats. Even though institutions at the international level could be required to address problems that arise, as was the case with the *Iranian Hostages Case* (1980), we would generally think of the system of diplomatic immunity as fairly well settled and widely accepted. Thus, there may be little need for formal international operating system provisions, and therefore little concern if such mechanisms are absent or deficient.

"Soft law" mechanisms

Finally, but far from least important, are so-called "soft law" mechanisms for ensuring norm compliance. Chinkin (1989: 50) points out that the term soft law encompasses a wide range, but also that it is an increasingly utilized tool:

> There is a wide diversity in the instruments of so-called soft law which makes the generic term a misleading simplification. Even a cursory examination of these diverse instruments inevitably exposes their many variables in form, language, subject matter, participants, addressees, purposes, follow up and monitoring procedures. These variables, coupled with the inherent contradictions in any concept of soft law, highlight the challenges presented to the structure and substance of the traditional legal order by the increasing use of soft law forms.

Despite the ambiguity, soft law mechanisms are broadly those that do not involve formal legal obligations or legal processes, but nevertheless represent a shared understanding or consensus about procedure or behavior among the parties. In the context of the operating system, informal or soft mechanisms for resolving jurisdictional disagreements (e.g., how to resolve disputes when overlapping jurisdiction is present) or disputes over substance (e.g., what diplomatic solutions are legitimized) represent soft law adaptations to inadequacies in hard law provisions. A growing body of empirical work shows that such informal mechanisms influence behavior (Dai, 2007; Shelton, 2000; Weiss and Jacobson, 1998; Chayes and Chayes, 1995).

As noted above, soft law mechanisms have multiple forms and purposes and we cannot describe all those variations here. Nevertheless, for illustration purposes, we describe a few of the ways in which soft law fills the gaps left by its hard law counterparts. Soft law can provide for both norms and their implementation when formal agreements are not possible or involve issues that are heretofore considered domestic concerns. For example, commodity agreements or those on the marketing of specific products, such as breast milk substitutes, provide a way to monitor and regulate behavior of international concern without resort to a treaty (Chinkin, 1989). Similarly, soft law is a vehicle to link international law to private entities regulated principally by domestic law, such as individuals and transnational corporations. The practices of corporate social responsibility are an example of how companies doing business across borders adhere to good labor practices and environmental protection by complying with domestic law in their worldwide operations (see Westfield, 2001–2; Bunn, 2004).

Soft law may also function as a supplement or follow-up to traditional operating system mechanisms. Indeed, as in the case of international environmental law, a treaty might provide for a framework convention that can be followed by protocols that generate soft law or practice in order to supplement the original text. Shelton (2000: 27) explained that: "Typically, the framework convention establishes a structure for further co-operation between the parties through monitoring and implementation procedures, exchanging data, and facilitating regulation."

Soft law fills in some gaps left by the formal operating system, but why would actors choose to rely on the former, which is sometimes ambiguous and may create multiple regimes? Abbott and Snidal (2000) identify a number of advantages of soft law. These include lower contracting or negotiating costs, especially in comparison to long and detailed legal agreements, such as those concerning trade negotiated under the auspices of the World Trade Organization, or the extended period prior to a treaty's entry into force experienced by such major international instruments as the Third United Nations Convention on the Law of the Sea. Soft law also entails fewer sovereignty costs, something that states reluctantly bear when signing hard legal agreements.

States also adopt soft law provisions in areas in which efforts have failed to produce hard law (Abbott and Snidal, 2000). Such guidelines could later be the basis for hard law, but nevertheless may function much as hard law does in the interim, albeit without the same obligations for compliance. Preservation of the world's forests through the Forest Stewardship Council is such an example. Loggers, foresters, environmentalists, and sociologists banded together to form the Forest Stewardship Council (FSC) in 1993. Its purpose was to provide a forum for dialogue on what constituted a sustainable forest and set forth principles and standards to guide "forest management towards sustainable outcomes." Acknowledging that achieving these goals requires the cooperation of a diverse group of actors, the Council encourages the use of its standards "while the discussion continues." The FSC reports that its standards are in use in almost sixty countries around the world, including the United States.[7]

Soft law therefore provides greater flexibility as states do not risk creating operating system institutions that turn out to be inappropriate, ineffective, or difficult to adapt or eliminate over time (Guzman, 2005). Soft law also allows executives to avoid problematic domestic political constraints and ratification procedures that could block the adoption of hard law (Guzman, 2005). Finally, soft law institutions and processes can be the product of compromises when states desire a particular international norm, but are reluctant to create the necessary operating system mechanisms that ensure its creation or effect.

Despite the challenges, Chinkin (2000: 42) observed that soft law is also a phenomenon that is here to stay because international affairs have outpaced the capabilities of traditional lawmaking machinery and that norm creation must occur "through international organizations, specialized agencies, programmes, and private bodies that do not fit the paradigm of Article 38(1) of the Statute of the ICJ." Dai finds that soft law can have particular influence because of "its potential ability to empower domestic constituents, who directly impact a government's rational self-interests" (Dai, 2007: 151). We might also find that over time, soft law hardens through practice or through implementation by international or national institutions.

Conclusion

The operating system does not always serve to facilitate the implementation and compliance of the rules embedded in the normative system. This is a cause for concern in that failed enforcement stifles the will of the international community. Yet we have argued in this chapter that the normative system does not depend on the operating system alone to ensure implementation and compliance. Various processes outside the international legal system come into play that fill some of the gaps left by the suboptimality of the operating system. Above, we outlined four

[7] See Forest Stewardship Council United States, www.fscus.org.

processes on how this occurs: (1) NGOs and transnational networks; (2) internalization of international law; (3) domestic legal and political processes; and (4) soft law mechanisms. The question remains whether this is a desirable outcome or not.

The use of the terms "gaps" or "suboptimality" implies a deficiency in the system, with all the pejorative elements associated with that. Yet, having national safeguards, soft law, and programs by interested actors is not necessarily undesirable and indeed could in some cases be superior (more efficient and cheaper) to having the same functions performed under a vibrant operating system (Guzman, 2008).

If neither the operating system nor the gap-filling processes ensure norm implementation or compliance, then problems arise. When one or the other perform the roles, it is probably better in most cases than having no mechanisms, whatever their source. The relative value of functions inside or outside the formal operating system depends on the effectiveness and efficiency of those options.

The operating system is probably better positioned to undertake its functions in a comprehensive fashion; the gap-filling processes in this chapter at best address one issue area and then often only address one aspect of that issue area. Our analysis indicates that none of the four adaptations alone is sufficient to ensure that international norms are adopted and actors continue to adhere to their prescriptions. Even in combination, a number of holes remain. Furthermore, because some of the adaptations are *ad hoc*, there is a tendency for periods of imbalance to persist until actors react. In addition, such *ad hoc* measures are not well suited to addressing new concerns or sudden changes in the international legal system. Finally, adaptations tend to be unevenly distributed across state members of the international legal system. Rarely will certain adaptations (i.e., internalization) spread to the almost 200 states in the world, leaving more of a patchwork of international norm compliance rather than blanket coverage. One might presume that legal systems in developed and democratic countries are more amenable to some adaptations than poorer and authoritarian governments. Although a network of NGOs provides better coverage than any single organization could, there will still be a collage of functions and some areas uncovered.

Despite their limitations, we also concluded that such adaptations could be superior to operating system mechanisms in a number of instances. For example, soft law mechanisms offer flexibility and greater acceptability advantages for states and this might make normative provisions more likely to be adopted in the first place. Furthermore, reliance on domestic legal and political institutions that are stronger and more developed than international structures allows greater access for a range of actors and more effective compliance mechanisms to ensure implementation of the norms. In areas in which an international agreement constitutes a framework or guiding principle or in which the shape of an international legal obligation is still in formation, such extra-legal mechanisms are useful precursors to more specific international standards and obligations.

Nevertheless, for individual experiences outside the traditional international law framework to help shape the development of a more formal international legal regime, such extra-legal activity needs to be monitored and assessed in a broader international setting. In 1997, Slaughter (1997) published "The Real New World Order", in which she concluded that the international governance model with a multipurpose international institution such as the United Nations at its center had built-in limits because "it requires a centralized rule-making authority, a hierarchy of institutions, and universal membership" (Slaughter, 1997: 183). In place of this, she observed that governance has moved into a transgovernmental order of "courts, regulatory agencies, executives, and even legislatures . . . networking with their counterparts abroad, creating a dense web of relations . . ." (Slaughter, 1997: 184). She argued that this can provide a much more expandable and flexible system of governance than is available through the classic system of states and intergovernmental organizations.

Our analysis of the international legal operating and normative systems suggests something quite similar. To understand how international law functions in the world, one must look beyond traditional legal institutions, processes, and mechanisms. This also suggests a refinement of legal education. Most law schools provide basic coverage of the international operating system with appropriate attention given to actors, subjects, courts, and jurisdiction principles. Yet standard public international law textbooks and courses largely ignore the vital roles that extra-systemic actors and processes play in keeping the international normative system functioning.

As befits the globalized environment in which international law now functions, we observe the increased complexity in the operation of international law and its component units. International law, of course, has never functioned in isolation from national or regional legal systems, but the volume of interactions that fall beyond the scope of traditional international law mechanisms has increased as transnational activity has changed with the increased flows of persons, goods, and capital across borders. Understanding how separate legal systems can best work together to provide order to these activities is both an opportunity and a challenge that international lawyers face today. Developing systematic and regularized means of drawing on the procedural and institutional mechanisms of other legal systems provides international law an unprecedented opportunity to increase its effectiveness and close the gap between norms and the operating system's capacity to give effect to those norms. This reliance cannot substitute for operating system change, but it can provide an important supplement to traditional operating system mechanisms. To do so effectively, however, will require the ability to evaluate such actions to ensure that individual applications add up to the sum of their parts. This, in turn, may signal the increased need for recognized and accepted dispute settlement mechanisms to carry out such evaluations.

5

The influence of the operating system on normative change

In the previous two chapters, we were concerned with how mechanisms, within and outside the international legal system, facilitated the successful implementation of international norms. Indeed, much of the focus of scholars and policymakers has been on how to ensure effective norms once they have been adopted. In the course of this enterprise, there is a tendency to ignore how the current shape of the international legal operating system influences the configuration of the international normative system. Accordingly, we reverse the causal arrow in this chapter and address that possibility.

If the configuration of the operating system were the only influence on normative system change, then the two systems would never be in a state of imbalance: only those norms that fit within the existing operating system would be adopted. From the last two chapters, we know that this is not the case. Furthermore, in Chapter 3, we noted that changes in the normative system could produce direct and sometimes relatively rapid changes in the operating system, although this was far from certain.

Reversing the causal arrow, we do not expect to find similarly strong relationships. Generally, the specific content of treaties, especially their normative prescriptions and proscriptions, will not be a function of the operating system provisions. Rather, one would expect that the preferences of those involved in drafting and signing the treaty, as well as the capabilities of those actors and the information available (Cook, 2004), determine the degree and direction of the cooperation. There is an extensive literature on cooperation and what makes states agree to treaty provisions (e.g., Axelrod and Keohane, 1985; Stein, 1990; Taylor, 1987; Young, 1989a; Young, 1989b; Goldsmith and Posner, 2005; Sandholtz and Stiles, 2009), and none refers to elements of the operating system *per se*. Furthermore, we recognize that such interests and other processes, such as those specified in the punctuated equilibrium theory, could be responsible for determining change in *both* the operating and normative systems. In this book, however, we are concerned only with the interaction of the two systems and not generally with exogenous influences such as actor preferences and their sources. Nevertheless, provisions of the two systems are usually created separately and at different times and to that extent the operating system could still have lagged and independent effects on the normative system even as interests and other factors have changed over time.

Thus, we anticipate that most of the influence from the operating system on the normative system will be indirect, for example influencing the configuration of actors involved in the rule creation, which in turn affects the specific sets of preferences that are brought to the table. Unfortunately, there are few clues from past work.

Insights from previous research

To our knowledge, previous research has not addressed the question of how the operating system conditions the normative system. Rather, the conceptual distinction between the two systems is underplayed or muddled in both the legal and political science literature. Hart's (1961) conception of primary and secondary rules, roughly analogous to our normative and operating systems, treats the latter as subordinate to the former. Accordingly, it is inconceivable in that framework that the mechanics of the operating system would influence the normative precepts.

On the political science side of the ledger, there are some references to compliance (see below) influencing the choice of norms, but there is a myopic focus on formal institutions to the ignorance of the other components that we have identified in the operating system. Too often, because operating and normative elements are subsumed in a given treaty, the treaty becomes the focus or unit of analysis and the external factors are used to account for the treaty. The interrelationship of what are seen as internal components of the agreement is therefore ignored.

There are only hints at which processes and key variables might exist in a relationship in which the operating system influences the configuration of the normative system. There is certainly an extensive literature on the origins and development of norms, but it does not address the question posed in this chapter. This is largely because operating system elements are ignored or the literature confounds the two systems. We have chosen not to review the norm generation literature *in toto*, but instead highlight only the points that might be relevant for our purposes.

Regime theory (for a summary, see Hasenclever, Mayer, and Rittberger, 1997) dominated the study of international cooperation in the 1980s and 1990s. The concept of a regime, however, includes both elements of what we refer to as the operating and normative systems respectively. Indeed, institutions are sometimes defined as norms, and it is difficult to disentangle the two, much less discern a causal relationship. As Goertz (2003:19) puts it, "for many purposes, norms, principles, decision-making procedures, and rules can be considered as synonymous." Theoretical approaches based on interest, knowledge, or power also do not readily lend themselves to insights about how structures condition norm formation, at least with respect to how we define the two systems. Nevertheless, there are a few relevant ideas in that research milieu. For example, Young (1989a) suggests that regimes reduce uncertainty and thereby facilitate future cooperation. This suggests that if operating system components produce this effect, then normative changes might result (an idea we develop in the next section). Indeed, Young (1989b) notes that one component of the operating system, compliance mechanisms, facilitated rule formation in the environmental area.

A second strand of relevant international relations literature concerns hegemony. As noted in Chapter 3, hegemonic stability theory (Kindleberger, 1973; Keohane, 1984; for a critique, see Pahre, 1999) argues that a system leader and its preferences define and shape international relations, in this case international legal provisions. If we accept for the moment the assumption of the hegemonic literature that the operating system reflects the hegemon's interests (Ikenberry and Kupchan, 1990), then new norms created in international law are likely to be only those consistent with the extant operating system. At first glance, this is of little help in addressing our query. The operating system does not condition the normative system; rather, they are joint outcomes of hegemonic preferences according to this theoretical approach. Nevertheless, this literature does imply that whoever controls the norm or rule-making machinery (who can make law) of the operating system determines the content of the normative system.

Hegemonic stability theory provides only a single and debatable answer to our question, but it does suggest that we should explore carefully how actors and their powers to make law more broadly condition new normative rules. Indeed, Raustiala (2005) notes that the preferences of powerful states often influence legal form. He also argues that even weak states can exercise power, most notably veto power over new rules, depending on the forum in which the rules are formulated and the issues in question.

Although quite different than hegemonic stability theorists on many dimensions, constructivist scholars also emphasize the influence of actors in the making of international norms. Constructivist works (e.g., Finnemore, 1996) tend to muddle the operating–normative system distinction because they define structure in terms of shared norms. Yet many constructivist works emphasize the roles of NGOs and other "policy entrepreneurs" in norm creation. Brunnée and Toope (2000) do not explicitly distinguish between operating and normative systems, but they recognize the "duality of structure" that is law, including international law. In particular, they note the intersection of institutions and norms: "structures constrain social action, but they also enable action, and in turn are affected and potentially altered by the friction of social action against the parameters of the structure" (Brunnée and Toope, 2000: 30). They also note that norm entrepreneurs and epistemic communities are important in the development of legal norms. This again raises the question of when and how the institutions of the operating system permit input from such actors in lawmaking.

Finally, the institutions literature, most often based on rational choice and sometimes outside of international relations, explores the relationships of structures and outcomes. Unfortunately, most of the institutions literature in American politics (e.g., Shepsle and Weingast, 1995) and international relations alike (Koremenos, Lipson, and Snidal, 2003; for a review, see Martin and Simmons, 1998; Rhodes, Binder, and Rockman, 2006) treats what we would regard as the operating system as endogenous. That is, institutions are instruments of majoritarian interests (in national democratic systems) or states involved in crafting laws (in the international system). The story told by rational choice theorists about international law (e.g., Guzman, 2008) is about the coordination, interests, and information. Other works focus on how norms lead to institutional change, but not the other way around. In any case, the independent influence of context is not addressed. Nevertheless, we do know anecdotally that rules of legislative process do indeed impact outcomes and may subvert majoritarian interests. In the US Congress, for example, the committee system may produce provisions in bills that would not appear if the legislation were drafted in the committee of the whole. Similarly, US Senate rules on cloture (specifically cutting off a filibuster) may have the effect of modifying legislation to appeal to a minority or block law creation altogether, even if supported by a majority. In international lawmaking, we need to be sensitive to the forums in which treaties are drafted and the rules and process of lawmaking therein.

Operating system influences

Setting the parameters of acceptability

At the most fundamental level, national constitutions set the parameters on what kinds of laws are permitted. Normally, we think of such documents as granting powers to make rules, but they also limit the scope of those powers and in some cases prohibit the creation of certain rules. For example, the Tenth Amendment to the US Constitution states: "The powers not delegated to the United States by the Constitution, nor prohibited by it to the States, are reserved to the States respectively, or to the people." This provision essentially excludes federal legislation on any subject that falls within the purview of a state's (e.g., Florida's) rights.

The unstructured character of the international system leaves it without the equivalent of a central defining document that forms the basis for all global governance. The prohibition against violations of *jus cogens* is one of the few principles in international law that corresponds to constitutional limits. Possible analogues to a constitutional document might be found in the charter or covenants of international organizations, especially general purpose organizations. The UN Charter lays out what might be called the fundamental principles and institutions for a significant portion of the international legal operating system. Similarly, various constitutive agreements of the European Union (e.g., Treaty of Rome, Maastricht Treaty) define the scope of this partnership among member states. Other major regional organizations, such as the African Union and the Organization of American States, have similar documents, albeit many are much less developed.

Such constitutional equivalents do not determine in a positive sense the content of new normative treaties, but they may exclude the adoption of certain normative elements. For example, the Charter of the Organization of African Unity (OAU) contained provisions supporting the non-interference in the internal affairs of states. This essentially precluded the creation of norms that would infringe on the exclusive domestic jurisdiction of states. Perhaps not surprisingly then, this continent has not adopted many human rights provisions (save those dealing with self-determination) as they would violate the Charter framework, even as preferences for such provisions have changed. So too have the organization members been reluctant to endorse armed humanitarian interventions in places such as the Sudan, although the African Union has fielded peacekeeping operations in both Sudan and Somalia.

Much as a national constitution defines the space for lawmaking, international organization charters rule out normative system changes that are "unconstitutional" or created *ultra vires* and thereby channel rule making into the directions permitted by these central documents. The seemingly limitless power of the United Nations Security Council to authorize and to mandate state action is an example of such a permitted venue for rule making.

In the absence of constitutional equivalents, broadly accepted state practice and processes can serve related gatekeeping functions. Most notable are those that provide for some type of judicial review. There are not, as yet, well-developed international courts to perform this function. The International Court of Justice has historically been under-utilized, has significant limits on its jurisdiction, and its rulings lack the impact of *stare decisis*. Still, ICJ usage has increased since 1990 and its opinions, while not becoming part of the "fabric" of the law, nonetheless are widely cited and influential on state behavior. The European Court of Justice is not hamstrung by such constraints, but it manages only a regional subset of the international legal operating system. A greater effect is evident from the emergence of standard practices, specifically reliance on arbitration.

The emergence of arbitration as an established means of settling disputes is an example of practice affecting the normative system by vesting individuals with certain judicial powers (note that this is different than direct lawmaking noted below). This practice has over time facilitated and produced substantive changes in international law, specifically with respect to international commerce. As a result, arbitration institutions such as the International Chamber of Commerce in Paris, the London Court of International Arbitration, and the Stockholm Chamber of Commerce have risen to prominence. Although the right of a private party to bring action against a government in an international tribunal over investment disputes now seems quite routine, Salacuse and Sullivan (2005) are correct to remind us that this is indeed a "revolutionary innovation" in international investment law. There is, for example, no similar right in international trade law. In the last decade, there has been a proliferation of such arbitration cases and rulings resulting both from the increase in the use of bilateral investment treaties and from the availability of dispute settlement mechanisms such as international commercial arbitration and the International Centre for the Settlement of Investment Disputes (ICSID). Treaty forms and mechanisms for dispute settlement are part of the operating system that has facilitated the flow of investment funds into developing countries.

This institutionalization of arbitration proceedings as part of international law's operating system has implications for the normative development of international investment and commercial law. The practices of these principal arbitration institutions influence the making of contracts, agreements, and treaties by signaling which provisions are consistent with prevailing international agreements and practice, thereby setting the parameters for the provisions of future agreements. As the London Court of International Arbitration notes, "Ad hoc clauses are frequently either inadequate or overly complex. By incorporating institutional rules into their contract, the parties have the comfort of a comprehensive and proven set of terms and conditions upon which they can rely, regardless of the seat of the arbitration; minimizing the scope for uncertainty and the opportunity for delaying or wrecking the process."[1] This might involve precluding certain provisions as well as suggesting to the parties that new elements will be received favorably by arbitration panels. The process involves an interactive cycle of contracts, awards and rulings, and new contracts, which is likely to accelerate in the future. The arbitration process is becoming fixed as part of the investment law landscape, "which in turn has increased the rate of publication of awards and accentuated public aspects of the arbitral process" (Rogers, 2005: 1004). These, in turn, shape future contracts, arbitrations, and awards.

One should not, however, make too much of the impact of this first process of parameter setting. Operating system frameworks are reflective of prevailing interests at the time of adoption and states choose limitations to norm adoption largely to exclude future changes in those norms; thus, the causal influence of the operating system is likely to come in the long run (if at all) from stickiness as states' preferences change and formerly excluded practices become desired (see Pierson, 2004); this is consistent with our punctuated equilibrium theory of change in which system stasis exercises a powerful influence against rapid and immediate change. Still, this path dependency is probably not as strong as in

---

[1] See www.lcia.org.

national policymaking given that institutions and rules are more formal and numerous in those legal systems.

Second, there are not that many overarching charters or covenants in existence and even these do not contain expansive rules and provisions so as to preclude numerous sets of actions. Furthermore, even the strong influence of international bodies conducting the equivalent of judicial review is very limited in geographic and substantive scope. Finally, the effects might be felt more in private international law than in its public counterpart. Thus, at least for the time being, this operating system influence is probably much less common than those elucidated below.

Clarifying credible commitment

A second way that the operating system influences the normative system is through clarifying whether credible commitment exists or not. States frequently share a common interest to incorporate a given norm in a treaty, but this is no guarantee that an agreement or one including the norm in question will result. States could have reason to fear that other parties will renege on performing actions required in the treaty, and therefore will be reluctant to sign or ratify a treaty without some assurance of compliance. Credible commitment theory has been applied most prominently to the termination of civil wars, but it has also been an important part of studies of international cooperation in general (Fearon, 1998).

With respect to international law, there are certainly numerous reasons, beyond convergent interests, why states agree to treaties, including the behavior of neighboring states (Simmons, 2000). Yet we posit that the existence of compliance institutions, one of the core elements of the operating system, is influential in whether treaty negotiations reach fruition. If states know that existing monitoring mechanisms, courts, or dispute resolution mechanisms exist, they will be more likely to commit to agreements (Downs, Rocke, and Barsoom, 1996). Indeed, the original purpose of creating institutions, such as tribunals, was to enhance the credibility of commitments by raising the costs of defection (Helfer and Slaughter, 2005). Young (1989a; 1989b) notes that compliance mechanisms reduced uncertainty and facilitated rule formation in the environmental area (see more generally, Guzman, 2008). In some issue areas (e.g., human rights), however, states may oppose strong monitoring and therefore be reluctant to create new rules in the face of an effective operating system. Broadly, institutions reduce uncertainty, conveying information about the likely effect of new rules (Kriehbiel, 1991), whether good or bad for individual state interests.

Proving that the operating system was critical in facilitating a normative agreement is difficult as it requires establishing that the treaty or treaty provision would not have been concluded otherwise except for the operating system rules that facilitated credible commitment. Even more difficult, cases in which agreements did not occur because of operating system deficiencies are "dogs that don't bark," and therefore not transparent. Still, one might offer a plausible candidate to illustrate the argument.

The Nuclear Non-Proliferation Treaty (NPT) might never have been signed had it not been for the presence of the International Atomic Energy Agency (IAEA) and its inspections protocol. This is not to say that the IAEA did not need to modify some of those mechanisms or that the organization has proven to be infallible in its duties. Rather, its existence gave underdeveloped and developed states assurance that NPT violations would be detected and that certain other rights (e.g., the right to nuclear energy) would be protected.

Institutions or existing arrangements also clarify the need for new lawmaking as illustrated by the review process that led up to the formulation of the 1997 Ottawa Convention on the Prohibition of the Use, Stockpiling, Production, and Transfer of Anti-Personnel Mines and on Their Destruction. This convention was an outgrowth of the 1980 Convention on Certain Conventional Weapons. Starting in 1993, the French government began a campaign to reduce their use and called for a review conference in 1995. When this conference failed to make any significant progress, NGOs and some states concluded that only a total ban could address compliance problems, eventually leading to the adoption of the Ottawa Treaty.[2]

This is a relatively simple argument, but we cannot expect the operating system to exercise a uniform effect on all treaty negotiations. First, we might initially anticipate that this influence will be less prominent in the security realm; with high stakes at risk, states may be reluctant to rely on operating system provisions, as opposed to self-help mechanisms, to ensure compliance with rules such as those in an arms control agreement. Thus, for example, states prefer to rely on their own satellite images and interpretation rather than those of an international agency or are reluctant to make advanced technology and the products of such

---

[2] See www.icbl.org/tools/faq/treaty/ottawa, "What is the Ottawa Process?", visited on January 8, 2008.

surveillance available to international organizations. Second, the effect also depends on the utility of less formal mechanisms for compliance. McAdams (1997) argues that the risk of detection is necessary for the emergence of norms, but some norms are virtually self-enforcing. If reciprocity, reputation, and "habit" (Henkin, 1968) are sufficient for compliance, then external credible commitments might not be necessary. For example, the fear of high costs from reciprocity have kept states from violating provisions on diplomatic immunity and chemical weapons usage, with a few exceptions, despite non-existent or weak monitoring mechanisms. Yet when these conditions are not present, the operating system needs to provide mechanisms to assure potential signatories that fellow parties will honor their obligations.

One might argue that parties could create their own compliance institutions and embed those provisions in the treaty. Yet this can be a costly enterprise in many cases and in any event does not always occur (see Chapter 3). It is even the case that extant arrangements and institutions will be insufficient to assure compliance and ultimately parties will need to rely on domestic political actors (Dai, 2007) or other mechanisms outside of the formal legal operating system (see Chapter 4), including national legal processes. Indeed, national governments still command governing capacity and "coercive and persuasive powers largely unmatched by international institutions" (Slaughter and Burke-White, 2006: 333). At the same time, the international components backstop the national ones in situations of transition or change. The key is the interaction between the international and the national that is required in order to give life to international obligations.

Providing flexibility

At the same time as operating system rules must facilitate compliance with provisions, so too must they permit some flexibility so that states are able to exit or modify agreements if perceived necessary. Absent such flexibility, states could also be unwilling to accept certain normative provisions. Two such elements are contained in the rules governing treaty acceptance and in practice: the possibility for parties to qualify their acceptance of an obligation through a reservation and the right to withdraw from a treaty. Although these are not generally regarded as encouraging strong and orderly relationships (Barnett and Finnemore (2004) refer to such things as "normalization of deviance"), in fact they could make any international cooperation and norm creation possible.

Any treaty or international rule involves some uncertainty about the benefits and costs of its implementation. A standard operating system rule, incorporated in most treaties (save territorial exchanges and selected other issues), is that parties are allowed to suspend participation or withdraw from the agreement under specified conditions and with adequate notice. For example, as noted by Guzman (2008), the International Covenant on Civil and Political Rights contains such a right in Article 4(1): "In time of public emergency which threatens the life of the nation and the existence of which is officially proclaimed, the States Parties to the present Covenant may take measures derogating from their obligations under the present Covenant to the extent strictly required by the exigencies of the situation . . ." Such "denunciation" clauses, notes Helfer (2005: 1599), actually promote the development of normative commitments: "All other things being equal, such clauses encourage the ratification of a treaty by a larger number of states than would be prepared to ratify in the absence of such a clause. They may also enable states to negotiate deeper or broader commitments than would be attainable for treaties without unilateral exit." We know that withdrawal is not just a theoretical matter, but is widely used by states. For the five-year period 2000–4, 220 withdrawals were reported from multilateral treaties registered with the United Nations (Helfer, 2005).

A second aspect of flexibility permitted by the operating system is the ability to make reservations. In like manner, reservations serve to inform the non-reserving states to a treaty "about reserving states' reputation and propensity to comply with treaties," and thereby strengthen rather than weaken a treaty regime by making possible broader participation and possibly deeper commitments (Helfer, 2006: 381). Most reservations have little direct impact on the normative content of the agreement (Gamble, 1980), but might be necessary for a state to ratify an agreement or for a treaty to receive the requisite number of parties to take effect. Substantive reservations alter the normative content of treaties, especially the responsibilities of the reserving party to all other parties. Yet these have been relatively minor; many have involved objections or clarifications of treaty language, such as Luxembourg's interpretation of the term "lawful sanctions" in the Torture Convention. Of greater significance for the normative system are attempts by states to sign onto parts of the agreement with which they agree, while relieving themselves of obligations to which they object. For example, the United States indicated in its reservation to the UN Convention to Combat Desertification that it would not have to make changes to existing land management practices and programs in order to meet its obligations, which seems to undermine the provisions relating to land-use planning.

In making states more likely to commit to agreements, reservations and exit clauses have a number of potential positive and negative consequences. To the extent that such provisions encourage non-compliance when compliance is counter-productive (e.g., following rules when they decrease the volume of trade flows), the effects may be beneficial (Guzman, 2008). Still, greater flexibility could diminish the level of actual commitment made by parties as the scope and depth of an agreement diminishes with the excessive use of reservations. It is possible that under such conditions, and with the prospect of states using liberal suspension or withdrawal clauses, participation actually decreases rather than is enhanced (Guzman, 2008).

Actor specification

A central part of the operating system is the specification of the rights and obligations of different kinds of actors. For our purposes here, the key concern is with the rules that designate which actors have what rights to make international law. Traditionally, this has been the exclusive purview of states. Yet over the past several decades, new actors have had input into the treaty-making process or in the case of some international organizations have direct power to create law (Alvarez, 2002; 2005). The specification of the lawmaking power of actors in the international legal operating system can have a significant impact on the actual provisions that appear in certain treaties. An example of this can be found in the framework protocol model introduced by the 1987 Montreal Protocol to the 1985 Vienna Convention for the Protection of the Ozone Layer. Brunnée (2004: 637) explains the approach and its consequences for treaty making: "This regime development is accomplished through regular meetings of the treaty's Conference of Parties (COP) and its various scientific and political subsidiary bodies. With an institutional core and ongoing regulatory agenda, modern MEAs (multilateral environmental agreements) therefore resemble international organizations in many respects." Treaty parties collectively gather information and work as a group to foster cooperation and consensus. This approach reduces the influence of individual states, no matter how powerful. "In addition, a range of techniques have evolved that facilitate treaty development by COP decision, reducing reliance on formal amendments and softening consent requirements in various ways" (Brunnée, 2004: 637).

Which specific actors and which kinds of actors legitimately participate in lawmaking can have an effect on the final provisions of a treaty or legally binding resolutions. We begin with the assumption that treaty provisions are the aggregated preferences of those involved in drafting the document and ultimately those who approve it, mediated by the power of those actors. A related assumption is that actors involved in rule creation also provide information that affects the choice of certain sets of provisions over others in the final draft. To the extent that the operating system allows more and varied actors into the process, there are resulting changes in the normative outcomes.

Even when the operating system restricts participation to states, it privileges subsets of states. Not surprisingly, the operating system rules are weighted in favor of the most powerful states in the international system at any given time. Hegemonic theories imply that the operating system should be consistent with the interests of the leading states, and Raustiala (2005) notes that the preferences of powerful states often influence legal form. Treaty rules that recognize the legality of imposed peace agreements, an exception to the standard invalidity of coerced agreements, are but one example. Powerful states also accrue advantage by virtue of their frequency of participation and strategic position in operating system institutions. This is evident in the WTO. As Shaffer (2004: 470) notes: "Not surprisingly, the United States and European Community remain by far the predominant users of the system, and thereby are most likely to advance their interests through the judicial process. As repeat players, the United States and EC strive not only to win individual cases. *They also play for rules.* They attempt to shape judicial interpretation of WTO rules over time" (emphasis added). Exogenous factors (size of markets, powerful interest groups, etc.) determine frequency of WTO usage, but such participation allows users to influence the normative system over time.

Although there has been an expansion in treaty-making participants beyond states, these are still subject to the consent of the other states participating in a negotiation or treaty according to the rules of the operating system. In the cases of sub-state entities, the state from which the entity emanates may also have to provide specific authorization for the participation of such groups in treaty making.

International organizations are another example of a new actor entering the treaty-making arena, but their participation has thus far been limited in scope. Most international organizations do not negotiate treaties on the same footing as states. For example, NATO is not permitted to be a party to international humanitarian law agreements. Furthermore, most international agreements concluded by international organizations are bilateral and only specify organization activities and legal status (Shaffer, 2004). Still, international organizations have played increasingly prominent roles in lawmaking. Alvarez (2005: 263) explains why this has occurred: "IO [international organization] law-making powers have expanded because their agents and organs have been given the benefit of a presumption – itself a creator of international institutional law – that they can accomplish legally whatever furthers a legitimate organizational purpose." No organ of an international organization has perhaps benefited more from this presumption than the UN Security Council.

In a related fashion, however, the emergence of independent inspection mechanisms in international financial institutions is also slowly having substantive effect on international law. Bradlow (2005: 410) describes how inspectors can influence legal standards:

> Legally, these mechanisms have turned out to be effective forums in which adversely affected persons can raise claims that relate to their rights as indigenous people or as involuntarily resettled people and in which they can challenge the interpretation and implementation of the internal policies and procedures of the MDBs [multilateral development banks]. Consequently, inspection mechanisms are slowly beginning to provide data and precedents that can influence the evolution of international human rights law, international environmental law and international administrative law. The inspection mechanisms may also ultimately influence the development of international financial law, as they investigate cases in which they are trying to determine the obligations of creditors towards those harmed by the projects they finance.

Constructivist works emphasize the roles of NGOs and other "policy entrepreneurs" in norm creation. In recent decades, NGOs have assumed greater roles in the construction of legal agreements, such as the UN Framework Convention for Climate Change. Indeed, NGOs favor more binding agreements, and the more so when there is heightened domestic interest in the subject area, in order to ensure ongoing access to information about implementation of the obligations as well as opportunities for ongoing comment and influence (Raustiala, 2005). Thus, these actors have significant stakes in formulating normative standards and hardening them in the legal system. Cakmak (2004) explores the area of human rights, but the author's analysis might easily apply broadly to most areas of international law. Cakmak (2004) goes so far as to suggest that NGOs have acquired virtual "sovereign rights" in the process of lawmaking. In any event, NGOs and related epistemic communities (Keck and Sikkink, 1998) influence normative outcomes in several fashions from several different sources of power granted to them in the operating system.

NGOs are sometimes permitted access to the lawmaking process in international organizations, and that is their primary gateway to influence the legal process (Charnovitz, 2006). For example, employer and business groups are given equal voice with governments in making labor agreements within the International Labor Organization (Ku, 2007). Occasionally, this is guaranteed formally, as in the provisions of Article 71 of the UN Charter: "The Economic and Social Council may make suitable arrangements for consultation with non-governmental organizations which are concerned with matters within its competence ..." Similar provisions exist in Article 70 for specialized agencies, allowing international organizations access to the lawmaking processes of other organizations. These provide "consultative" status for those actors, but do not give them a place at the table. Although Article 71 applies only to ECOSOC, the practice has spread throughout the UN system and beyond. Few international organizations lack such a process and although there is yet no legal duty to consult NGOs, there is some movement in that direction (Charnovitz, 2006).

A stronger legal basis for participation is found in "observer" status, which may entitle NGOs to admittance and participation to all meetings (Koenig, 1991). At other times, the roles of NGOs and other actors in the lawmaking process have evolved gradually and more informally. NGOs are now regularly part of international conferences, including those that draft international agreements. As noted below, they are regularly a part of deliberations in drafting treaties, although they do not have voting rights and cannot become parties to the treaty.

As the operating system has opened its door to NGO (and other actor) participation, those actors have assumed a number of roles. First, they play an agenda-setting role in bringing topics or issues to the attention of the state members (Aviel, 2000). This does not ensure that new norms will be created, but it does mean that some norms would not otherwise be codified, or at least not at a particular point in time, without the impetus of NGOs. Second, NGOs can submit statements or make presentations in the course of treaty drafting. One might expect that their greatest influence will occur on more technical matters in which the expertise of the organizations grants greater legitimacy to NGO input. The net result is that provisions of a treaty more closely coincide with NGO preferences than would otherwise be the case without their participation because NGOs are more focused on a specific issue area and therefore more able to respond rapidly to opportunities to promote norms in those areas. They might also be involved in the drafting of convention language, either directly or indirectly through alternative operating system structures. For example, Cakmak (2004; see also Breen, 2003) notes that NGOs formed the *Ad Hoc* NGO Group on the Drafting of the Convention on the Rights of the Child and actually contributed substantive articles to the final convention. Finally, NGOs can submit friends-of-the-court briefs, with such access permitted in almost all international courts except the International Court of Justice (Charnovitz, 2006; Shelton, 1994).

Perhaps the most notable, and certainly the most cited, instance of NGOs influencing normative treaties concerns the so-called Ottawa Treaty, officially the Ottawa Convention on the Prohibition of the Use, Stockpiling, Production, and Transfer of Anti-Personnel Mines and on Their Destruction. Rutherford (2000) details the influence of NGOs in all aspects of that treaty. NGOs highlighted the damaging effects of landmines at international conferences as well as outside the operating system through media campaigns. Price (1998) recounts the influential domestic political forces that NGOs created by linking up with veterans organizations, thereby making the elimination of landmines a broad-based political issue that reached across the political divide in many countries. This agenda-setting laid the basis for eventual drafting of the landmine ban, despite the opposition of some states, such as the United States.

Forum specification

Related to actor specification, the operating system also defines the institutions or forums in which law is made. In the United States, for example, the Constitution specifies that all appropriation bills must originate in the House of Representatives and that international agreements must be ratified by the President, subject to advice and consent of the Senate. In the international legal arena, the operating system is more diffuse. Technically, any two states can create international legal obligations between themselves, with direct negotiations being the most common forum for this. Still, generic elements of the operating system influence the making of law regardless of context (something referred to as "bureaucratic universalism" by Barnett and Finnemore, 2004), with sometimes undesirable effects. Yet the most significant treaties and other law (custom, binding resolutions) arise from multilateral interactions in forums whose structures and rules are part of the operating system. Indeed, over half of all multilateral treaties are attributable to forums in the UN system (Alvarez, 2005). Thus, subsystem rules of the international legal operating system have important effects. As rules change within forums, so too will policies (Martin and Simmons, 1998); as one moves across forums with different rules, outcomes will also change.

There are several ways that characteristics of the operating system with respect to lawmaking forums influence final outcomes in the form of normative treaties. First, such forums determine which kinds of actors may participate and in what fashions. These aspects are discussed in the previous section. Institutional rules inherently define these processes and will tend to favor some actors over others (Baumgartner and Jones, 1993).

Second, every forum carries with it certain norms that condition the expectations and participation of those involved in the treaty drafting. Cook (2004) notes that actors rely on institutional rules and information to develop expectations. Although these elements were developed by the participants in the past, they are not necessarily changed easily and they may be very "sticky" as they affect future deliberations. Once again, stasis in the system conditions the prospects for and content of change. For example, negotiations on trade under the auspices of GATT/WTO include a series of norms (e.g., major interests, development) that will affect specific provisions of any final treaty (Finlayson and Zacher, 1981). In particular, the major interests norm will produce an agreement whose precise subjects and specific provisions will be more closely aligned with the interests of leading states (and others most affected by the treaty) than they will be for other parties, even as the agreement was negotiated in a large multilateral setting.

Third, agenda-setting power differs across forums, and this influences what issues are possible subjects (or not) for new legal rules. Indeed, those actors who are most influential in the creation of those forums often have built in such advantages for themselves (Gruber, 2005). For example, agenda control will lead to different outcomes when rules are discussed in the WTO versus UNCTAD given the powers of different coalitions in those bodies (Shaffer, 2005).

The institutional arrangements also influence the kinds of provisions that find their way into final drafts of agreements. UN bodies, such as the International Law Commission, include participation from different states, many of whom may have few direct interests in most provisions. Yet these bodies operate on principles of consensus, even though a treaty will not become binding on any state other than a signatory. Bargaining in such forums produces treaty provisions that are necessary to promote that consensus. This could mean that the language of the document is deliberately vague, as are many articles of the Covenant on Civil and Political Rights, so as to facilitate multiple and self-interested interpretations. It may also produce "package deals" in which articles or subsections are added to a treaty to secure the support of a certain group of states. For example, the Convention on the Law of the Sea, negotiated at the Third UN Conference on the Law of the Sea, includes guarantees for access to the high seas by landlocked states, a provision designed to secure the support of that set of conference participants. Some forums might include members with only certain preferences or those in a given direction (Baumgartner and Jones, 1993); this may make consensus and therefore an agreement easier. There might be a tradeoff between the breadth of membership and the strength of commitment exacted in any agreement (Guzman, 2008).

Because where international law is made helps determine what law is made, strategic actors may seek to have law created in certain forums as opposed to other alternatives when such options exist. We usually associate the process of "forum shopping" (Weintraub, 2002) with litigants searching for the optimal venue in which to file suit. Yet shifting forums is also applicable earlier in the legal process when actors are seeking to create law (Shaffer, 2005). Some forums are better suited to the interests of certain states than others. With its historically underdeveloped institutions, there is less "layering" (Thelen, 2004) or multiple forums performing similar functions than in domestic politics. Nevertheless, there are still some opportunities for forum shopping. Stiles (2006) provides an excellent illustration, discussing anti-terrorism law and the United Nations, and by implication how actors may use or abuse the operating system to promote their interests. The UN General Assembly, through its Sixth Committee, had worked for a number of years on drafting conventions dealing with terrorism. Yet its procedures for operating on consensus and its track record of taking actions, such as trying to carve out exceptions to terrorism norms for national liberation groups, made it an anathema to major power states. Not surprisingly, after the 9/11 attacks, the United States and the United Kingdom sought to use the Security Council, a forum much friendlier to their interests and subject to their control, to develop new legal rules on terrorism. The success of efforts to draft rules on terrorism will depend on which forum is privileged and any convention emanating from one of those two bodies is likely to contain very different provisions from a convention emanating from the other.

We can see another example in the adoption of the World Health Organization's (WHO) Framework Convention on Tobacco Control. Crow (2004) notes that by connecting the health issue to the human rights operating system, tobacco control could then be brought under the established human rights institutions to advance the development of the norm of tobacco control; such institutions would include the European Court of Human Rights, the United Nations Human Rights Committee, and the Inter-American Commission and Court of Human Rights. These examples show how in providing several strategic options for lawmaking, the operating system influences the likelihood and kinds of outcomes in international lawmaking.

Finally, there is the possibility that the operating system processes that take place within treaty-making forums lead to a redefinition of the interests and values of the treatymakers (Haas, 1990). This may involve problem redefinition, such that new laws are created to address concerns that were previously less salient but are now at the forefront. This may not have occurred with respect to UNESCO, which remained stagnant and consequently created few new standards, but is evident in a number of human rights organizations in which rights for women and indigenous peoples were adopted. It can also be the case that actors were transformed by their participation in international forums and thereby created new rules on a variety of issues that would otherwise not have been manifest. Yet, it is very difficult to document this transformation of interests, much less then to tie that change to the adoption of specific normative standards.

Direct lawmaking

The final process by which the operating system affects the development of the normative system might seem a bit surprising: institutions of the operating system create new normative laws. This involves more than empowering particular actors to make laws or allowing certain bodies to craft agreements. It also includes the creation of law as part of the normal procedural functioning of the operating system rather than from statutory authority.

In several cases, states have transferred treaty-making authority to supranational entities such as the European Union. For example, the

EU's member states have given it treaty-making competence with respect to fisheries (Hollis, 2005). Still, there are instances in which the operating system has permitted international organizations to construct normative standards. For example, under Article 28 of the 1944 Convention on International Civil Aviation, the International Civil Aviation Organization (ICAO) is

> authorized to promulgate international standards in relation to matters such as communications systems, rules of the air, and air traffic control practices as part of a state's obligations under the Convention. Similarly, the World Health Organization has the authority to adopt regulations on various health matters that bind all members except for those that notify their rejection of, or reservations to, the regulations within a set period of time. (Hollis, 2005: 168)

Another example of such law creation comes from international tribunals. International courts do not have the same powers as many domestic courts and technically cannot make the law *per se*; the absence of *stare decisis* on the international level limits the last influence that judicial action may have on the law. Traditional operating system rules establish that court decisions can be used as evidence of custom, but are not lawmaking in and of themselves. Rape as a war crime might have existed under customary law, but its existence was murky at best. It was only when the crime was recognized by the Yugoslav and Rwandan war crimes tribunals that one might be able truly to say it is international law, especially given that (1) rape is rarely if ever mentioned in legal lists of such crimes, and (2) no international court had ever convicted an individual for rape as a component of genocide before this was done by the Rwandan tribunal in *Prosecutor* v. *Akayesu* (1998).[3]

The process of lawmaking sometimes thrusts authority onto adjudicatory bodies, if only out of necessity. Such is the case with the WTO. Shaffer (2004: 470) explains:

> The difficulty of amending or interpreting WTO law through the WTO political process enhances the impact of WTO jurisprudence. WTO law requires consensus to modify, resulting in a rigid legislative system, with rule modifications occurring through infrequent negotiating rounds. Because of the complex bargaining process, rules often are drafted in a vague manner, thereby delegating *de facto* power to the WTO dispute settlement system to effectively make WTO law through interpretation.

---

[3] Case no. ICTR-96–4–7, Judgment (September 2, 1998), available at www.ictr.org.

Danner finds evidence of judicial lawmaking in a number of different courts. Specifically, she notes: "The International Court of Justice has reshaped the law on transboundary resources, including rivers and fish stocks. The Iran–US Claims Tribunal has clarified the international law of unlawful expropriation. Most of these decisions have been subsequently accepted as valid by states, despite their often weak textual or customary law bases" (Danner, 2006: 47–8). Yet Danner claims that much of the effect is likely to be manifest in temporary international courts. Her argument is that this is most appropriate as a mechanism for revision of treaties when those agreements are old and no longer reflect current conditions, and there is little prospect for revision any time soon. The European Court of Justice (ECJ) has played a significant, if originally unintended, role in policymaking. Article 177 of the 1958 Treaty of Rome – the preliminary ruling procedure – allowed national courts to ask the ECJ for rulings. This generated a steady flow of cases that allowed the court to give more expansive rulings (Martin and Simmons, 1998).

Ginsburg (2005) indicates a broader effect, arguing that judicial lawmaking is "inevitable." Primarily, he notes that courts and related institutions make laws in several different ways. Judicial decisions have increasingly been used by subsequent courts to guide decisions, even though precedent is not explicitly an established rule (e.g., see Article 59 of the International Court of Justice Statute). The ICJ can also issue advisory opinions, providing another avenue to reinterpret the law or establish new principles. Furthermore, courts have the power to interpret treaties and detect custom. Such judicial lawmaking, however, is not unlimited. States can still "overrule" judicial actions by subsequent contrary action or constrain ("discipline") tribunals who make undesirable law, thereby limiting future judicial lawmaking.

Conclusion

This chapter explored the ways that the operating system influences the normative system. The result was the identification of six processes through which the operating system might affect which norms are adopted as well as the specific configurations of those norms: (1) setting the parameters of acceptability; (2) clarifying credible commitment; (3) providing flexibility; (4) actor specification; (5) forum specification; and (6) direct lawmaking. Although we do not contend that the operating system exercises a dominant influence on new treaties, we do contend that models based solely on interests, power, and information are incomplete in accounting for how international cooperation is achieved and structured.

There are several implications from the finding that the operating system influences the normative system. As indicated in Chapter 2, most of the trends in the operating system are toward expansion, in the number and kind of actors, in the creation of new courts, and the scope of international lawmaking. One might suspect that this will continue well into the future. This suggests that the operating system will exercise a greater influence on future lawmaking. Much of this may be unintended, but nevertheless real. For example, a court created for a specific purpose, such as the International Criminal Court, could play a critical role in the development and application of international humanitarian law. The desirability of this reality is already being debated (see Posner and Yoo, 2005 and the response by Helfer and Slaughter, 2005) but that reality is not in question.

6

Implications and future directions

Classic international legal analyses have been largely descriptive – what the law is – or prescriptive – what the law should be. This was acceptable for the purposes of the legal training and perhaps only slightly less so for public discourse on legal policymaking. It is, however, wholly inadequate for understanding how international law conditions behavior and the processes by which international legal change actually occurs. From a scholarly standpoint, such an understanding is essential to build theory that can account for how, when, and why international law changes (or, just as importantly, does not change). From a policymaking standpoint, elucidating these processes is essential for anticipating changes (or lack thereof) and formulating strategies to facilitate change in the face of compelling international problems.

When legal scholars have undertaken systematic analyses of international law, their models and analyses often are based on those developed for national or municipal legal systems. These do not generally fit well with the unique character of the international legal system, which lacks a central legislative body, a developed judicial system, and other elements that we traditionally associate with domestic legal systems. Rather than a mirror image of other legal arrangements, international law is better understood as one segment among several overlapping layers of legal systems. As the International Law Commission described: "international law regimes are always partial in the sense that they regulate only some aspects of State behavior while presuming the presence of a large number of other rules in order to function at all" (United Nations General Assembly, 2006: 94).

Furthermore, analyses of legal systems (such as autopoietic systems, see Teubner, 1988; 1993; Luhmann, 2004) have focused too much attention on the boundaries of legal systems and not enough on the permeability of those borders, much less what occurs inside those borders. Social scientific analyses, more conducive to dynamic and causal analyses, have historically ignored issues of international law in favor of other aspects of international relations such as war and trade. This has begun to change since the turn of the twenty-first century.

In response to the limitations of past international legal scholarship, we developed a new framework for analyzing international law, based on our division of the international legal system into two component parts: operating and normative systems respectively. We then developed a theory of legal change for those two subsystems. Summaries of our argument and theory are given below.

Summarizing the argument and theory

The book was motivated by several concerns:

- To understand the capacity of the international legal system to give effect to norms and the conditions that trigger adaptation and give rise to system-wide change.
- To recognize the multilevel character of the contemporary international legal system and how practices at different levels of the legal system (international, national, subnational, and private) fill gaps to give norms effect and to produce sustained change in both the operating and normative systems.
- To capture the cumulative effect of system-wide changes that enable the international legal system to meet the new demands and requirements of global governance.

The failure to understand these issues partially accounts for a broad impression that international law does not work or ultimately only works for the powerful as some form of political cover or legitimation. Indeed, our analysis shows that international law norms can operate at a suboptimal level for long periods of time, but that they can, nevertheless, function. Our analysis further shows that international law is more complex and multilayered than an exclusive focus on state-to-state actions might suggest. Both the volume of transnational activity and the number of public and private actors involved have exploded in the last few decades. Scholars of international law have been slow in trying to understand these interactions on a system-wide basis (United Nations General Assembly, 2006). As a result, focus has been on international norms as they take effect on the international stage without adequate system-wide attention to the activities taking place beyond the state-to-state level or formally outside the legal system. Our study reveals that international law can reach deeply into municipal legal systems and draw on the resources and structures of national, subnational, and private law.

The point of departure for our analysis is the view that the international legal system divides into two interrelated subsystem components: the operating and normative systems respectively. The former signifies legal rules that deal with how international law functions, specifically laying out the sources of laws, rights and obligations of actors, jurisdictional delineation, and mechanisms for dispute resolution. The latter subsystem deals with issue-specific prescriptions and prohibitions on topics such as human rights and the use of force. This is in contrast to the view that regards international law as an undifferentiated set of regulations that exist largely independent of one another.

Over time, the breadth of the two subsystems has increased dramatically. The number and character of forums for dispute resolution have expanded, even in the private realm; for example, there is the development in international commercial arbitration to allow for the settlement of investor–state disputes. Most notably, the kinds of actors and their accompanying rights and obligations have dramatically changed in the last century. For example, the operating system now includes the recognition of individuals as actors within the international legal system both in human rights and in international investments. Similarly, international organizations have become complex norm-generating systems of their own. They began by governing their own internal affairs such as personnel, and moved to implement state-sanctioned mandates; then they encouraged focus on particular issue areas and subsequently facilitated the drafting of legal instruments to address those areas (see Alvarez, 2005). This has led writers such as Charney (1993: 547) to recognize such forums as the United Nations General Assembly as having a special role to "advance and formalize the international lawmaking process." The broader application of universal jurisdiction is also consistent with the expansion of the operating system. Similarly, the normative system has deepened and expanded its boundaries. With respect to the latter, international law now covers new areas such as governance of cyberspace and includes such related issues as the protection of software licenses. Furthermore, the legal rules in established areas such as human rights and the environment are now more numerous and detailed than only a few decades ago.

The operating and normative systems work together to give us international law, but may develop at different rates. Actors often seek to pursue objectives beyond those provided for in existing norms. The development of human rights law is an example in which states initially set out to achieve acknowledgement that human rights, such as those enumerated in international instruments such as the International Covenant on Civil and Political Rights (ICCPR), existed and should be protected. States then moved further into monitoring the behavior of those accepting these obligations through regular reporting, and the Human Rights Committee was set up to receive and to review these reports.[1] The review function subsequently became an interpretive one that clarified ambiguities in the ICCPR. In addition, for states that accept the provisions of Optional Protocol I to the ICCPR, the Human Rights Committee can receive complaints from individuals in those states alleging a violation of their ICCPR rights. Still, for the most part, monitoring and sanctioning of human rights violations was largely left in the hands of those actors – states – most likely to be the perpetrators; this is the proverbial fox responsible for the safety of the hen house. This gap has been narrowed outside the legal system by the ongoing monitoring and actions of non-governmental organizations and provisions in selected national laws, to name two examples.

When the operating and normative systems are not aligned, an imbalance occurs. The international legal system then functions suboptimally, but nevertheless functions even during periods of imbalance. In the case of European human rights, for example, the level of protection afforded nationals of Council of Europe member states is much higher than for the nationals of non-member states, many of whom would not permit the level of international scrutiny of their conduct required by the European Convention on Human Rights. Such suboptimal conditions can remain for long periods of time before a permanent change occurs. Thus, imbalances lead to norms that are not effectively implemented or monitored as well as circumstances in which operating system provisions are underused (e.g., certain adjudicatory forums).

What accounts for the differential rates of change in the operating and normative systems, and accordingly when might we expect imbalances to occur and persist? Moving from the taxonomy of the two systems to a causal explanation, we employ a punctuated equilibrium theory of legal change. In keeping with this approach, we note long periods of little or no system-wide change that are followed by abrupt transformations when conditions are right. Generally, our theory of international legal change is predicated on the following components:

---

[1] The Human Rights Committee is a body of independent experts charged with monitoring the implementation of the International Covenant on Civil and Political Rights by state parties. All state parties are obligated to provide regular reports to the Committee on how rights are being implemented.

- International law within issue areas is generally static and resistant to change.
- Major international legal change occurs infrequently and often rapidly.
- Political shocks and related events provide the impetus for, but are no guarantee of, international legal change.

Within this theoretical framework, we focused on the interaction of the operating and normative systems. The first step was to identify the conditions under which new normative rules precipitated changes in the operating system. Other approaches assume an automatic restoration of the balance between the two systems. Our model, consistent with illustrative examples and an extended case study of genocide law, indicates that operating system change often does not occur, or does so in a delayed fashion, in response to normative change. Specifically, the following are necessary, but not sufficient, conditions for such alterations in the operating system:

- Necessity – the extant operating system must be insufficient, incompatible, or ineffective to handle the requirements of the new norm.
- Political shocks – major changes in the international environment must create the opportunity for policy change in a normally static environment characterized by inertia.
- Leading states – although they cannot impose change, leading states must not actively oppose necessary operating system change.
- Domestic political influences – such considerations may block operating system change or limit its applicability to a less than universal set of states or geographic regions.

Not surprisingly, these conditions are often not present simultaneously, and therefore international legal change is infrequent. Accordingly, there is an imbalance between the operating and normative systems. The imbalance may also persist even after operating system change, as alterations may not be fully effective or adequately extensive. Is the international legal system doomed to the attendant problems associated with this imbalance? To some extent, it is. Yet there are numerous adaptations outside of the formal legal system that redress the gaps left by the imbalance between the two systems.

The international political system and its constituent actors have moved to take actions that make international law more efficient by substituting for inadequate or non-existent monitoring mechanisms in the operating system as well as creating rules in different forums and venues that serve to promote new international legal norms. In particular, we identified four processes by which this gap-filling occurs:

- NGOs and transnational networks – the actions of private organizations and networks have been particularly important in monitoring legal norm compliance.
- Internalization – national courts and processes often take responsibility for ensuring compliance.
- Domestic legal and political processes – formal (laws) and informal (public opinion) safeguards are often consistent with, and provide support for, international legal norms.
- Soft law – shared understandings and non-legal agreements often accomplish what an inadequate operating system cannot.

Finally, we reversed the causal arrow and examined how the operating system conditioned changes in the normative system, an approach generally ignored by other theoretical formulations. A variety of important influences (power, interests) affect which norms are adopted and their configuration. Nevertheless, there are subtle ways in which the operating system affects normative change:

- Setting the parameters of acceptability – limiting the scope and direction of normative change, including excluding certain options.
- Clarifying credible commitment – enhancing or undermining faith that possible agreements might be observed thereby affecting the probability that such agreements will be adopted.
- Providing flexibility – permitting some maneuvering room (e.g., reservations, withdrawal clauses) that increases the likelihood that hesitant states will come to agreement as well as providing the means for states to indicate the degree to which they are willing to be bound.
- Actor specification – the rights, obligations, and identities of players in the formulation of normative rules will affect the content of those rules.
- Forum specification – the forum in which the normative rules are drafted will affect the content of those rules.
- Direct lawmaking – some institutions of the operating system can create normative rules.

The full picture of our description of international law is a system that is characterized by stability, but punctuated by rapid and dramatic change. It is also a system in which the internal processes of the operating and normative systems are influenced by external actors and national processes as the system borders are increasingly permeable.

Policy implications

What policy implications follow from an international legal system that is dynamic, but in which major changes are rare? Unlike other formulations that imply a self-regulating character to law, we see a significant role for agency in the formulation of new norms and operating rules. Recognizing the interaction of the operating and normative systems, strategic actors (especially states) can attempt certain moves that would enhance their own interests and maximize the achievement of their preferred outcomes. Given this assumption, there are a number of implications and recommendations that flow from our theory.

From the perspective of norm making, international law is desirable and should be effective. Because political shocks and the other conditions for change are infrequent and not often coterminous, there may be few opportunities to make substantial changes in international law. Most obviously, actors must seize opportunities when they occur, lest they not reappear again for a number of years. In the context of normative treaty-making, actors face something of a dilemma. On the one hand, the limited opportunities available for change suggest that actors should pursue "broader" and "deeper" agreements, incorporating as much as possible in any agreement; the Law of the Sea Convention is an example of a comprehensive treaty. This ensures that all that actors desire to accomplish can be done at once, rather than counting on future negotiations and agreements to fill out the set of desired changes. On the other hand, attempting to negotiate an omnibus agreement will further delay any changes and runs the risk of the whole process collapsing and therefore no new law being adopted.

Even given a substantial normative change, there is still the challenge of making sure that actors comply with the norms and that disputes are resolved peacefully and effectively. Following our approach, the best way to ensure an operating–normative system balance is to assess the level of available operating system capacity and to adopt normative provisions that maximize operating capacity from the outset. Thus, treaties can (as indeed many do) include reference to the relevant dispute settlement mechanisms or institutions (e.g., ICJ or International Criminal Court) or practices (e.g., universal jurisdiction) that would support the norm. Alternatively, the treaty could create new institutions or practices (e.g., International Seabed Authority), providing for those in the treaty text. The alternative is to rely on actors to create the necessary infrastructure and processes at a later time. Our analysis, however, reveals this could be a long wait, even if such rules come to fruition. The extra time needed to negotiate operating system changes in treaty formulation should be shorter than the time that it takes to facilitate such system change subsequently and separately. Which option is adopted may depend on available extra-systemic mechanisms to carry out some of the operating system functions, although these have some inherent limitations and are often outside of the decision-makers' control.

Strategic actors might also choose the forum in which new norms are created in order to manipulate their scope and content. In drafting treaties, coalitions of less developed states and interested NGOs might seek to use organs of the United Nations for drafting treaties where majority voting rules, observer status for NGOs, and other machinery generally blunts some of the influence of major power states. In contrast, more powerful actors might choose to deliberate new norms in arenas more favorable to their interests and in which they have more control over outcomes. As noted in Chapter 5, states such as the UK and the US chose to build new terrorism law in the UN Security Council where they have veto power rather than taking the matter to the General Assembly. States could also battle over rules for lawmaking in a given forum – such as the rule of unanimity or consensus – in order to guarantee more favorable outcomes.

The same might be true for choosing forums under which disputes are adjudicated. These behaviors assume that there is a range of institutional choices available, something not yet as true of international relations as in national political processes. As the number of operating system institutions proliferates, one can expect greater "forum shopping" by states with respect to both normative rule creation and dispute resolution. These phenomena are already seen with respect to litigation in the Inter-American legal system because there exist multiple venues in which to press claims. At the international level, national and regional alternatives exist for states, corporations, and even individuals in addition to a multitude of global forums, with significant variation across issue areas.

Our analysis also suggests a greater role for non-systemic factors in an increasingly permeable international legal system. Much of this is discussed below as evidence of future trends. Yet various actors and processes will play important roles in the formulation, implementation, and compliance of legal norms. As new norms are created by states, they must recognize that how these norms become part of the system and all their components (monitoring, compliance, dispute resolution) will increasingly be less under exclusive state control. Thus, there is more uncertainty for states. In a globalized world, however, non-state actors will have enhanced opportunities to become part of the international legal operating system as well as play extra-systemic roles in guiding the future of international law.

One implication of our analysis stems from the stickiness of operating and normative system components. From a policymaking perspective, such components may have unintended and downstream consequences not envisioned by their creators. Thus, the creation of the ICC may someday lead to the reformulation of what crimes constitute war crimes or crimes against humanity, even those that are not contained in the original statute or in other international agreements (see Article 121 of the Rome Statute of the International Criminal Court that allows state parties to the Statute to amend the Statute seven years after its entry into force). Similarly, a norm in the area of human rights could stimulate the creation of new monitoring institutions or follow-up meetings that later inspire similar institutions or processes in other normative areas.

One might also consider the potential behavior of actors who benefit from the underdevelopment of the normative system and imbalances that occur when the operating system is inadequate to serve the normative system. That is, some actors do not want international law to constrain their behavior. Such "insincere" players might be assuaged if the operating system is inadequate to deal with some normative precepts and this imbalance lingers for years or indefinitely. This provides some incentive to sign treaties or agree to certain rules without fear that they will be strictly enforced. China's acceptance of certain human rights provisions is one such example.

In addition, the flexibility provided by the operating system, most notably in allowing treaty reservations, provides further assurance to reluctant and/or insincere parties. In an effort to protect the integrity of such delicately balanced packages as the 1982 Law of the Sea Convention, a convention may forbid reservations; in fact, that agreement prohibits reservations at Article 309. Yet, such a strategy in treaty making could have the effect of driving away potential signatories. There is a tradeoff between restricting reservations and gaining parties, and drafters need to find the proper equilibrium points: too little flexibility and the treaty could lack the requisite number of signatories to take effect or leave out key states (Gamble, 1980); too much flexibility and states are able to gut the purpose or effectiveness of an instrument.

Insincere states can also sign onto a norm, but then work to block or undermine the necessary operating system changes to give it effect. This is an especially attractive strategy for a coalition of leading or powerful states. Nevertheless, such states are vulnerable to gap-filling activities by others outside of the system. For example, NGOs might pick up the slack left by an underdeveloped operating system. In the human rights case, NGO reporting may lead to considerable embarrassment and loss of international reputation even if no legal institutions exist to hold perpetrators responsible. Democratic states are particularly vulnerable to gap-filling activities. Domestic public opinion, local NGOs, and national court systems tie the hands of insincere leaders, even as international monitoring and compliance mechanisms lag. These could account for why democratic states are reluctant to sign human rights treaties, even if their compliance record would be quite good, and why authoritarian states are just as likely to become parties to such agreements as they might not have to fear monitoring or detection of violations (see Hathaway, 2007). This reality suggests that successful treaties will need some form of follow-up or reporting requirement to hold political systems and leaders accountable with regard to the fulfillment of a country's international obligations.

Thinking about the future

As we discussed in an earlier chapter, both the operating and normative systems have expanded dramatically in the last few decades. There is little reason to believe that such expansion will not continue in the near and medium term. Yet it is very difficult to foretell the exact elements of these new laws or their timing, given the myriad interests affecting the content of new normative laws and the unpredictability of political shocks that provide windows of opportunity for change. Our theory is not designed to make such precise predictions in any case, as its strength lies in general explanations for legal change.

Although it is perhaps too early to tell, the importance of major power states in the international legal system seems to be declining. The United States holds the status of the only superpower and yet it has been less able to shape international law than global powers of the past. Its ability to block change might also diminish in the future, although a coalition of the US and rising states such as China may be successful in holding off normative or operating change championed by others. The rise in the importance of other actors, including NGOs and individuals, in operating system functions has weakened state influence in general and that of major states in particular. Such actors also play significant roles outside the formal legal system in law formulation, monitoring, and compliance processes.

As the normative system develops further, albeit usually sporadically but sometimes dramatically, it will be hard for the operating system to keep up. As both systems change, several challenges arise that represent barriers and opportunities to effectiveness. Although a full rendering of all such challenges is beyond the scope of this study, we concentrate on three of the more important ones: fragmentation, public–private interconnections, and the domestic–international interface.

Addressing the fragmentation of international law

Our approach highlighted the adaptation that the international legal system undertakes if it finds existing conceptual, procedural, and structural capacities inadequate to achieve its normative objectives. Nevertheless, the range of adaptation as well as the volume of law have created concern that international law is fragmenting from the weight of specialization and the increase in the number of institutions whose actions have international legal effect; the latter include international courts, international organizations, and other lawmaking or standard-setting bodies. Such fragmentation comes, in part, from different preferences, which in turn lead to the adoption of different rules and institutions (Alter and Meunier, 2009).

Some of our analysis has implied that new operating system adaptations have improved the operation of the system, and indeed this is usually true at the micro-level. Yet the operating system may become less coherent when viewed from a macro-perspective. This seems particularly disturbing when conflicting or competing practices result. As the International Law Commission Report on the Fragmentation of International Law (United Nations General Assembly, 2006: 14) states: "Very often new rules or regimes develop precisely in order to deviate from what was earlier provided by the general law. When such deviations become general and frequent, the unity of law suffers." The analogy might made to a computer that uses different operating systems and often incompatible software to run different programs. For example, individuals and corporations have standing to press claims in the European Court of Justice, but do not have similar rights in most global adjudicatory proceedings, which remain the exclusive purview of states. Various human rights standards can also diverge across regions, such as prohibitions against capital punishment in some areas and acceptance of it in others. In this way, the divergence of laws across national systems is becoming mirrored in global law and regional subsystems. There are also differences across issue areas as institutions and processes are created for narrow issue areas and therefore lack broader applicability; for example, NGOs have varying degrees of rights according to different forums and issue areas, with particular weakness in the security area.

Functional specialization, closer cooperation and even integration on a regional basis, and the proliferation of lawmaking venues can contribute to multiple and sometimes competing norms. This is not necessarily a new phenomena, although it is more frequent in contemporary times. For example, during the period between World War I and World War II, one might find potentially conflicting obligations restricting the use of force in the League of Nations Covenant (not to resort to war without trying to settle the dispute peacefully first), the 1928 Pact of Paris (to renounce war as an instrument of national policy), and individual neutrality agreements concluded by states (the League Covenant required that "Should any Member of the League resort to war in disregard of its covenants under Articles 12, 13, and 15, it shall ipso facto be deemed to have committed an act of war against all other Members of the League" which would seem to preclude the possibility of neutrality).

It would take a major reorganization and consolidation in order to streamline the operating and normative systems respectively. This kind of effort would likely be rare and very slow given the processes of change in international law. Such an objective prompted the work of the Third United Nations Conference on the Law of the Sea, an effort to bring together provisions of earlier maritime treaties with any customary practice. Revisions in just a single subject area required nine years of negotiation to produce a text in 1982 and it was another twelve years before the convention entered into force in 1994. Broader regional integration could solve some problems at one level, but promote fragmentation problems across regions and globally; European Union trade rules illustrate this dilemma. Still, the use of existing operating system components for new norms could reduce the potential conflict by using standard operating institutions and processes.

Given the delays and uncertainty in transformation, states might purposely bypass the existing system. The short-lived effort during the Korean War to use the UN General Assembly as an alternative to the UN Security Council when it became deadlocked because of a veto is an example of this. Of course, when the political tide turned in the UN General Assembly, the US and the UK, who had proposed the Uniting for

Peace Resolution in 1950, retreated to the Security Council where each held the veto. It is therefore not clear which option – staying within an existing operating system or innovation – would produce the most effective arrangement for norm compliance. In any event, whatever theoretically might be attractive would not matter if states chose to behave differently.

It is in understanding the contours and depth of this dynamic that the International Law Commission has taken on a monitoring and restatement project to confirm acceptance by states of practices and principles that are prevalent in the contemporary international legal system. Examples of topics that fall into this study are: what sources are covered by general international law; how does general international law appear in the practice of domestic courts and tribunals; and how does general international law function "spontaneously"? (United Nations General Assembly, 2006: 256). This is essentially a prospective "tune-up" to existing operating system measures on the sources and application of international law. Extending the computer analogy, this step is less about reformatting the hard disk than it is about ensuring that it is properly partitioned and the rules for space allocation are proper.

Such a review and understanding of the system-wide significance of specific practices could be very important in recognizing when practical adaptations such as enforcing the judgments of foreign courts or arbitration panels in domestic courts are effective as extra-systemic mechanisms. As we see from the string of death penalty cases that have gone before the US Supreme Court, however, the US had breached its treaty obligations, but the Court declined to enforce the judgment (see *Medellin v. Texas* 2008). Although confined to the US, this shows both the inconsistency in practice in this important area and how the enforcement of international judgments through national courts cannot be assumed. A counter-example may be found in the practice of the European Court of Human Rights in which there has generally been a very good rate of national compliance with ECHR decisions.

Is fragmentation necessarily a fault that needs to be corrected? Competing norms, practices, and institutions have a role to play by "staying in the background" and "controlling the way the later and more specific rules are being interpreted and applied" (United Nations General Assembly, 2006: 22). In the *Southern Bluefin Tuna Case* (2000), Japan had argued that the 1993 Convention on the Conservation of the Southern Bluefin Tuna applied to the situation as *lex specialis* and *lex posterior*, excluding the application of the 1982 UN Convention on the

Law of the Sea. The tribunal decided that this was not the case and that both the 1993 Convention on the Conservation of the Southern Bluefin Tuna and the 1982 UN Convention on the Law of the Sea applied (United Nations General Assembly, 2006: 21). Nevertheless, transaction costs associated with such contradictions make subsequent change harder and slower, much as incompatible software and viruses limit the effectiveness of computers, even as individual applications become more efficient.

In its conclusion (United Nations General Assembly, 2006: 248), the International Law Commission noted that:

> Fragmentation moves international law in the direction of legal pluralism but does this, as the present report has sought to emphasize, by constantly using the resources of general international law, especially the rules of the Vienna Convention on Treaties, customary law, and "general principles of law recognized by civilized nations." One principal conclusion of this report has been that the emergence of special treaty-regimes (which should not be called "self-contained") has not seriously undermined legal security, predictability or the equality of legal subjects. The techniques of *lex specialis* or *lex posterior*, of *inter se* agreements and of the superior position given to peremptory norms and the (so far under-elaborated) notion of "obligations owed to the international community as a whole" provide a basic professional tool-box that is able to respond in a flexible way to most substantive fragmentation problems.

This conclusion envisages a stabilizing role that is not unlike the one we describe for international law's operating system although our emphasis is on its effect on performance and the ILC's interest seems to be a general one – ensuring international law's coherence as a legal system.

Public–private partnerships

Individuals and private concerns have sought and developed a greater role in international legal operations. How can these be reconciled with an operating system that is still state-centered and where formal organizations play important roles? Some innovations in the human rights and investment areas provide models for further expansion, such that private matters become public and individuals become more important actors. Both individuals and private entities have gained the right to complain against the actions of governments through treaties. The growing body of complaints that these systems have produced are providing a basis for modifying state behavior and are independent sources for interpreting treaties as complaints or questions are reviewed by bodies such as the

Human Rights Committee. All state parties are obligated to provide regular reports to the Committee on how rights are being implemented. "In addition to the reporting procedure, Article 41 of the Covenant [the ICCPR] provides for the Committee to consider inter-state complaints." The Covenant's First Optional Protocol gives the Committee competence to examine individual complaints with regard to alleged violations of the Covenant by States parties to the protocol.[2]

Other public institutions that were set up to provide remedy to private complaints are the arbitral tribunals of the International Centre for the Settlement of Investment Disputes (ICSID). ICSID was created by the Convention on the Settlement of Investment Disputes between States and Nationals of Other States. It presently has more than 140 parties and enables private investors to sue states for failure to live up to the obligations of an investment treaty. The existence of ICSID allows private investors to enter into dispute settlement directly with states through arbitration or conciliation without getting another state to pursue the claim (see Fauchald, 2008). This has established and institutionalized what could be an important precedent where private entities – in this case investors – can sit as equals with states in a dispute settlement proceeding. Through July 2009, 167 cases have been concluded before ICSID tribunals.[3]

These activities add to the operating capacity of international law by including the legally significant statements of these new monitoring and dispute settlement mechanisms. In effect, they represent cases of what we have identified as extra-systemic gap-filling actions, even though many exist in subsidiary fashion or at the margins of the system. The volume of activity can make a difference in the level of overall influence that it might have even if these institutions are not formally setting precedents as is the case with ICSID decisions. As the volume of such activity increases, however, the operating system, or at least certain issue-specific institutions in the operating system, might need to take more steps to accommodate such input.

Issues in which private actions have public global consequences will be another area where international law will be called upon to stretch its operating capacities. Extant operating system mechanisms are not designed to deal with many of these challenges. Groundwork for addressing such issues has also been laid through the work of organizations like

[2] See www2.ohchr.org/english/law/ccpr-one.htm.
[3] See http://icsid.worldbank.org/ICSID/.

the Hague Conference on Private International Law. This is an inter-governmental organization that was set up "to work for the progressive unification of the rules of private international law." Its thirty-nine conventions have principally focused on three broad areas: International Protection of Children, International Family and Family Property Relations, International Legal Cooperation and Litigation, and International Commercial and Financial Law. These conventions have addressed a host of complicated cross-border issues relating to the recognition of marriages and divorces, inter-country adoption of children as well as maintenance obligations towards children, the recognition of judgments, service of judicial and extrajudicial documents, choice of court, recognition of the legal personality of foreign companies, and the like.[4]

Domestic institutions and international obligations

When new norms are created, states often create new institutions, albeit after some delay to implement, monitor and enforce provisions associated with the norm. Yet, many of these institutions still lack some capacity to carry out all the necessary operating system responsibilities. As we noted above, operating system change often reduces, but does not eliminate, suboptimality. Yet experience has demonstrated that centralizing all activities in one organization may also not be very effective (see Slaughter, 2004) and counter-intuitively might not be the most efficient way to achieve the purposes of the normative system. We noted that a number of different national and subnational processes have filled the gaps, many of which are important but do not necessarily receive a lot of recognition. As Sassen (2006: 419) concludes:

> critical components of authority deployed in the making of the territorial state are shifting toward becoming strong capabilities for detaching that authority from its exclusive territory and onto multiple bordering systems. Insofar as many of these systems are operating inside the nation-state, they may be obscuring the fact that a significant switch has happened.

The net result can be "a space in which the strict dichotomy between domestic and international has largely broken down, in which administrative functions are performed in often complex interplays between

---

[4] A full list of conventions is available at the Hague Conference website at www.hcch.net/index_en.php?act=conventions.listing.

officials and institutions on different levels, and in which regulation may be highly effective despite its predominantly non-binding forms" (Krisch and Kingsbury, 2006: 1).

The wider range of international law subjects that now rely on domestic structures to come into force means that larger numbers of government officials at all levels and in all branches of government are being exposed to, and are being called upon to work in, international law. The scope and intensity of these relationships are such that some imagine a world of networked groups who share interests and responsibilities within their own countries or jurisdictions (Slaughter, 2004). This should make responding to international law's needs easier as more people and institutions gain experience working with international law. Further, international law itself may be increasingly in a position to influence more aspects of other legal systems (see Brunnée, 2004).

How will the international legal system deal with multiple layers of governance, relying more on national processes to supplement the international operating system? The European Union, for example, has opted for the approach of "subsidiarity" in which functions remain at the local level if that is where they can be most effectively addressed. This practice is sound not only because centralization can be costly, but also because it can be a political liability if it appears that decisions affecting people's lives are being taken by unelected geographically remote bureaucrats. The 2005 rejection of the European Constitution by Dutch voters is an example where concerns about job losses and the ability of a small country to thrive in a community where the larger countries would dominate caused up to 61.6 percent of Dutch voters to reject this Constitution even though a major benefit of the Constitution was to streamline decision making.

Still, even for well-developed institutions such as the European Union, demands on regional operating systems might be greater than their capacities. For example, the European Court of Human Rights is trying to reduce the backlog it faces in individual complaints and cases by seeking "to bolster domestic mechanisms for remedying Convention violations at home, obviating the need for aggrieved individuals to seek relief at the regional level" (Helfer, 2008b: 159). The Court has also tried to facilitate the domestic remedies by being more specific in its rulings as to the appropriate remedy. International criminal law provides a further example in which the varied character of crime and its potential appearance in any location around the world could make the more developed domestic criminal law system better suited to addressing most of international crime, reserving only the most serious cases when the domestic system fails to act (see Aceves, 2000).

Yet national capacities vary tremendously. Relying on regional, national, and subnational legal systems is fine when dealing with developed states, but inherently problematic when the international system depends on more politicized and lesser developed legal systems that lack transparency and legitimacy. For domestic institutions to play an effective role in carrying out international obligations, their actions need to be coordinated and subject to some form of review, preferably external. The relationship between national governments and international institutions is present in monitoring requirements, dispute settlement, and interpretive pronouncements. These arrangements could become even more prominent in the future as the process for operating system change is slow and sporadic, but the need for norm implementation and compliance is more immediate.

It is not clear, however, that domestic legal processes to ensure international obligations will have many spillover effects outside that state's borders. In addition, as we can see from the debates about the appropriate reliance on "foreign law" by the US Supreme Court (most evident in *Roper* v. *Simmons* 2005 and discussed in Waldron, 2005; Larsen, 2004; and Slaughter, 2004), the desirability for effective international law might not be a guiding factor in the national decision-making process and therefore national courts cannot be relied on all the time to implement international law or to do so effectively. At the same time, practice at the national level and across boundaries affects the interpretation of the law, even if it does not create new law or completely replace operating system procedures at the global level. For example, enough of a transnational judicial dialogue has taken place on the death penalty for at least one scholar to claim that "[national] courts are helping to shape a customary international law norm on cruel or inhuman punishment to include limitations (or an outright prohibition) of the death penalty" (Waters, 2007: 478).

Related to this is the ongoing problem of the international accountability of individuals through international criminal law. Thus far, it may only be the most serious of crimes that are prosecuted internationally, such as genocide in Bosnia or in Darfur. This is not to say that crimes such as drug and human trafficking cannot be pursued in international legal forums. Yet the stickiness of international arrangements means that change is difficult at the international level. We have already demonstrated that a lag can exist between normative innovation and institutional adaptation. There also may be a lag between adaptation and subsequent functionality and effectiveness; for example, the International Criminal Court only came into existence fully in 2002, and in 2009 has yet to carry out its first prosecution to the end. Given such circumstances, national and subnational institutions, or even *ad hoc* components of the international operating system, might substitute until the global or regional institutions are mature.

The triggering mechanism for the involvement of domestic institutions is often the incorporation of some international standard into the domestic law of the country. A classic example is the Constitution of South Africa that has incorporated international human rights; this equips the Constitutional Court of South Africa to implement these rights. Buergenthal (2006) noted that many European and Latin American countries regard treaty provisions, particularly of the regional human rights conventions, as self-executing. In other cases, such as that of the United Kingdom, specific legislative acts bring international human rights law into domestic law with the result of "mak[ing] it possible for international human rights treaties and the decisions of international tribunals applying these instruments to have a direct impact on the domestic administration of justice" (Buergenthal, 2006: 806).

As the forces of globalization have increased the volume of transnational activity and the number of transnational actors, this selective partnering whereby a domestic legal institution enforces or acts on the basis of an international norm will increase. The key challenge will be in understanding the multiple ways by which these partnerships and particularly the *ad hoc* arrangements born of necessity become part of international law's operating system. Formally incorporating international law standards into national law is the most classic example of a relationship between international and national laws. In this way, the international law is given effect by the national system as part of its own law. Increasingly, human rights are taking on this character with many countries adopting the international human rights standards as part of the constitutional guarantee of individual rights in these countries (see Buergenthal, 1997).

Maintaining the capacity of international law's operating system

As international law becomes a more complex system that reaches more deeply into states and touches individual lives in more ways, it will require additional capacity to match its normative directions. We see that the normative system can still perform without full operating capacity. Yet, we also see that it performs suboptimally or relies on

adaptations to carry out its functions. These aspects have led international lawyers to be concerned about fragmentation or other stresses in
the system. In fact, our study has shown that using international law is
vital to maintaining a robust operating system even if broad system-wide
changes are infrequent and often only follow some sort of shock. To draw
once again on computer analogies, where international law finds itself
today is not unlike the move from Web 1.0 to the present Web 2.0. Web
1.0 was characterized by static pages that followed a strict hierarchy
determined by the author or publisher of the page. User interactions
were passive. In the Web 2.0 environment, interactivity and participation
are encouraged and users contribute content and even knowledge as
elements within a site are combined to produce new insight. The characteristic is a lack of hierarchy and less ability to control the content. The
challenge of this rich environment is for the user to be able to discern the
authentic from the less accurate or reliable. One only needs to think of a
system such as Wikipedia to have a sense of this phenomenon. For
international law, this means that efforts to use instruments such as
treaties are valuable even if a state ultimately concludes that it will opt
out of a treaty regime or attach reservations to its acceptance of those
obligations. The experience of opting out and making reservations adds
to the overall knowledge about how states behave with regard to treaty
obligations.

This ongoing process, punctuated by shocks, is what will provide
international law with guidance on how to adapt to the intensified
transnational legal environment. Understanding the existing capacity
of the operating system, addressing its suboptimalities, and applying a
functional test to determine when change has occurred will go a long way
not only to recognizing the strength and dynamism of international law,
but also to identifying the most effective means of meeting normative
objectives. This analysis focuses the scholar and practitioner less on
abstract philosophy than on system-wide functionality. It will facilitate
change by drawing readily on the existing tenets of the operating system
and stretching them to the limit, after which practices from outside the
international legal system may be adapted for use. Understanding the
function of the operating system also increases the speed of normative
change and reduces transaction costs by making available elements of an
existing, familiar, and proven system even if it has inherent limits to how
much it might deliver. The ability to assess the effectiveness of the system
or identify its inadequacies will also help discover areas in need of
change, even as change may be difficult, slow, and suboptimal.

Such widely shared observations in turn can help to foster needed change, thereby sustaining international law's role as an important and dynamic part of global governance. Not only does this provide international law with the capacity to recognize and to undertake the change, but it also provides a possible range of tested solutions through the adaptations that can become part of the operating system when the opportunity for system-wide change occurs. If such new capacities have already been proven and used, even though they were previously employed outside the operating system, accepting them as part of the operating system and folding them into existing system mechanisms becomes much easier. The creation of the International Criminal Court provides a recent example of such an operating system change. The mass killings and violence of World War II and then of the 1990s led to the desire for some international system of accountability for those committing such atrocities. *Ad hoc* solutions through the Nuremberg, Tokyo, former Yugoslavia, and Rwanda international tribunals to address the crimes committed during those conflicts provided the experience and the content to establish a permanent international criminal court, even as conditions were right for the creation of one. Subsequent mass killings facilitated the environment for a major operating system change to establish an International Criminal Court in 1998 and made possible the pursuit of personal criminal responsibility against a sitting head of government such as President al Bashir of Sudan in 2008.

The operating system can also track and evaluate performance in a structured way. This occurs as it either validates the adequacy of its operating capacity to give effect to a norm or identifies the system's inadequacy. In the case of inadequacy, any extra-systemic adaptations undertaken to overcome the suboptimal performance could be among the possible solutions available for adoption by the operating system when the opportunity for change occurs. Because it cannot be easily predicted when such opportunities might arise, it is useful to have as many options as possible from which to choose. Therefore, addressing suboptimalities ultimately strengthens the system by recognizing the need for change and by developing extra-systemic adaptations for possible adoption. These adaptations therefore not only provide a short-term boost to existing operating system capacity, but they also help test different options for longer-term system-wide change.

It is therefore no longer enough to look within the formal confines of international law to understand its operation. In order to capture its full capacity, we must look outside of international law to find the full range of practices and possible options to strengthen international law's operating system. Not all adaptations will or should become part of the operating system, but in today's rapidly changing and globalized legal environment, the greater the range of options, the greater the likelihood of an effective upgrade or enhancement when the opportunity for system-wide change occurs.

In this view, each international law action contributes separately to the development of a specific norm as well as more generally to the overall capacity of international law to function effectively through a strong operating system. International law may not work perfectly at all times – far from it – but at worst actors will be able to understand what alternatives outside the international legal system are necessary to achieve compliance with existing norms or new norms. Our approach not only captures international law's inherent dynamism, but also more accurately depicts its adaptability and capacity for change.

REFERENCES

Abbott, K. W. 1999. "International Relations Theory, International Law, and the Regime Governing Atrocities in Internal Conflicts," *American Journal of International Law* 93 (2): 361–79

Abbott, K. W. and D. Snidal 2000. "Hard and Soft Law in International Governance," *International Organization* 54 (3): 421–56

Aceves, W. J. 2000. "Liberalism and International Legal Scholarship: The *Pinochet Case* and the Move Toward a Universal System of Transnational Law Litigation," *Harvard International Law Journal* 41 (1): 129–84

Adler, E. and P. M. Haas 1992. "Conclusion: Epistemic Communities, World Order, and the Creation of a Reflective Research Program," *International Organization* 46 (1): 367–90

Alston, L. 2000. "A Framework for Understanding the New Institutional Economics," unpublished paper

Alter, K. and S. Meunier 2009. "The Politics of International Regime Complexity," *Perspectives on Politics* 7 (1): 13–24

Alvarez, J. 2002. "The New Treaty Makers," *Boston College International and Comparative Law Review* 25 (2): 213–34

2005. *International Organizations as Law-makers.* Oxford: Oxford University Press

American Society of International Law 1998. *Trilateral Perspectives on International Legal Issues: From Theory into Practice.* Ardsley, NY: Transnational Publishers

Anghie, A. 2004. *Imperialism, Sovereignty and the Making of International Law.* Cambridge: Cambridge University Press

Annan, K. 2000. *We the Peoples: The Role of the United Nations in the 21st Century.* New York: United Nations

Arend, A. 1999. *Legal Rules and International Society.* Oxford: Oxford University Press

Arrieta, J. I. 2000. *Governance Structures within the Catholic Church.* Montreal: Wilson & Lafleur

Arzt, D. and I. Lukashuk 1995. "Participants in International Legal Relations," in L. F. Damrosch, G. Danilenko, and R. Mullerson (eds.), *Beyond Confrontation: International Law for the Post-Cold War Era.* Boulder, CO: Westview Press, pp. 61–92

Aust, A. 2005. *Handbook of International Law*. Cambridge: Cambridge University Press

Avdeyera, O. 2007. "When Do States Comply with International Treaties? Policies on Violence against Women in Post-Communist Countries," *International Studies Quarterly* 51 (4): 877–900

Aviel, J. F. 2000. "Placing Human Rights and Environmental Issues on ASEAN Agenda: The Role of Non-Governmental Organizations," *Asian Journal of Political Science* 8 (2): 17–34

Aviram, A. 2004. "A Paradox of Spontaneous Formation: The Evolution of Private Legal Systems," *Yale Law and Policy Review* 22 (1): 1–68

Axelrod, R. and R. Keohane 1985. "Achieving Cooperation Under Anarchy: Strategies and Institutions," in K. Oye (ed.), *Cooperation Under Anarchy*. Princeton: Princeton University Press, pp. 226–54

Barnett, M. 1995. "The United Nations and Global Security: The Norm is Mightier than the Sword," *Ethics and International Affairs* 9: 37–54

Barnett, M. and M. Finnemore 2004. *Rules for the World: International Organizations in Global Politics*. Ithaca, NY: Cornell University Press

Barrett, S. 2003. *Environment and Statecraft: The Strategy of Environmental Treaty-making*. Oxford: Oxford University Press

2007. *Why Cooperate? The Incentive to Supply Global Public Goods*. Oxford: Oxford University Press

Baumgartner, F. and B. Jones 1993. *Agendas and Instability in American Politics*. Chicago: University of Chicago Press

Beck, R. 1996. "International Law and International Relations: The Prospects for Interdisciplinary Collaboration," in R. Beck, A. Arend, and R. Vander Lugt (eds.), *International Rules: Approaches from International Law and International Relations*. New York: Oxford University Press, pp. 3–33

Bederman, D. J. 2001. *International Law in Antiquity*. Cambridge: Cambridge University Press

2002. *The Spirit of International Law*. Athens, GA: University of Georgia Press

Bentham, J. 1970. *Collected Works of Jeremy Bentham*. J. H. Burns and H. L. A. Hart (eds.). London: Athlone Press

Berman, P. S. 2005. *The Globalization of International Law*. London: Ashgate

2007a. "Global Legal Pluralism," *Southern California Law Review* 80 (6): 1155–1238

2007b. "A Pluralist Approach to International Law," *Yale Journal of International Law* 32 (2): 301–29

Bianchi, A. 1999. "Immunity and Human Rights: The *Pinochet Case*," *European Journal of International Law* 10 (2): 237–77

Bodin, J. 1992. *On Sovereignty: Four Chapters from the Six Books of the Commonwealth*, (ed. and trans.) J. H. Franklin. New York: Cambridge University Press

Boulding, K. 1985. *The World as a Total System*. Beverly Hills, CA: Sage Publications

Boutros-Ghali, B. 1995. *An Agenda for Peace*. New York: United Nations

Bradlow, D. 2005. "Private Complainants and International Organizations: A Comparative Study of the Independent Inspection Mechanisms in International Financial Institutions," *Georgetown Journal of International Law* 36 (2): 403–94

Breen, C. 2003. "The Role of NGOs in the Formulation of and Compliance with the Optional Protocol to the Convention on the Rights of the Child on Involvement of Children in Armed Conflict," *Human Rights Quarterly* 25 (2): 453–81

Brierly, J. L. 1963. *The Law of Nations: An Introduction to the International Law of Peace*, 6th edn. Oxford: Clarendon Press

Brunnée, J. 2004. "The United States and International Environmental Law: Living with an Elephant," *European Journal of International Law* 15 (4): 617–49

Brunnée, J. and S. J. Toope 2000. "International Law and Constructivism: Elements of an International Theory of International Law," *Columbia Journal of Transnational Law* 39 (1): 19–74

Buergenthal, T. 1997. "Modern Constitutions and Human Rights Treaties," *Columbia Journal of Transnational Law* 36 (1/2): 211–24

  2006. "The Evolving International Human Rights System," *American Journal of International Law* 100 (4): 783–807

Bull, H. 1977. *The Anarchical Society*. New York: Columbia University Press

Bunn, I. D. 2004. "Global Advocacy for Corporate Accountability: Transatlantic Perspectives from the NGO Community," *American University International Law Review* 19 (6): 1256–1306

Burci, G. L. 2005. "Institutional Adaptation without Reform: WHO and the Challenges of Globalization," *International Organizations Law Review* 2: 137–43

Burke-White, W. 2002. "A Community of Courts: Toward a System of International Criminal Law Enforcement," *Michigan Journal of International Law* 24: 1–101

Burley (Slaughter), A. M. and W. Mattli 1993. "Europe before the Court: A Political Theory of Legal Integration," *International Organization* 47 (1): 41–76

Cakmak, C. 2004. "The Role of Non-Governmental Organizations (NGOs) in the Norm Creation Process in the Field of Human Rights," *Alternatives: Turkish Journal of International Relations* 3 (1): 100–22

Calabresi, G. 1961. "Some Thoughts on Risk Distribution and the Law," *Yale Law Journal* 70 (3): 499–553

Capoccia, G. and D. Keleman 2007. "The Study of Critical Junctures. Theory, Narrative, and Counterfactuals in Historical Institutionalism," *World Politics* 59 (April): 341–69

Carr, E. H. 1964. *The Twenty Years' Crisis: 1919–1939*. New York: Harper & Row

Cassese, A. 1986. *International Law in a Divided World*. Oxford: Clarendon Press

Charlesworth, H., C. M. Chinkin, and S. Wright 1999. "Feminist Methods in International Law," *American Journal of International Law* 93 (2): 379–94

Charney, J. I. 1993. "Universal International Law," *American Journal of International Law* 87 (4): 529–51

1999. "The Proliferation of Courts and Tribunals: Piercing Together the Puzzle," *New York University Journal of International Law* 31: 697–708

Charnovitz, S. 2006. "Nongovernmental Organizations and International Law," *American Journal of International Law* 100 (2): 348–72

Chayes, A. and A. H. Chayes 1993. "On Compliance," *International Organization* 47 (2): 175–205

1995. *The New Sovereignty: Compliance with International Regulatory Agreements*. Cambridge, MA: Harvard University Press

Chayes, A., T. Ehrlich, and A. Lowenfeld 1968. *International Legal Process: Materials for an Introductory Course*. Boston: Little, Brown and Company

Chinkin, C. M. 1989. "The Challenge of Soft Law: Development and Change in International Law," *International and Comparative Law Quarterly* 38: 850–66

2000. "Normative Development in the International Legal System," in D. Shelton (ed.), *Commitment and Compliance: The Role of Non-binding Norms in the International Legal System*. Oxford: Oxford University Press, pp. 21–42

Cioffi-Revilla, C. 1998. "The Political Uncertainty of Interstate Rivalries: A Punctuated Equilibrium Model," in P. F. Diehl (ed.), *The Dynamics of Enduring Rivalries*. Urbana, IL: University of Illinois Press, pp. 64–97

Claude, I. L. 1966. "Collective Legitimization as a Political Function of the United Nations," *International Organization* 20 (2): 367–79

Coase, R. 1960. "The Problem of Social Cost," *Journal of Law and Economics* 3 (1): 1–44

Cohen, C. P. 1990. "The Role of Nongovernmental Organizations in the Drafting of the Convention on the Rights of the Child," *Human Rights Quarterly* 12 (1): 137–47

Cohen, M., J. March, and J. Olsen 1972. "A Garbage Can Model of Organizational Choice," *Administrative Science Quarterly* 17 (1): 1–25

Colaresi, M. 2001. "Shocks to the System: Great Power Rivalry and the Leadership Long-cycle," *Journal of Conflict Resolution* 45 (5): 569–93

Cook, R. 2004. "Dynamic Content: The Strategic Contingency of International Law," *Duke Journal of Comparative and International Law* 14 (1): 89–123

Cooter, R. and T. Ulen 1987. *Law and Economics*. Reading, MA: Addison Wesley Longman

Cover, R. 1983. "The Supreme Court, 1982 Term – Foreword: Nomos and Narrative," *Harvard Law Review* 97 (1): 4–68

Cox, R. W. and H. K. Jacobson 1973. *The Anatomy of Influence: Decision Making in International Organization*. New Haven, CT: Yale University Press

Crawford, J. 2002. *The International Law Commission's Articles on State Responsibility*. Cambridge: Cambridge University Press

Crow, M. E. 2004. "Smokescreens and State Responsibility: Using Human Rights Strategies to Promote Global Tobacco Controls," *Yale Journal of International Law* 29 (1): 209–50

Dahl, R. A. 1998. *On Democracy*. New Haven, CT: Yale University Press

Dai, X. 2007. *International Institutions and National Policies*. Cambridge: Cambridge University Press

Damrosch, L. 2004. "Brief of International Law Experts and Former Diplomats as *Amici Curiae* in Support of Petitioner," Appeal from the District Court of Oklahoma, County, State of Oklahoma, CF-1993–4302

Damrosch, L. F. and B. H. Oxman 2004. "Editors' Introduction to Agora: The United States Constitution and International Law," *American Journal of International Law* 98 (1): 42–3

Danner, A. M. 2006. "When Courts Make Law: How the International Criminal Tribunal Recast the Law of War," *Vanderbilt Law Review* 59 (1): 1–57

Deehr, M. 1991. "A Proposal for the International Monitoring of Potential Genocide Conditions," *Wisconsin International Law Journal* 9 (2): 491–514

Dessler, D. 1989. "What's at Stake in the Agent–Structure Debate?" *International Organization* 43 (2): 441–73

Deutsch, K. and J. D. Singer 1964. "Multipolar Power Systems and International Stability," *World Politics* 16 (3): 390–406

Diehl, P. F. 2001. "International Law: Stepchild in Social Science Research," *International Studies Review* 3 (1): 4–9

Diehl, P. F. and G. Goertz 2000. *War and Peace in International Rivalry*. Ann Arbor: University of Michigan Press

Downs, G., D. Rocke, and P. Barsoom 1996. "Is the Good News about Compliance Good News about Cooperation?" *International Organization* 50 (3): 379–406

Dubinsky, P. 2005. "Human Rights Law Meets Private Law Harmonization," *Yale Journal of International Law* 30 (1): 211–317

Duffield, J. 2003. "The Limits of Rational Design," *International Organization* 57 (2): 413–30

Dunoff, J. and J. Trachtman 1999. "The Law and Economics of Humanitarian Law Violations in Internal Conflict," *American Journal of International Law* 93 (2): 394–409

Durant, R. and P. F. Diehl 1989. "Agendas, Alternatives and Public Policy: Lessons from the US Foreign Policy Arena," *Journal of Public Policy* 9 (2): 179–205

Eldredge, N. 1985. *Time Frames: The Evolution of Punctuated Equilibria*. Princeton: Princeton University Press

1995. *Reinventing Darwin: The Great Evolutionary Debate*. New York: Wiley

Ellickson, R. 1991. *Order Without Law. How Neighbors Settle Disputes*. Cambridge, MA: Harvard University Press

Evans, P. B., H. K. Jacobson, and R. Putnam 1993 (eds.). *Double-Edged Diplomacy: International Bargaining and Domestic Politics*. Berkeley: University of California Press

Fauchald, O. K. 2008. "The Legal Reasoning of ICSID Tribunals: An Empirical Analysis," *European Journal of International Law* 19 (2): 301–64

Fawcett, J. E. S. 1968. *The Law of Nations*. New York: Basic Books

Fearon, J. 1998. "Bargaining, Enforcement, and International Cooperation," *International Organization* 52 (2): 269–305

Ferstman, C. 1997. "Domestic Trials for Genocide and Crimes Against Humanity: The Example of Rwanda," *African Journal of International and Comparative Law* 9 (4): 857–77

Finlayson, J. and M. Zacher 1981. "The GATT and the Regulation of Trade Barriers: Regime Dynamics and Functions," *International Organization* 35 (4): 561–602

Finnemore, M. 1996. *National Interests in International Society*. Ithaca, NY: Cornell University Press

Franck, T. M. 1990. *The Power of Legitimacy among Nations*. Oxford: Oxford University Press

Friedmann, W. 1966. *The Changing Structure of International Law*. New York: Columbia University Press

Gamble, J. K. 1980. "Reservations to Multilateral Treaties: A Macroscopic View of State Practice," *American Journal of International Law* 74 (2): 372–94

   2006. "The Comprehensive Statistical Database of Multilateral Treaties (CSDMT) Project." Paper presented at the Shambaugh Conference, "Building Synergies: Institutions and Cooperation in World Politics," Iowa City, IA

Genco, S. 1980. "Integration Theory and System Change in Western Europe: The Neglected Role of Systems Transformation Episodes," in O. Holsti, R. Siverson, and A. L. George (eds.), *Change in the International System*. Boulder, CO: Westview, pp. 55–80

George, A. L. 1979. "The Causal Nexus between Cognitive Beliefs and Decision-Making Behavior: The 'Operational Code' Belief System," in L. Falkowski (ed.), *Psychological Models in International Politics*. Boulder, CO: Westview, pp. 104–24

George, A. L. and T. McKeown 1985. "Case Studies and Theories of Organizational Decision Making," in R. Coulam and R. A. Smith (eds.), *Advances in Information Processing in Organizations*, vol. II, *Research on Public Organizations*. Greenwich, CT: JAI Press, pp. 21–58

Gilligan, M. 2006. "Is Enforcement Necessary for Effectiveness? A Model of the International Criminal Regime," *International Organization* 60 (4): 935–67

Ginsburg, T. 2005. "Bounded Discretion in International Judicial Lawmaking," *Virginia Journal of International Law* 45 (3): 631–73

2006. "Locking in Democracy. Constitutions, Commitment, and International Law," *International Law and Politics* 38: 707–59

Giorgia, G. 1992. "Positivism and Dualism in Dionisio Anzilotti," *European Journal of International Law* 3 (1): 123–38

Goertz, G. 2003. *International Norms and Decision Making: A Punctuated Equilibrium Model.* Oxford: Rowman and Littlefield

Goertz, G. and P. F. Diehl 1992. "Toward a Theory of International Norms: Some Conceptual and Measurement Issues," *Journal of Conflict Resolution* 36 (4): 634–64

Goertz, G., B. Jones, and P. F. Diehl 2005. "Maintenance Processes in International Rivalries," *Journal of Conflict Resolution* 49 (5): 742–69

Goertz, G. and H. Starr 2002. *Necessary Conditions: Theory, Methodology, and Applications.* Lanham, MD: Rowman and Littlefield

Goldsmith, J. and E. Posner 2005. *The Limits of International Law.* Oxford: Oxford University Press

Goldstein, J., M. Kahler, R. O. Keohane, and A. M. Slaughter 2000. "Legalization and World Politics," *International Organization* 54 (3): 401–758

Gould, S. J. 1983. *Hen's Teeth and Horse's Toes.* New York: W. W. Norton

Gould, S. J. and N. Eldredge 1993. "Punctuated Equilibrium Comes of Age," *Nature* 366: 223–7

Green, S. 1997. "A Campaign to Sweep Away Danger," *Chronicle of Philanthropy* (20 October): 60

Gross, L. 1948. "The Peace of Westphalia, 1648–1948," *American Journal of International Law* 42 (1): 20–41

Grotius, H. 1925. "De jure belli ac pacis. Libri tres," (trans.) F. W. Kelwey, in J. B. Scott (ed.), *The Classics of International Law.* Oxford: Clarendon Press

Gruber, L. 2005. "Power Politics and the Institutionalization of International Relations," in M. Barnett and R. Duvall (eds.), *Power in Global Governance.* Cambridge: Cambridge University Press, pp. 102–29

Guzman, A. 2005. "The Design of International Agreements," *European Journal of International Law* 16 (4): 579–612

2008. *How International Law Works. A Rational Choice Theory.* Oxford: Oxford University Press

Haas, E. 1990. *When Knowledge is Power: Three Models of Change in International Organizations.* Berkeley: University of California Press

Haas, P. M. 1992. "Introduction: Epistemic Communities and International Policy Coordination," *International Organization* 46 (1): 1–35

Hall, P. and K. Thelen 2006. "Institutional Change in Varieties of Capitalism." Paper presented for the Europeanists Conference, Chicago

Halperin, M. 1974. *Bureaucratic Politics and Foreign Policy.* Washington, DC: Brookings Institution

Hart, H. L. A. 1961. *The Concept of Law.* Oxford: Clarendon Press

1994. *The Concept of Law*, 2nd edn. Oxford: Clarendon Press

Hasenclever, A., P. Mayer, and V. Rittberger 1997. *Theories of International Regimes*. Cambridge: Cambridge University Press

Hathaway, O. A. 2007. "Why Do Countries Commit to Human Rights Treaties?" *Journal of Conflict Resolution* 51 (4): 588–621

Hawkins, D. 2004. "Explaining Costly International Institutions: Persuasion and Enforceable Human Rights Norms," *International Studies Quarterly* 48: 779–804

Heldring, F. 1988. "Can the US Dollar Survive as a World Reserve Currency?" *Annals of the American Academy of Political and Social Science* 500: 23–32

Helfer, L. R. 2005. "Exiting Treaties," *Virginia Law Review* 91 (7): 1579–1648

2006. "Response: Not Fully Committed? Reservations, Risk, and Treaty Design," *Yale Journal of International Law* 31 (2): 367–82

2008a. "Nonconsensual International Lawmaking," *Illinois Law Review* 102 (1): 71–125

2008b. "Redesigning the European Court of Human Rights: Embeddedness as a Deep Structural Principle of the European Human Rights Regime," *European Journal of International Law* 19 (1): 125–59

Helfer, L. and A. M. Slaughter 2005. "Why States Create International Tribunals: A Response to Professors Posner and Yoo," *California Law Review* 93 (3): 901–56

Henkin, L. 1968. *How Nations Behave: Law and Foreign Policy*. New York: Columbia University Press

1995. *International Law: Politics and Values*. Dordrecht, Netherlands: Martinus Nijhoff Publishers

Henkin, L. and J. L. Hargrove 1994 (eds.). *Human Rights: An Agenda for the Next Century*. Washington, DC: American Society for International Law

Higgins, R. 1968. "Policy Considerations and the International Judicial Process," *International and Comparative Law Quarterly* 17 (1): 58–84

1994. *Problems and Process: International Law and How We Use It*. Oxford: Clarendon Press

Hollis, D. B. 2005. "Why State Consent Still Matters: Non-State Actors, Treaties, and the Changing Sources of International Law," *Berkeley Journal of International Law* 23 (1): 137–74

Huntington, S. P. 1991. *The Third Wave*. Norman, OK: University of Oklahoma Press

Ikenberry, G. J. and C. Kupchan 1990. "Socialization and Hegemonic Power," *International Organization* 44 (3): 283–315

International Law Association, 1998. Committee on Cultural Heritage. *Report of the Sixty-Eighth Conference*. Available at http://whc.unesco.org/archive/repcom99.htm

Janis, M. W. 1988/1993. *An Introduction to International Law*. Boston: Little, Brown and Company

Jennings, R. Y. 1938. "The *Caroline* and *McLeod* Cases," *American Journal of International Law* 32 (10): 82–99

Jervis, R. 1997. *System Effects: Complexity in Political and Social Life*. Princeton, NJ: Princeton University Press

Joyner, C. C. 2006. "International Law Is as International Theory Does?" *American Journal of International Law* 100 (1): 248–58

2007. "The Responsibility to Protect: Humanitarian Concerns and the Lawfulness of Armed Intervention," *Virginia Journal of International Law* 47 (3): 693–724

Kader, D. 1991. "Progress and Limitations in Basic Genocide Law," in I. Charny (ed.), *Genocide: A Critical Bibliographical Review*, vol. II. London: Mansell, pp. 141–5

Kaldor, M. 2003. *Global Civil Society: An Answer to War*. Cambridge: Polity Press

Kaplan, M. A. 1957. *System and Process in International Politics*. New York: Wiley

Keck, M. E. and K. Sikkink 1998. *Activists Beyond Borders: Advocacy Networks in International Politics*. Ithaca, NY: Cornell University Press

Kegley, C. 2008. *World Politics: Trend and Transformation*. Boston, MA: Thomson/Wadsworth

Kennedy, D. 1986. "Primitive Legal Scholarship," *Harvard Journal of International Law* 27 (1): 1–98

1997. "New Approaches to Comparative Law: Comparativism and International Governance," *Utah Law Review* 2: 545–637

Kennedy, D. and C. Tennant 1994. "New Approaches to International Law: A Bibliography," *Harvard Journal of International Law* 35 (2): 417–60

Kent, H. S. K. 1954. "The Historical Origins of the Three-Mile Limit," *American Journal of International Law* 48 (4): 537–53

Keohane, R. 1980. "The Theory of Hegemonic Stability and Changes in International Economic Regimes, 1967–1977," in O. Holsti, R. Siverson, and A. George (eds.), *Change in the International System*. Boulder, CO: Westview Press, pp. 131–62

1984. *After Hegemony: Cooperation and Discord in the World Political Economy*. Princeton, NJ: Princeton University Press

1986 (ed.). *Neorealism and Its Critics*. New York: Columbia University Press

Keohane, R. and J. Nye 2000. "Introduction," in J. Nye and J. D. Donahue (eds.), *Governance in a Globalizing World*. Washington, DC: Brookings Institution Press, pp. 18–20

Kindleberger, C. 1973. *The World in Depression, 1929–1939*. London: Penguin Press

Kingdon, J. W. 1995. *Agendas, Alternatives, and Public Policies*. New York: Harper Collins

Kirsch, P. 2007. "The Role of the International Criminal Court in Enforcing International Criminal Law," *American University International Law Review* 22: 539–47

Kissinger, H. 2001. "The Pitfalls of Universal Jurisdiction," *Foreign Affairs* 80 (4): 86–96

Klir, G. and B. Yuan 1995. *Fuzzy Sets and Fuzzy Logic: Theory and Applications.* New York: Prentice-Hall

Klotz, A. 1995. *Norms in International Relations: The Struggle against Apartheid.* Ithaca, NY: Cornell University Press

Koenig, C. 1991. "Observer Status for the ICRC at the United Nations: A Legal Viewpoint," *International Review of the Red Cross* 280: 37–48

Koh, H. 1997. "Why Do Nations Obey International Law?" *Yale Law Journal* 106: 2599–659
    2002. "Opening Remarks: Transnational Legal Process Illuminated," in M. Likosky (ed.), *Transnational Legal Process: Globalisation and Power Disparities.* London: Butterworths, pp. 327–32

Konig, T. and S. Hug 2000. "Ratifying Maastricht," *European Union Politics* 1 (1): 93–124

Koremenos, B., C. Lipson, and D. Snidal 2003 (eds.). *The Rational Design of International Institutions.* Cambridge: Cambridge University Press

Koskienniemi, M. 2001. *The Gentle Civilizer of Nations: The Rise and Fall of International Law 1870–1960.* Cambridge: Cambridge University Press

Krasner, S. 1983 (ed.). *International Regimes.* Ithaca, NY: Cornell University Press
    1984. "Approaches to the State: Alternative Conceptions and Historical Dynamics," *Comparative Politics* 16 (2): 223–46

Kriehbiel, K. 1991. *Information and Legislative Organization.* Ann Arbor: University of Michigan Press

Krisch, N. and B. Kingsbury 2006. "Introduction: Global Governance and Global Administrative Law in the International Legal Order," *European Journal of International Law* 17 (1): 1–13

Ku, C. 2007. "Strengthening International Law's Capacity to Govern through Multilayered Strategic Partnerships," *South African Yearbook of International Law* 33: 107–23

Ku, C. and C. Borgen 2000. "American Lawyers and International Competence," *Dickinson Journal of International Law* 18 (3): 493–515

Ku, C. and J.K. Gamble 2000. "International Law – New Actors and New Technologies: Center Stage for NGOs?" *Law and Policy in International Business* 32 (2): 221–62

Ku, C. and H.K. Jacobson 2003. *Democratic Accountability and the Use of Force in International Law.* Cambridge: Cambridge University Press

Ku, C. and T. Weiss 1998. *Towards Understanding Global Governance: The International Law and International Relations Toolbox*. Waterloo, ON: Academic Council on the United Nations System

Larsen, J. 2004. "Importing Constitutional Norms from a 'Wider Civilization': *Lawrence* and the Rehnquist Court's Use of Foreign and International Law in Domestic Constitutional Interpretation," *Ohio State Law Journal*, 65: 1283–1327

Lasswell, H. and M. McDougal 1992. *Jurisprudence for a Free Society: Studies in Law, Science, and Policy*. Dordrecht: Kluwer Law

Lazlo, E. 1983. *General Systems Theory*. New York: Braziller

Leben, C. 1998. "Hans Kelsen and the Advancement of International Law," *European Journal of International Law* 9 (2): 287–305

LeBlanc, L. 1991. *The United States and the Genocide Convention*. Durham, NC: Duke University Press

Lippman, M. 1998. "The Convention on the Prevention and Punishment of the Crime of Genocide: Fifty Years Later," *Arizona Journal of International and Comparative Law* 15: 415–514

Luhmann, N. 1988. "The Unity of the Legal System," in G. Teubner (ed.), *Autopoietic Law: A New Approach to Law and Society*. Berlin: Walter de Gruyter, pp. 12–35

2004. *Law as a Social System*. Oxford: Oxford University Press

March, J. G. and H. A. Simon 1958. *Organizations*. New York: Wiley

Martens, G. F. von 1803. *The Law of Nations, Founded on the Treaties and Customs of the Modern Nations of Europe: With the Science of National Law, Covenant, Power, etc. to Which is Added, a Complete List of all the Treaties, Conventions, Compacts, Declarations, etc. from the Year 1731 to 1802 Inclusive, Indicating the Several Works in Which They are to be Found*. London: E. Jeffrey

Martin, L. and B. Simmons 1998 (eds.). *International Institutions. An International Organization Reader*. Cambridge, MA: MIT Press

Martin de Agar, J. T. 2007. *Handbook on Canon Law*. Montreal: Wilson & Lafleur

Mathews, J. T. 1997. "Power Shift," *Foreign Affairs* 76 (1): 50–66

McAdams, R. H. 1997. "The Origin, Development, and Regulation of Norms," *Michigan Law Review* 96 (2): 338–433

McDougal, H. and D. Lasswell 1959. "The Identification and Appraisal of Diverse Systems of Public Order," *American Journal of International Law* 53 (1): 1–29

Mearsheimer, J. 1994–5. "The False Promise of International Institutions," *International Security* 19 (3): 5–49

Miller, J. and S. Page 2007. *Complex Adaptive Systems*. Princeton: Princeton University Press

Mingst, K. 2003. "Domestic Political Factors and Decisions to Use Military Forces," in C. Ku and H. K. Jacobson (eds.), *Democratic Accountability and the Use of Force in International Law.* Cambridge: Cambridge University Press, pp. 61–80

Mitchell, R. 2002. "A Quantitative Approach to Evaluating International Environmental Regimes," *Global Environmental Politics* 2 (4): 58–83

Moore, S. 1973. "Law and Social Change: The Semi-Autonomous Social Field as an Appropriate Field of Study," *Law and Society Review* 7: 719–46

Morgenthau, H. 1948. *Politics among Nations: The Struggle for Power and Peace.* New York: Knopf

Murphy, P. 2008. "Excluding Justice or Facilitating Justice? International Criminal Law Would Benefit From Rules of Evidence," *International Journal of Evidence and Proof* 12: 1–31

Nussbaum, A. 1954. *A Concise History of the Law of Nations.* New York: Macmillan

O'Connell, M. E. 1999. "New International Legal Process," *American Journal of International Law* 93 (2): 334–51

Onuma, Y. 2003. "International Law in and with International Politics: The Functions of International Law in International Society," *European Journal of International Law* 14 (1): 105–39

Oppenheim, L. 1955. *International Law: A Treatise,* 8th edn. H. Lauterpacht (ed.). New York: David McKay Company, vol. I

Otto, D. 1996. "Nongovernmental Organizations in the United Nations System: The Emerging Role of Civil Society," *Human Rights Quarterly* 18 (1): 17–41

Page, S. 2006. "Path Dependence," *Quarterly Journal of Political Science* 1 (1): 87–115

Pahre, R. 1999. *Leading Questions: How Hegemony Affects the International Political Economy.* Ann Arbor: University of Michigan Press

  2006 (ed.). *Democratic Foreign Policy Making: Problems of Divided Government and International Cooperation.* New York: Palgrave

Peterson, M. J. 1992. "Whalers, Cetologists, and the International Management of Whaling," *International Organization* 46 (1): 147–86

Pevehouse, J., T. Nordstrom, and K. Warnke 2004. "The COW-2 International Organizations Dataset Version 2.0," *Conflict Management and Peace Science* 21 (2): 101–19

Pierson, P. 2004. *Politics in Time: History, Institutions, and Social Analysis.* Princeton, NJ: Princeton University Press

Posner, E. and J. Yoo 2005. "Judicial Independence in International Tribunals," *California Law Review* 93 (2): 957–73

Posner, M. 2005/6. "President's Letter," *Human Rights First 2005/06 Annual Report*

Posner, R. 2007. *Economic Analysis of Law.* New York: Aspen Publishers

Price, R. 1998. "Reversing the Gun Sights: Transnational Civil Society Targets Land Mines," *International Organization* 52 (3): 613–44

Ratner, S. and J. S. Abrams 1997. *Accountability for Human Rights Atrocities in International Law: Beyond the Nuremberg Legacy.* Oxford: Clarendon Press

Ratner, S. and A. M. Slaughter 1999. "Appraising the Methods of International Law: A Prospectus for Readers," *American Journal of International Law* 93 (2): 291–302

Raustiala, K. 2005. "Form and Substance in International Agreements," *American Journal of International Law* 99 (3): 581–614

Reisman, M. W. and A. Armstrong 2006. "The Past and Future of the Claim of Pre-emptive Self-defense," *American Journal of International Law* 100 (3): 525–50

Reus-Smit, C. 2004. "The Politics of International Law," in C. Reus-Smit (ed.), *The Politics of International Law*. Cambridge: Cambridge University Press, pp. 14–44

Rhodes, R., S. Binder, and B. Rockman 2006. *Oxford Handbook of Political Science*. Oxford: Oxford University Press

Roberts, Adam 1999. "NATO's Humanitarian War," *Survival* 3. 102–23

Roberts, Anthea 2001. "Traditional and Modern Approaches to Customary International Law: A Reconciliation," *American Journal of International Law* 95 (3): 757–91

Rogers, C. A. 2005. "The Vocation of the International Arbitrator," *American University International Law Review* 20 (5): 957–1020

Root, E. 1911. "The Function of Private Codification in International Law," *American Journal of International Law* 5 (3): 577–89

Rottleuthner, H. 1988. "Biological Metaphors in Legal Thought," in G. Teubner (ed.), *Autopoietic Law: A New Approach to Law and Society*. Berlin: Walter de Gruyter, pp. 97–127

Rovine, A. 1976. *Digest of United States Practice in International Law*. Washington, DC: Office of the Legal Advisor, Department of State

Rutherford, K. R. 2000. "The Evolving Arms Control Agenda: Implications of the Role of NGOs in Banning Antipersonnel Landmines," *World Politics* 5 (3): 74–114

Saint Augustine 1958. *City of God*. V. J. Bourke (ed.). New York: Image Books

Salacuse, J. W. and N. P. Sullivan 2005. "Do BITs Really Work? An Evaluation of Bilateral Investment Treaties and Their Grand Bargain," *Harvard International Law Journal* 46 (1): 67–130

Sandholtz, W. and K. Stiles 2009. *International Norms and Cycles of Change*. Oxford: Oxford University Press

Sandholtz, W. and A. S. Sweet 2004. "Law, Politics, and Global Governance," in C. Reus-Smit (ed.), *The Politics of International Law*. Cambridge: Cambridge University Press, pp. 238–71

Sassen, S. 2006. *Territory, Authority, Rights: From Medieval to Global Assemblages*. Princeton, NJ: Princeton University Press

Satzer, J. 2007. "Explaining the Decreased Use of International Courts: The Case of the ICJ," *Review of Law and Economics* 3 (1): 11–36

Scelle, G. 1932. *Droit International Public*. Paris: Les Éditions Dorat Montchretien

Schachter, O. 1991. *International Law in Theory and Practice*. Dordrecht: Martinus Nijhoff Publishers

Selden, J. 2003. *Of the Dominion, or, Ownership of the Sea*. (trans.) M. Nedham. Clark, NJ: Lawbook Exchange

Shaffer. G. 2004. "Recognizing Public Goods in WTO Dispute Settlement: Who Participates? Who Decides? The Case of TRIPS and Pharmaceutical Patent Protection," *Journal of International Economic Law* 7 (2): 459–82

2005. "Power, Governance, and the WTO: A Comparative Institutional Approach," in M. Barnett and R. Duvall (eds.), *Power in Global Governance*. Cambridge: Cambridge University Press, pp. 130–60

Shanks, C., H. K. Jacobson, and J. H. Kaplan 1996. "Inertia and Change in the Constellation of International Governmental Organizations, 1981–1992," *International Organization* 50 (3): 593–627

Shaw, M. 2008. *International Law*, 6th edn. Cambridge: Cambridge University Press

Shelton, D. 1994. "The Participation of Nongovernmental Organizations in International Judicial Proceedings," *American Journal of International Law* 88: 611–42

2000 (ed.). *Commitment and Compliance: The Role of Non-binding Norms in the International Legal System*. Oxford: Oxford University Press

2006. *Remedies in International Human Rights Law*, 2nd edn. Oxford: Oxford University Press

Shepsle, K. A. and B. Weingast 1995. *Positive Theories of Congressional Institutions*. Ann Arbor: University of Michigan Press

Sikkink, K. 1993. "Human Rights, Principled Issue-Networks, and Sovereignty in Latin America," *International Organization* 47 (3): 411–41

1998. "Transnational Politics, International Relations Theory, and Human Rights," *PS: Political Science and Politics* 31 (3): 517–21

Simma, B. 1995. "The Contribution of Alfred Verdross to the Theory of International Law," *European Journal of International Law* 6 (1): 33–54

Simma, B. and A. Paulus 1999. "The Responsibility of Individuals for Human Rights Abuses in Internal Conflicts: A Positivist View," *American Journal of International Law* 93 (2): 302–16

Simmons, B. 2000. "International Law and State Behavior: Commitment and Compliance in International Monetary Affairs," *American Political Science Review* 94 (4): 819–35

2001. "International Law – Stepchild in Social Science Research? A Rejoinder to Paul Diehl," *International Studies Review* 3 (1): 9–14

Singer, J. D. and M. Wallace 1970. "Inter-Governmental Organization and the Preservation of Peace, 1816–1965: Some Bivariate Relationships," *International Organization* 24 (3): 520–47

Siverson, R. 1980. "War and Change in the International System," in O. Holsti, R. Siverson, and A. L. George (eds.), *Change in the International System*. Boulder, CO: Westview Press, pp. 211–29

Slaughter, A. M. 1993. "Regulating the World: Multilateralism, International Law, and the Projection of the New Deal Regulatory State," in J. G. Ruggie (ed.), *Multilateralism Matters: The Theory and Praxis of an Institutional Form*. New York: Columbia University Press, pp. 125–56

  1997. "The Real New World Order," *Foreign Affairs* 76: 183–98

  1998. "International Law and International Relations Theory: A New Generation of Interdisciplinary Scholarship," *American Journal of International Law* 92 (3): 367–97

  2004. *A New World Order*. Princeton, NJ: Princeton University Press

Slaughter, A. M. and D. Bosco 2002. "Plaintiff's Diplomacy," *Foreign Affairs* 79 (5): 102–17

Slaughter, A. M. and W. Burke-White 2006. "The Future of International Law is Domestic (or, the European Way of Law)," *Harvard International Law Journal* 47 (2): 327–52

Stein, A. 1990. *Why Nations Cooperate: Circumstances and Choices in International Relations*. Ithaca, NY: Cornell University Press

Steinbrunner, J. 1974. *The Cybernetic Theory of Decision: New Dimensions of Political Analysis*. Princeton, NJ: Princeton University Press

Stiles, K. W. 2006. "The Power of Procedure and the Procedures of the Powerful: Anti-Terror Law in the United States," *Journal of Peace Research* 43 (1): 37–54

Streeck, W. and K. Thelen 2005. "Introduction: Institutional Change in Advanced Political Economies," in W. Streeck and K. Thelen (eds.), *Beyond Continuity: Institutional Change in Advanced Political Economies*. Oxford: Oxford University Press, pp. 1–39

Sylvest, C. 2004. "International Law in Nineteenth-Century Britain," *British Yearbook of International Law* 75: 9–70

Taft, W. H., IV and T. B. Buchwald 2003. "Preemption, Iraq, and International Law," *American Journal of International Law* 97 (3): 557 63

Taylor, P. 1987. "Prescribing for the Reform of International Organization: The Logic of Argument for Change," *Review of International Studies* 13: 19–38

Teubner, G. 1988. (ed.) *Autopoietic Law: A New Approach to Law and Society*. Berlin: Walter de Gruyter

  1993. *Law as an Autopoietic System*. Oxford: Blackwell

Thelen, K. 2004. *How Institutions Evolve*. Cambridge: Cambridge University Press

  2006. "Institutions and Social Change: The Evolution of Vocational Training in Germany," in I. Shapiro, S. Skowronek, and D. Galvin (eds.), *Rethinking Political Institutions: The Art of the State*. New York: New York University Press, pp. 135–70

Thelen, K. and S. Steinmo 1992. "Historical Institutionalism in Comparative Politics," in S. Steinmo, K. Thelen, and F. Longstreth (eds.), *Structuring Politics: Historical Institutionalism in Comparative Analysis*. Cambridge: Cambridge University Press, pp. 1–32

Thierry, H. 1990. "The Thought of George Scelle," *European Journal of International Law* 1 (1/2): 193–209

Tipson, F. S. 1974. 'The Lasswell–McDougal Enterprise: Toward a World Order of Human Dignity," *Virginia Journal of International Law* 14: 535–85

Trachtman, J. 2008. *The Economic Structure of International Law*. Harvard University Press

Tsebelis, G. 2002. *Veto Players: How Political Institutions Work*. Princeton: Princeton University Press

United Nations General Assembly 2006. "Fragmentation of International Law: Difficulties Arising from the Diversification and Expansion of International Law," Report of the Study Group of the International Law Commission. Finalized by M. Koskienniemi (April 13), A/CN.4/L.682.0

Van Schaack, B. 1997. "Crime of Political Genocide: Repairing the Convention's Blindspot," *Yale Law Journal* 106 (7): 2259–91

Vick, D. 2002. "The Human Rights Act and the British Constitution," *Texas International Law Journal* 37: 329–72

Waldron, J. 2005. "Foreign Law and Modern *Ius Gentium*," *Harvard Law Review* 119: 129–47

Walker, T. A. 1893. *The Science of International Law*, Cambridge: Cambridge University Press

Waltz, K. 1964. "The Stability of a Bipolar World," *Daedalus* 93 (3): 881–909
    1979. *Theory of International Politics*. New York: McGraw Hill

Waters, M. 2007. "Normativity in the 'New' Schools: Assessing the Legitimacy of International Legal Norms Created by Domestic Courts," *Yale Journal of International Law* 32: 455–84

Weil, P. 1983. "Towards Relative Normality in International Law," *American Journal of International Law* 77 (3): 413–42

Weintraub, R. 2002. "Introduction to Symposium on International Forum Shopping," *Texas International Law Journal* 37 (3): 463–67

Weiss, E. B. and H. K. Jacobson 1998. *Engaging Countries: Strengthening Compliance with International Environmental Accords*. Cambridge, MA: MIT Press

Weiss, T. 2007. *Humanitarian Intervention: Ideas in Action*. Cambridge: Polity Press

Weiss, T. and T. Shaw 1998 (eds.). *Beyond UN-Subcontracting: Task-Sharing with Regional Security Arrangements and Service Providing NGOs*. London: Macmillan

Wendt, A. 2003. "Driving with the Rearview Mirror: On the Rational Science of Institutional Design," in B. Koremenos, C. Lipson, and D. Snidal (eds.), *The Rational Design of International Institutions*. Cambridge: Cambridge University Press, pp. 259–90

Westfield, E. 2001–2. "Globalization, Governance, and Multinational Enterprise Responsibility: Corporate Codes of Conduct in the 21st Century," *Virginia Journal of International Law* 42: 1075–1108

Whewell, W. 1853. "Editor's Preface," in W. Whewell (ed.), *Hugo Grotius, De Jure Belli et Pacis Libri Tres*. Cambridge: Cambridge University Press

Widmaier, W., M. Blyth, and L. Seabrooke 2007. "Exogenous Shocks or Endogenous Constructions? The Meaning of Wars and Crises," *International Studies Quarterly* 51 (4): 747–59

Wiessner, S. and A. Willard 1999. "Policy-Oriented Jurisprudence and Human Rights Abuses in Internal Conflict: Toward a World Public Order of Human Dignity," *American Journal of International Law* 93 (2): 316–34

Wolff, C. 1934. "Introduction," in O. Nippold (ed.), J. Drake (trans.), *Jus Gentium Methodo Scientifica Pertractatum*. Oxford: Clarendon Press

Young, O. 1989a. *International Cooperation: Building Regimes for Natural Resources and the Environment*. Ithaca, NY: Cornell University Press

　1989b. "The Politics of International Regime Formation: Managing Natural Resources and the Environment," *International Organization* 43 (3): 349–76

Zartman, I. W. 2000. "Ripeness: The Hurting Stalemate and Beyond," in P. Stern and D. Druckman (eds.), *International Conflict Resolution after the Cold War*. Washington: National Academy Press, pp. 225–50

Zimmermann, H.-J. 2001. *Fuzzy Set Theory and Its Applications*, 4th edn. Dordrecht: Kluwer International

Zinnes, D. 1980. "Prerequisites for the Study of System Transformation," in O. Holsti, R. Siverson, and A. L. George (eds.), *Change in the International System*. Boulder, CO: Westview Press, pp. 3–21

INDEX

Abbott, K. W., 124
Abu Ghraib, 121
actors and subjects in international law
  corporations, 32, 39
  extra-systemic adaptations to
    systemic imbalance, 104–5
  in Genocide Convention and
    genocide norm, 99–102
  individuals, 32, 39, 99–102, 164–6
  insincere players, 159
  international organizations, 29, 38
  NGOs, 38
  normative change influenced by
    operating system regarding,
    140–4
  in operating system, 31–3, 38–9, 140–4
  policy implications, 157–60
  states, 32, 99–102
ad hoc tribunals. *See* tribunals
Adler, E., 109
African Union, 133, 134
agents and subjects. *See* actors and
    subjects in international law
Alien Tort Claims Act (US), 118
Alvarez, J., 142
*American Journal of International
    Law,* 116
Andean Court of Justice, 30
Annan, Kofi, 112
Anzilotti, Dionisio, 16
arbitration, 134–5, 165
Arctic Council, 107
Armenian massacres of WWI, 90
Augustine of Hippo, 8
Australia, domestic concerns about
    commitment of troops in, 121
autopoietic systems theory, 51

balance/equilibrium, 53–9. *See also*
    punctuated equilibrium theory
  courts and other compliance
    institutions, presence or lack
    of, 55–7
  defined, 53
  different configurations of operative
    and normative systems, 55–7
  ensuring, 157
  impacts of imbalance, 57–9
  inherent unlikeliness of, 54–5
  operating system inadequate to serve
    normative system change,
    imbalance due to, 159, 160
  systemic imbalance. *See* extra-
    systemic adaptations to
    systemic imbalance
Barnett, M., 44, 145
Barrett, S., 6
Al Bashir (President of Sudan),
    indictment of, 171
Baumgartner, F., 62
Beck, R., 16
Bederman, D. J., 7, 11
Belgium, universal jurisdiction in, 118
Bentham, Jeremy, 12
Berman, P. S., 19
Bodin, Jean, 9
Bosnia. *See* Yugoslavia, former
boundaries of international law system,
    52–3
Bradlow, D., 142
Britain. *See* United Kingdom
Brunnée, J., 87, 132, 140
Buergenthal, T., 169
Burci, Gian Luca, 110
bureaucratic universalism, 145